D1015557

"It is the unfortunate habit of books on illness and recovery to rely heavily on sanitized clichés. The downs are very down, the ups sky-high. This honest and carefully observed account avoids preconceived notions of the complicated path toward an organ transplant. Describing the stages of the affliction in detail, it makes you feel as if you were there, suffering a pain you had heard about but never really visualized, aware that death is no longer just a concept but could come at any time, and experiencing the complex emotions that come with being saved because someone else died. For readers who have not been close to a wasting disease, it will be an eye-opener, horrifying but in the end inspiring, a tale of courage being tested all day and every day."

—Reg Green, author of *The Nicholas Effect: A Boy's Gift to the World*

"Ana and Isa Stenzel were born against odds of 1.8 billion to one; identical twins of a Japanese mother and German father, with the crippling disease cystic fibrosis. Continuing against even greater odds, they succeeded in education and in living, and the long odds of listing for and receiving double lung transplants. These improbable events are, in fact, true and provide a fascinating and enlightening read. The beauty and the pain of the human condition continue to amaze us. This account is a winner in every respect."

—Bruce Reitz, M.D., Cardiothoracic Surgeon and Norman E. Shumway Professor at Stanford University School of Medicine

"This is a great book for professionals in healthcare, biology, and biotech. I first met Ana and Isa when they were Stanford college students. They were two of the more than 900 cystic fibrosis patients who volunteered to participate in the clinical study that established the benefits of inhaled Pulmozyme. I have always taught doctors in training that our patients inspire us and that we learn so much when we really listen to them. Readers of this book will be inspired by their story. They will learn much about cystic fibrosis and about life. They will learn that it is not the number of days that we live that matters, it is what we do with every day that we are fortunate to have."

—Steven Shak, M.D., Chief Medical Officer at Genomic Health and Inventor of Pulmozyme

"This is an excellent narrative that takes us through the twists and turns of high-tech medicine and transplantation. Written with insight and courage, this is a book to use with students of medical anthropology and those interested in culture and healing."

—Elizabeth Strober, Medical Anthropologist
and Lecturer at Seattle University

"Isabel and Anabel: twins with CF. Each author is unique, authentic. And each is a mirror to the other, offering the reader intimate insight into life with cystic fibrosis. These two women reveal their histories with candor and compassion. They help us find strength within ourselves and from our communities to rise above difficulty and breathe the freshness of each new day. Those with chronic illness will find a voice in this book for the daily challenges they themselves face and for the rich joys of life that others may take for granted. I read this book in one sitting—and now I revisit the pages to keep in touch with their compelling story."

—Carroll Jenkins, Executive Director of Cystic Fibrosis Research, Inc.

"One of the hardest and earliest lessons we learn is that life isn't fair. Perhaps for that reason I don't usually take to inspirational books, which often attempt to portray a particular example of misfortune as a special gift, to be appreciated for its character-building qualities, or failing that, for an advantage so mysterious that no mere mortal can discern what it might be. Fortunately, the genre is transcended by *The Power of Two*, an astonishing account by twin sisters born with a genetic disease that should have killed them in infancy, and almost did. But they survived that and numerous other close calls and are now in their thirties, with degrees from Stanford University, newly transplanted lungs, and a gift for writing that takes us directly into their lives. This is an intimate, brutally honest, and compelling memoir."

—Jeffrey Wine, Professor of Psychology and Pediatrics
and Former Director of the Program in Human Biology at
Stanford University's Cystic Fibrosis Research Laboratory

The Power of Two

The Power of Two

A Twin Triumph over Cystic Fibrosis

Isabel Stenzel Byrnes & Anabel Stenzel

University of Missouri Press   Columbia and London

Library of Congress Cataloging-in-Publication Data

Stenzel Byrnes, Isabel, 1972–
    The power of two : a twin triumph over cystic fibrosis / Isabel Stenzel Byrnes and
Anabel Stenzel.
        p.   cm.
    Summary: "Born in 1972, twins who share this life-threatening disease give an hon-
est portrayal of their struggle to live normal lives, their interdependence, day-to-day
health care, the impact of chronic illness on marriage and family, and the importance
of a support network to continuing survival"—Provided by publisher.
    Includes bibliographical references and index.
    ISBN: 978-0-8262-1754-7 (alk. paper)
  1. Stenzel Byrnes, Isabel, 1972—Health.   2. Stenzel, Anabel, 1972—Health.
3. Cystic fibrosis—Patients—United States—Biography.   4. Cystic fibrosis—
Patients—United States—Family relationships.   5. Twins—United States—
Biography.   I. Stenzel, Anabel, 1972–   II. Title.
    RC858.C95B97   2007
    362.196'3720092—dc22
    [B]   2007028962

Designer: Jennifer Cropp
Typesetter: The Composing Room of Michigan, Inc.
Printer and binder: The Maple-Vail Book Manufacturing Group
Typefaces: Palatino, Eplica, Rage Joi, and Demian

For permissions, see page 293.

Contents

Acknowledgments

This book could not have been accomplished without the support of countless individuals who believed in this story. First and foremost, we are extremely grateful for the hours of editing by Andrew Byrnes, who helped make this book what it is. We are also deeply indebted to Daniel Lazar, of Writer's House, who worked so hard on our behalf. The challenging process of writing a book began with many writing courses, and we are indebted to the teachers who have inspired and taught us how to write: Sheila Dunec, Alan Acosta, the Women on Writing Conference at Skyline College and Isa's writing group members, Jackie, Leslie, and Elaine. We are grateful for the editing and feedback by Bob Crabb, Dixie Redfearn, Robert Rohde, Stacey Collver, Sylvie Parkin, Beth Sufian, and Pat Rose, and for the endorsements by Dr. Jeffrey Wine, Dr. Bruce Reitz, Dr. Howard Dean, Reg Green, Boomer Esiason, Dr. Steven Shak, Carroll Jenkins, and Frank Deford. Most of all, we are grateful to Gary Kass, Beth Chandler, Karen Renner, Eve Crawford, Beverly Jarrett, Sara Davis, and the entire University of Missouri Press staff for believing in *The Power of Two*.

On a personal note, we are grateful to God for the blessings we've received to write this book. Everything we are and have done is a testament to something greater than ourselves. We'd like to thank our family for their patience and support as we poured out our secrets for the world to see. Thank you to our mother for pushing us to write as kids and to our dad, who accepted his description in the book so openly. We would also like to acknowledge our brother, Ryuta, who endured and showed that he cared in the most unique ways. We are grateful for the cheerleading efforts of the entire Byrnes extended family. Thanks goes to our friends and medical caregivers, who have allowed us to share their story in this book. We are grateful to Naomi Takeuchi for her guidance with Japanese vocabulary and to Ian Bullock for his support with our Web site.

Though hardly a comprehensive list, we'd like to thank the following supporters: Dr. Noreen Henig, Danielle Targan, Josh Wagner, Nancy El Sonbaty, Sally Cha, Betty Mednick, Mac Stearns, Jerry Cahill, Michelle Compton, Nahara Mau, the Jenkins family, the Robinsons and Modlins, the extended Stenzel family, Kathleen Flynn, Grace Chang, Judy and Alan Wester, Cathy Olmo, Dr. Ramona Doyle and all of our friends at the Pacific Athletic Club, Red Morton Jazzercise, Team Northern California-Nevada, the Stanford Lung Transplant Support Group, USACFA, Genentech, Inc., TRIO, and CFRI Retreat. We would especially like to acknowledge the California Transplant Donor Network and our donor families, who, in their time of grief, gave unconditionally so that we might live to write this book. Thank you to our many, many friends from the cystic fibrosis community, especially our Cystic Fibrosis Research, Inc. family, who provided inspiration, knowledge, medical education, and life lessons. This also includes the staff of Southern California and Northern California Cystic Fibrosis Summer Camp, Genentech's Heroes of Hope Program, the Cystic Fibrosis Foundation, and the Breathing Room. We are forever grateful to the countless healthcare providers who have sustained us at the Cystic Fibrosis Centers at Kaiser Hospitals in Los Angeles, Santa Clara, and Oakland, and to our health-care providers at Stanford University Medical Center and Lucile Packard Children's Hospital at Stanford.

We are tremendously thankful for the people and organizations who have given us permission to reprint their work: Hal Leonard Corporation, the Breathing Room, Jimmy Perkins at Why Are You Following Me Music, LLC, Jesse Winchester and Keith Case and Associates, Alfred Publishing, Frank Deford, Howard Auzenne, Lifetouch Studios, Sheree Rose and Music Services, Inc.

This book is written in memory of all our friends who've died of CF before us. May their lives be remembered in our words.

"The Power of Two"

So we're okay, we're fine
Baby I'm here to stop your crying
Chase all the ghosts from your head
I'm stronger than the monster beneath your bed
Smarter than the tricks played on your heart
Look at them together then we'll take them apart
Adding up the total of a love that's true
Multiply life by the power of two

Indigo Girls—Emily Saliers and Amy Ray—1995

Isa percussing Ana's back, from The Breathing
Room, entitled "Therapy," 1998

Therapy

An endless rhythmic beat
A sort of faint knocking in the distance.
The hands of a mutual therapist
Pounding hard on the delicate chest
Beating delicately on the hard chest.

A cruel and merciless treatment
Squenching our precious time on this earth.
Depleting such valuable energy from our souls
As the timer ticks away—anyway.

Faster! Faster!
Harder! Harder!
Day in, day out
A mindless routine sets in.

The anxiety of every breath grows stronger
With each cupped pound.
The aching back, sore muscles.
The bleeding hands gloved for protection
The cup overflows.
What meaning gives this bizarre and undignified practice
To the core of our existence?

"I love you!" says the beating rhythm.
With each beat a reminder that you are no burden
A cherished moment of togetherness
Of deep connection between you and me.
A synchronicity of beating arms
Is a synchronicity of love and affection.

Isabel Stenzel Byrnes, 1998

Symbiosis—(l to r) Ana and Isa inserting port needles, 1996

Symbiosis

I am Cystic.
You are Fibrosis.
We are cystic fibrosis.
The genes we share give us the same face,
the same body, the same cough,
the same hospital room.
The love grows stronger with every beat
on the chest, with every pierce of the heart.
As I hurt you and you hurt me, we fight
together to keep each other alive.

Isabel Stenzel, 1996
From The Breathing Room

For those who gave us extraordinary lives:

our parents,
Reiner and Hatsuko

&

our organ donors,
James Dorn and Xavier Cervantes

The Power of Two

Authors' Note

This memoir is based on our memories and journal entries of true events. Some of the chronological sequences of events and persons have been altered to support the flow of the story. Some of the names in this story have been changed to protect the privacy of the individuals.

A portion of the proceeds of this book will be donated to cystic fibrosis research.

Introduction

Isa

I rushed from the chilled outside air into the warmth of the women's locker room. Ana followed me. I had swum eighty laps, and she, one hundred. My muscles trembled, but I felt victorious. Eight months had passed since my lung transplant, and now I swam with new breath that made me glide through the water with ease. Ana's presence motivated me; she had trained with the Masters Swimming team and now sped through the water with fervent determination.

Modesty made me avert my eyes from the naked women who surrounded me, drying their hair, lounging in the jacuzzi, and passing from showers to bathroom stalls to locker stations. I couldn't help but think that the women's bodies were beautiful, mostly fit but of all shapes and sizes. My mind wandered. *Everyone is locked into mortal bodies that carry them through life. In this gym, everyone works hard to keep their bodies going.*

The showers were crowded, and Ana and I removed our swimsuits and jumped into an open shower together. As children, we had felt mortified at being naked in the YMCA locker room or in the hot springs in Japan. Years later, as grown women, we had come to suppress that deeply engrained Japanese shame and show our bodies with only a tinge of embarrassment.

As I washed my hair, I stared at Ana's body. Her torso was covered with war wounds. A centipedelike scar covered her entire belly as a reminder of our diagnosis at birth of cystic fibrosis (CF). Across her chest, curving under her breasts, was the mirror image of my own familiar "clam-shell incision," a mark of the lung transplant that had saved her life and ended her cystic fibrosis four years ago.

1

"I can't believe you already swam eighty laps!" Ana said. "I didn't do that until I was two years posttransplant." Our subtle competition never ceased.

After our shower, we grabbed towels from a shelf next to an alcove surrounded by mirrors. I gazed at my reflection, imagining the stares of other women, but I hesitated to cover myself. *This is who I am. I don't need to hide my own scar.*

A lady brushing her hair stepped toward us and inquired if we were twins; pointing at our matching scars, she went a step further and asked if we were Siamese twins.

Ana and I laughed and glanced at each other.

I said, "Oh, no, we're not. We just both had lung transplants."

The woman reacted with the amazement we had come to expect when we shared our story.

Though we'd never been mistaken for Siamese twins before, everywhere we went, people noticed us for being twins. We were truly identical, inseparable, each of us half of a pair. Some people called us "duplicates," "peas in a pod," or even "bookends." In fact, we were mirror-image identical twins, with moles on opposing sides of our bodies and missing teeth and naturally open sinus cavities on opposite sides of our skulls. Our friends tried to distinguish our physical differences: "Isa has a round face; Ana's is more narrow. Ana has a scar on her belly, and Isa has an outie. Isa has bangs, and Ana doesn't."

To those who know us well, though, there are glaring personality differences: "Isa is passive and more quiet; Ana is more outspoken and assertive. Isa has a brighter disposition; Ana has a more serious style with an edge. Ana is more intellectual; Isa is more humanistic. Ana is more social; Isa is more dependent. Isa is prudish and reserved; Ana has a rebellious, naughty flare. Ana is more self-sacrificing; Isa is more selfish. Ana is angrier; Isa is more forgiving. Ana is the advocate; Isa is the follower. Ana's the bitch. Isa's the sweetie pie." But despite such differences, our twinness made us closer than an old married couple. I could complete Ana's sentences and read her thoughts. I inhaled when she exhaled. We were, in essence, one person, complete with polar temperaments in two separate bodies that faced the world in unison.

The stranger's curiosity in the locker room reminded us how far we had come. In a way we *had* been conjoined at the chest. The lung disease with which we were both born forced us to stick together. We followed each other as children, to college, on travels abroad, to graduate school, and, finally, to the same workplace. We struggled with feeling different only to find solace in sharing those differences with each other. Our drive for independent identity was squelched as we acknowledged the deep-seated need to rely on each other for emotional and physical survival. Our coming-of-age story is one of twin lives intricately influenced by chronic illness, the blending of cultures, and developmental challenges.

Being saved by lung transplants marked a crossroads in our lives. We have an old life—one of growing up with chronic illness—and a new life—one of opportunities and gifts we never before imagined possible. We are writing this family memoir to pay tribute to our first life and to all the remarkable people who have shaped our experience.

Part 1

The Early Years

Chapter 1

One in 1.8 Billion

Isa

When Mama talked to Ana and me about our birth, she would recite the Japanese proverb, *"Kafuku wa azanaeru nawa no gotoshi* (Luck and misfortune are interwoven together like a rope)." Luck intervened at the divine moment when the zygote split and we became two, yet misfortune lurked in our genes. "This has made our lives more colorful," Mama explained.

Mama's labor pains started six weeks too early, on a chilly January morning in 1972. Our unsuspecting father, Reiner Ludwig Stenzel, was out of town at a physics conference, so our mother, Hatsuko ("Hat-skoh") Arima Stenzel, drove herself the forty-five minutes to Kaiser Hospital on Sunset Boulevard in the heart of Hollywood, California. A few hours before the delivery, a young resident thought he discerned two heartbeats and ordered an X-ray.

The X-ray confirmed twins. Mama's first reaction was disappointment. According to her grandmother in Japan, elegant women had single babies; it was not honorable to have twins because it was animallike. Japanese mothers of twins often hid them or gave one away. But Mama had suspected what was to come. Her firstborn, a son, Ryuta ("Ryoo-tah"), had weighed nearly nine pounds, so she had tried to watch her weight when she became pregnant eleven months after Ryuta was born. But her belly grew and grew.

Mama, always the more cautious of our parents, was more concerned than elated at the news. How would they manage with three babies in diapers? How would they survive financially?

She called our father at his conference to tell him the news. He was thrilled and saw twins as twice the blessing. He knew they would manage somehow. After calling his parents in Germany, he left his conference and came home right away.

Mama said the delivery was easy. "Twin A," Anabel Mariko, or Ana, weighed five pounds. "Twin B," Isabel Yuriko, or Isa, was born two minutes later and weighed half a pound more. After holding the two identical babies, Mama felt pleased. Being a mother of twins would be fun.

But three days later, as Mama prepared to leave the hospital, she and Dad received bad news. Ana had not yet passed her meconium, a newborn's first bowel movement. Her stomach was distended like a watermelon, and the doctors told my parents that she needed emergency surgery to repair the meconium ileus, or bowel blockage. Although Ana had only a fifty-fifty chance of surviving the procedure, without it she could suffer an intestinal rupture, which would cause an infection, and die.

Mama visited the nursery before Ana's surgery. As she held Ana in a tight embrace, she sobbed uncontrollably at the thought of losing her. She prayed to God that he would not take away her baby and promised to do anything to protect her. She told me she cried harder when she saw me in the next incubator and imagined my life without my twin.

Ana survived the surgery, but the blockage caused her paper-thin intestine to burst, and the surgeon could not fully seal the damaged openings. His attempts left a reckless incision across her entire abdomen. Ana was fixed with a colostomy bag, an external plastic pouch, which collected her stools for twelve months.

Because meconium ileus is a hallmark of cystic fibrosis (CF), the neonatal physician and director of Kaiser's Special Problems Clinic, Dr. Patrick Robbie, was asked to consult with my parents. Dr. Robbie was a stocky Irish American who resembled Santa Claus, although his demeanor was often stern and paternalistic instead of jolly and generous. He told my parents he suspected that Ana had this serious genetic disease. Since we were twins, he wanted to perform a "sweat test" on both of us, which, if abnormal, would prove CF.

Ana and I were wrapped in plastic, and, as our tiny bodies began to perspire, beads of our sweat were collected in small vials.

The "sweat test" demonstrated that both Ana and I had sodium chloride levels twice the level normally found in healthy children, and our diagnosis was confirmed. Dr. Robbie informed our parents that CF was a uniformly fatal disease and that we would be lucky if we reached our tenth birthday.

He explained that CF is an autosomal recessive genetic disease, meaning that both parents must carry the gene and, if they do, they have a one-in-four chance of having a child with CF with each pregnancy. CF is most common in people of Northern European descent; about one in twenty-five carries the gene. In Japanese, or any Asians, though, CF is extremely rare. At the time, the data showed that only one in ninety thousand Asians carried the CF gene.

My father, a physicist, loved statistics. He quickly did the math: with one-in-two-hundred odds of having identical twins, the odds of having half-Japanese twins with CF were roughly one in 1.8 billion.

Dr. Robbie gave Mama an article on cystic fibrosis from a Japanese journal and a pamphlet written in English. Upon first glance at the article, Mama read that in the few cases of Japanese CF infants, all had died within the first few months of life. As they left the consultation, Dr. Robbie told my parents, "You are in this together. You will have to work very hard to keep your twins alive."

My parents visited a local library, where, in a trancelike state, they pored over all the information they could find about CF. They read that it was a relatively newly discovered disease, having been first reported in 1938 by Dorothy Andersen in New York City. The basic CF defect, which affects approximately one in twenty-five hundred Caucasian children in the United States, involves an abnormal transport of salt and water across epithelial cells in the lungs, digestive tract, and sweat glands. CF patients lose a large amount of salt in their sweat, the basis for the German proverb, "The child will soon die whose forehead tastes salty when kissed." The salt imbalance leads to the production of thick, sticky mucus that blocks the airways of the lungs and the pancreatic ducts in the digestive tract, among other passages. The thick secretions in the lungs harbor bacteria that cause chronic, progressive lung infections and, eventually, lung failure. The blocked ducts in the pancreas lead to malabsorption, nutritional deficiencies, and in later life, diabetes.

It would be seventeen years after our birth before scientists discovered that a gene mutation on chromosome seven created an altered protein that prevented salt and water from passing through the cells normally, causing this subtle yet deadly defect. It would be thirty-five years after our birth that California would start screening all newborns for CF, to detect and treat babies early on.

Before we were born, my parents had never heard of CF. My German father and Japanese mother knew that many relatives in their war-torn countries had died of pneumonia and diarrhea, two classic symptoms of CF, but they never could be sure if CF had run in their families. Mama tried to make sense of why she would have such a rare gene. Later, she told us that she had called her mother in Japan after our diagnosis and asked her if she had any Caucasian ancestors. Our grandmother reacted defensively. "Of course, not, Hatsuko. We are pure Japanese! Maybe the gene is from your father's side. He lost seven of his eleven siblings, you know. Many died of pneumonia. But I am from the Honda clan, and we are an honorable family of pure Samurai blood."

After our diagnosis, a negative sweat test confirmed that Ryuta was perfectly healthy. Ryuta's chubbiness epitomized health, and he even won second place in Santa Monica's "Biggest Baby Contest" in 1970. Firm, stocky legs and round cheeks obscured his half-Asian features. His Japanese name, which translates to "big and strong," fit him well.

I stayed in the hospital for six weeks and came home before my sister. Mama breast-fed me, learned to give me medications, and bathed and changed me. She managed all this while chasing Ryuta and still visiting Ana at Kaiser. She and Dad prepared the nursery for two. Ana came home six weeks later, having recovered from her surgery. Twenty-one-month-old Ryuta asked Mama, "More babies come home?"

"No, Ryu-chan. There are only two," she replied and hugged him, relieved that at least her son would not die young.

Mama often told us how much she struggled in the first few months after we were born. Whether she did it to vent, to validate her own strength in overcoming adversity, or to instill guilt in us, she repeated her stories often: how we'd wake up several times a night; how when one of us started crying, the other followed, competing in decibels for her attention; how Ana's colostomy bag often came undone, and watery stool smeared all over Ana and the bedding; how the smell of the nursery stung her nostrils (loose, foul-smelling stools are diagnostic criteria for CF); how our shrill, deafening cries of hunger would crescendo as she scrambled to add powdered digestive enzymes to our bottles of formula; how we gained weight so slowly—even if we ate voraciously—that it took over a year for each of us to reach ten pounds.

Mama felt more like a nurse than a mother, with laundry, medications, doctor's visits, changing and bathing consuming her while we provided little affection in return. Most of all, she told us how she had to dismiss Ryuta's cries for attention because she was too occupied with and exhausted by our needs.

Dad helped when he could. The pressures of his academic career at that time forced him to work two jobs—one in plasma physics as an assistant professor at the University of California, Los Angeles, and one at a technical research company. He was in charge of dropping Ryuta off and picking him up from day care. Obsessed by his work, he once forgot to pick up Ryu-ta. That was just the beginning of Mama's resentment that he did not do enough for the family.

After several months, Mama recorded a tearful plea for help and mailed the cassette tape to her mother. My grandmother, whom we called Oba-chan, took a leave of absence from her job in Tokyo and came to Los Ange-les to become our second caregiver. Often she cared for Ryuta while Mama tended to us twins. Obachan changed our diapers, fed us, and bathed us. Her presence that year lifted my mother's spirits. She had someone with whom she could speak Japanese and share her fears.

"I don't know why we have such bad luck," Mama said to Obachan one day as they changed our diapers again. Mama changed Ana's, since it had to be sealed carefully so as to not disturb the colostomy bag.

"This is not bad luck," Obachan replied. "You must find joy from these beautiful babies. Whatever challenge awaits you will only make you stronger. That is what I learned from my life."

Obachan stayed with us until we were one year old; then she returned to Tokyo, but she returned every summer to help Mama care for us as we be-came active toddlers. She taught us our first words in Japanese and pre-pared Japanese foods that became our first solids. "I always changed your diaper first and Ana-chan would get so upset," she would tell me years lat-er, "because changing her bag was more complicated." Alongside a less-stressed mother, Obachan nurtured us with affection.

When we were older, Mama told us how, in those early days, she had wondered why fate had given her this challenge. Her mother's presence re-minded her of her former life in Japan, which seemed so distant, though only eight years had passed since she had arrived in America to study. She had never imagined her decision to come to America and marry my father would lead to raising sick children. Her dreams of graduate school were shattered, and the future seemed bleak. She loved her babies intensely and wanted to give them everything she had, but she still dreaded the growing burden they would be. Caring for the twins was so much work, she often thought, and they would die young anyway.

Beside Mama's bed sat a faded brown photo of her father, Sukehisa Ari-ma, standing beside his wife, our grandmother, Tazuko, and their four chil-dren. As a child I often gazed at my grandfather's narrow face, his wire-rimmed glasses, and his formal western-style suit. Mama said this was the last photograph taken before he was drafted into the Japanese army in May 1945. Her family lived in Manchuria, China, conquered by Japan, where Sukehisa worked at a Japanese bank. He survived the war but was sent by the Russians to a prisoner-of-war camp in Siberia. His clothes were stolen while he was taking a bath. He caught pneumonia as a result and died in December 1945. Mama told us how Obachan struggled to raise her children all alone. The oldest, Juichi, was eight, and the youngest, Sukeyoshi, was only six months old when their father died. Mama had to be strong like her mother.

Although Mama and Dad were from different worlds, they shared a youthful spirit and ambitious dreams of freedom and adventure far from home, in America. They remembered their impressions as children of the American soldiers who had occupied Japan and Germany after the war. Mama remembered the Hershey's chocolates that GIs had given her; Dad recalled an American soldier who had saved his life by snatching a clumsy five-year-old from the path of a racing U.S. military police jeep in 1945.

After the atomic bomb was dropped on Hiroshima in August 1945, the Japanese surrendered, and our grandmother fled Manchuria with her children. The family traveled on foot through Korea until they reached the Sea of Japan, where Japanese boats waited. The journey took months, and they often had to walk at night to decrease their visibility among the antagonistic Korean and Chinese civilians. Mama recalled dodging stones thrown by people who hated her because she was Japanese. Even after returning to Japan, Obachan was often ridiculed for being *hikiagesha,* a refugee from a defeated imperial colony. Only the American soldiers had shown her kindness.

After the war Obachan opened and managed a successful inn outside of Tokyo on property her mother owned. Visitors from America befriended the Arima family in the late 1950s and invited Mama to study in the States. Obachan agreed to let Mama go to America, but only if her oldest brother, Juichi, accompanied her. Mama had just finished her undergraduate studies in psychology at Waseda University and was ready for a change. After being accepted into a master's degree program in child development at Pacific Oaks College in Pasadena, California, she boarded a ship bound for America in the summer of 1964. Juichi, also on board, would continue on from the West Coast to Detroit, where he planned to study design.

A year later, on a different continent, Dad was making plans to come to America. He had received an engineering degree from Braunschweig University in Germany and been offered a scholarship to study in the United States. He was accepted for graduate studies at the California Institute of Technology, also in Pasadena, California. He told us that after traveling by propeller airplane across the Atlantic to New York, his first vision of America was the skyline of Manhattan and Lady Liberty. A seventy-two-hour bus trip brought him to Los Angeles. Restless by nature, he sat in the bus

watching the American countryside, admiring the open spaces of the Mid-
west and wondering what this new land would offer him. When he arrived
in Los Angeles, the Watts riots were erupting, and he was shocked by
the racial tension, protests, and police barricades. *This is the true Wild West,*
he thought.

Dad met Mama at a Rotary Club-sponsored party for international students. Mama was wooed by Dad's romantic and gentleman-like qualities
and his handsome, sharp features. His slight build made him look like a
high school student, and his shy, sweet, and well-mannered intellectualism
charmed her. She was also impressed with his drive, ability to fix things,
and love of nature and hiking. Mama was a petite woman with a round face
whose narrow smile tamed her thick, wiry Betty Boop hair. She always had
a cheerful smile. An aura of clueless confusion made her vulnerable; Dad
prided himself on teaching her things. He admired her skills as a cook, her
sociability, and her generous, helpful nature. Their relationship quickly became serious.

Dad proposed in 1966, and although Mama tentatively accepted his proposal, she remained ambivalent about their relationship. She didn't know
what it meant to be in love or if he was the one. His tendencies to become
absorbed in his studies and to respond to her intimate questions with an
uncomfortable laugh made her wonder if he could meet her needs. She also
worried about whether an interracial marriage would work. Interracial
marriage was still controversial; it was illegal in seventeen states until 1967,
when the Supreme Court declared those state bans unconstitutional. Fa-
therless and living with three brothers who couldn't understand her had
created a desperate yearning within Mama to find a man who would listen, appreciate, and love her.

Mama returned to Japan for one year to contemplate Dad's proposal. In
Japan she felt allegiance to her family but also felt distant from them. She
wondered where she belonged. She knew that if she stayed in Japan, there
would be limited opportunities for her as a woman to put her education
into practice in the workplace. Obachan told her, "If you stay here, there
will be nothing for you to do except get married. If you go to America to be
with Reiner, maybe you can make something of your life." She was right.
A different life would await Mama in America, but living there would be
complex; it took great effort for her just to grasp the English language.

One year and many love letters later, Mama agreed to marry Dad. They
filed for international marriage certificates in Tokyo and Berlin. They were
married on a hot and humid August day in 1967 just outside of Tokyo. The
wedding ceremony was all in Japanese, none of which Dad could understand, except for the part when he said, "I do."

Upon returning to the United States, the newlyweds moved into an apartment in Santa Monica, where the air was fresh and cool and the Pacific Ocean was visible from their windows. Dad received his Ph.D. in electrical engineering in June 1970, just a few weeks before the birth of the couple's son, who arrived on Father's Day. The robust newborn was given the German name of Andreas by his father and the Japanese name of Ryuta by his mother. Dad was offered a research and teaching position in the physics department at UCLA. When Mama learned that she was expecting a second child, she and Dad rented a home in the coastal suburb of Pacific Palisades, which was, at that time, an idyllic town populated by middle-class Caucasian families. Their life as an American family had begun.

Chapter 2

First Memories

Isa

When I grow up I want to have a family and be a writer.

—Isa, age eight

I awoke and noticed my right hand felt strange. It was taped tightly to a cushioned board, where an upside-down paper cup had been carefully positioned to cover an IV needle that was anchored in a vein. My eyes traveled past the needle and traced the length of a long stretch of clear tubing that ran to a pump that stood next to my crib. The pump was attached to a pole. A light on the machine blinked as fluid dripped into the tubing from a large glass bottle suspended from the top of the pole. I looked down at my unfamiliar pajamas—blue cotton with colorful clowns. They itched. I could hear a noisy baby nearby. I inhaled the faint scent of disinfectant.

I sat up to see where I was. I scanned the room, but Mama wasn't around. I couldn't remember how long I had been here. With my free hand, I rubbed my chest, which ached from coughing. I remembered that Mama had told me I had to go to the hospital because my lungs "had bad germs in them."

I lifted my left hand and slid it across the yellowish plastic tarp that loomed above me like a rectangular bubble. As I moved my legs between the stiff bedsheets, the plastic mattress crinkled and squeaked beneath me. I pushed against the thick clear covering that surrounded me. At my eye level, where the plastic tarp ended, my five-year-old fingers grasped the cold, shiny silver bars that surrounded me. Still feverish from pneumonia, I saw that I was actually suspended in midair, my cage several feet off the ground. My olive hands pulled and pushed. I tried to break out, creating a clatter.

A wrinkled old nurse in a white uniform entered the room. "Now, Isabel. I see you're awake. Don't worry, your mother will be back tomorrow," she said in a soft singsong voice. She examined me with beady blue eyes with scarily small pupils. Her gray, frizzy hair was tucked under a white cap that looked like an origami creation. "We'll take good care of you here. Now you be a good girl and stay in bed."

I didn't want to be a good girl. I wanted to go home. I wanted my Mama, and I said so. The nurse pointed her wrinkled finger at me and said that I was too big to want my Mama and that I should get used to being here. She told me I should feel lucky that it was the first time I was in the hospital and that she would take good care of me. But I didn't feel very lucky. She flicked on the TV and left.

I didn't understand what she meant. Sitting in my bubble bed, all I wanted was my Mama. It felt like my first days of preschool, when Mama had left me and I had cried and cried.

Through the plastic hood, the TV's picture looked distorted, but I could see Tom and Jerry. The little mouse ran around trying to escape the big gray cat. Piano music, the kind Mama practiced every morning, played in the background. I was annoyed at Tom, always chasing the poor innocent mouse. *What did Jerry ever do to that cat?* I wondered. *Why doesn't that mean Tom just leave Jerry alone?*

While I was in the hospital, a man came three times a day and put a mask on my face. He had a long mustache and wore a white coat. He explained that the cold steam that rose out of the mask would help open my lungs and allow me to breathe better. After I breathed in the steam, he hit me on the back. It hurt at first, but I got used to it, and his clapping made me cough. He smiled when I coughed, saying what a good girl I was for doing my therapies.

The day before I left the hospital, Mama came with Ana, and we went down to the respiratory therapy clinic. I lay on a tilted hospital bed while Mama learned how to do chest percussion, what the mustached man in the white coat had done for me. With intense concentration, Mama watched as the respiratory therapist placed me in various positions—lying flat, sitting up, lying on my side—while she was instructed to clap my back to help dislodge the thick mucus in my lungs. Her heavy clapping created a popping sound, and the skin on my back burned from the sting of her blows. In those *interminable* minutes, I let my mind wander to ignore the sting. *What did I do wrong? Maybe if I was a good girl, we could stop this.*

But Mama did not stop. She compliantly worked on eleven positions, clapping and draining the five lobes of the lungs at various angles.

I looked up to see the stares of the other patients, who must have thought it strange for a mother to be hitting her child in such a way. When I was finished, it was Ana's turn. Mama shook out her arms to relieve her aching muscles and repeated her practice on Ana. Dr. Robbie had prescribed the therapy three times per day, every day, for the rest of our lives.

The day after I came home from the hospital, a man delivered two black-and-silver machines, which had plastic tubes connecting various valves and water pipes.

"Look what you get to do!" Mama and Dad exclaimed. "Isn't this fun? This is what makes you special."

The novelty of therapy wore off quickly. Soon, Ana and I squirmed and complained about starting our therapies. We envied Ryuta, who could keep playing outside while we were held hostage inside, sitting side by side with misty masks on our faces, waiting for it to be over. The routine became painfully boring. The cool steam clouded my vision and condensed into droplets that collected on my eyebrows and lashes. The elastic straps pinched my cheeks, irritating my skin. The mask was connected to a long white hose that protruded like an elephant's trunk. It was attached to a buzzing machine called an ultrasonic nebulizer. If I tried to get up and move around, the hose became disconnected, and Mama usually scolded me to sit still. Sometimes the salty fog would tickle my throat and make me wheeze, setting off a coughing spell. When Ana or I whined, Dad explained that we had to be good girls and do therapy every day to stay healthy. "For every treatment you miss is one day less of your life," he warned. To make the time go faster, he read us German fables like *Max und Moritz*.

After twenty minutes, the timer rang and we happily removed the masks. Then it was time to go to Mama and Dad's bedroom. Mama and Dad shared the task of chest percussion. I lay next to Ana, both of us propped on a pile of pillows in a slanted position to drain the mucus from our lungs. With the timer again set, this time for thirty minutes, the minutes were punctuated by the *pop, pop, pop* of cupped hands hitting our backs. The sounds echoed throughout the house. It hurt my stomach when Dad's leathery hands slipped below my ribcage and made my back ache when Mama's bony hands smacked my spine.

Eventually, the vibrations made me cough, and Mama passed me tissues to spit into. I hated to cough and wished it would be over. "*Mo-ii*," I begged in Japanese for this to finish, but Mama or Dad would just keep pounding away. So I just lay there, trying not to cry.

Sometimes Mama complained to Dad that she was too tired to do more. Then Dad took over, sitting between us, hitting Ana on one side and me on the other side with his strong arms, like an albatross flapping his powerful wings. When the timer rang, Dad scratched our backs, his thick fingers digging into my bony shoulders. At last, something that felt good.

Chapter 3

Kaiser Visits

Isa

> At age six, Ana and I were admitted for five weeks with fungus in the lungs. We met a girl with CF who was very sick. She was really nice. She drew us pictures and had a kind family. I remember we used to throw pieces of bubble gum to and from our beds. It was very sad to find out later she didn't live very long.
>
> —Isa, age fourteen

When we were six, Ana and I developed fungal infections in our lungs that led to our being hospitalized together for the first time. We were placed in the same room on Kaiser's pediatric ward, 7 North, a circular wing with colorful pictures on the walls and orange-and-yellow curtains between the beds. From the windows we could see the smoggy horizon, the skyscrapers of downtown Los Angeles, and Kaiser's many clinic buildings and parking structures.

The infections were particularly difficult to treat, and our five-week stay was unusually long. With nothing to fill our days but respiratory treatments, intravenous infusions, and meals, we quickly became restless. We felt fine, and we complained to each other about being bored. We were tired of walking around the ward repeatedly. We wished we could go outside. We memorized every detail of the walls in our rooms: the sockets, the pattern of the floors, the stains on the curtains.

One day the sunshine outside beckoned me, and I could no longer stand the temptation. I darted out of bed and climbed a chair by the window. In the distance I could see the Hollywood sign and the Griffith Observatory up in the hills. The windows of the pediatric rooms were clamped. I grabbed a clamp and lifted it and pushed open the window as wide as it would go, several inches. A gentle breeze came through.

"It opened! We got air! Real air!" I exclaimed to Ana. I pressed my face against the opening and took a deep breath; I could smell the exhaust of cars rushing along Sunset Boulevard down below. Ana joined me, and we both reached out and waved our skinny arms outside to feel pure sunshine on our skin.

Suddenly, we heard Dr. Robbie's voice from outside our room. We pulled our arms inside and rushed back to our beds. As often happened, Dr. Robbie had brought by a group of medical residents. My attention perked up— I loved to eavesdrop. I could hear them talking, mumbling complicated words about CF and our treatments. Sometimes the doctors talked about our race and how novel it was that Asians had CF. They would come inside and ask us questions and be amazed at our precocious understanding of our disease. That day, they joked with us, and we had fun with them. I was disappointed when our new hospital friends left the room. We got more attention in the hospital than at home.

Years later, Mama told us how our lengthy hospitalizations had confused Ryuta. This particular time, he was eight years old, and he ran to our next-door neighbor Sue's home after school and told her that we had died. Sue came over immediately to offer her condolences. Mama told her that we were fine and felt so bad that she had forgotten to explain how we were doing to Ryuta. She was determined to include him more.

Later that week, Ana and I were sitting at the nurse's station, which was at one end of a long hallway that led to the elevator. Kids weren't allowed to walk down the hallway because that was considered leaving the pediatric floor. That day, we both jumped up with excitement when the elevator doors opened up and we saw Mama and Ryuta coming to visit. But when they stepped out of the elevator, the security guard stopped them and said, "You can't bring your boy here."

Mama explained how Ryuta hadn't seen his sisters in three weeks and that they had driven an hour to get there. Ryuta stood there, staring down at his feet. The security guard looked unaffected. He picked at his nails while Mama told her story, then he nonchalantly explained how kids under twelve were not allowed. From where we stood at the end of the hallway we could see that Mama's face was getting red. She ranted more about how much we missed our brother and how we weren't going to be discharged anytime soon, but the guard mumbled something about the rules and the safety of the patients. Finally, Mama began to lead Ryuta to the adjacent waiting room. Then the security guard stopped her and told her that she couldn't leave her boy alone; there had to be parental supervision at all times. Raising her voice, Mama demanded to talk to the supervisor, and she said how unfair the rules were. We could hear her shrill voice down the hall loud and clear. Apparently the supervisor was off that day so there was nobody higher up to complain to. She turned to us with defeated eyes and sighed. She walked toward us, leaving Ryuta near the elevator, and stood there halfway between us. I wanted her to come over and hug me. She stopped, looked at Ryuta, then turned to us. Then she said, "Mama and Ryu-chan cannot stay long, because of these awful rules. You talk to your brother from here."

We yelled to our brother from down the hall and pushed our IV poles to the very edge of the hall, hesitant, as if an invisible electric fence would shock us if we stepped into the forbidden zone. We waved briskly, and he waved back with a weak smile. The nurses still wouldn't let us leave the floor.

We could hear Mama reassure Ryuta that we looked well and that we were well taken care of. She explained to him about the IVs in our hands and pointed to the bags of medicine that dangled from our poles. We wanted to ask Ryuta about his Legos, his bike riding, and our pets, but it was hard to have a conversation with him by yelling down the long hallway. So, after we had all exchanged a few words, Mama and Ryuta left.

As the weeks passed, the hospital began to feel like a foreign land, distant from our family and friends. My parents tried to visit often, but the drive was just too long for them to come every day. Sometimes it felt like they were forgetting about us. When our parents did visit, they brought only food and books. Later, I learned that Mama didn't want us to associate being sick with being spoiled and lavished with gifts. We were thrilled when our neighbor Sue visited us and gave us a whole market bag full of candies, toys, and coloring books.

One day, we met a girl named Cheryl. Her mom pushed her wheelchair into our room and introduced her with enthusiasm. Cheryl was ten years old and also had cystic fibrosis.

Ana and I gazed at Cheryl. Under her pink Snoopy pajamas, she was emaciated, and her tiny frame sagged in the wheelchair. She was wearing a massive green oxygen mask. A heavy green tank sat between her chicken legs. Her hair was stringy and wet, and I could see droplets of sweat on her forehead. She gazed at us, expressionless, as her chest shook vigorously from her struggle to breathe. Her toes hung over the edge of the chair's footrest. They were strangely swollen, round and blue. We later learned about clubbed fingers and toes, a classic sign of a lack of oxygen and very typical of kids with CF.

That evening, Ana and I were making our rounds of 7 North. I could see that Cheryl's room was an isolation room, for really sick kids. In the dimness of the room's light, I could see her mom sliding a lubricated tube down her throat. When we asked a nurse about it, she explained that Cheryl had become too weak to cough, and her mom was helping to suction mucus from her lungs.

A few days later, as we walked the halls, I noticed that Cheryl's room was empty. Ana and I approached Sally, our favorite nurse. We asked where Cheryl was because we wanted to see if she wanted to play. Sally crouched down so we could see her pale face and stringy long black hair at eye level. Her tone was serious.

She put her warm arms around both of us and said, "Cheryl went to Heaven last night."

Ana asked what that meant, and Sally explained that she was with God now, that she wasn't here anymore, and that she had gone to a better place.

I didn't understand.

On the day we were finally discharged, Dad announced a surprise during the drive home. When the car was parked in the driveway, Mama and Dad took each of us by our hands from the car and said, "Close your eyes!" as they proudly directed us into the little pantry next to our kitchen. The room smelled of vinegar.

Dad instructed us to open our eyes.

I explored the room. They had remodeled the pantry into our very own little "therapy room." Just as I stepped toward a brand-new brown vinyl recliner, Ryuta, who had followed us in, pushed me aside and marched ahead. He plopped himself onto the recliner and pushed back on the arms with his hands to let his feet fling forward.

"Isn't this neat? I wanna watch TV in here!"

"Wait!" I protested.

Just then Dad grabbed Ryuta's arm, scolding him to get out of our chair. He yanked Ryuta up and shoved him aside. "This is not your room. It belongs to your sisters." Ryuta retreated to the corner and pouted.

Ignoring Ryuta, I ran my fingers across the new wallpaper: yellow-and-green stripes adorned with large flowers that were embossed with fuzzy felt. I climbed into the recliner, and my skin stuck to the vinyl, making a slurping sound. In reclining position, the chair was perfect for chest percussion. On one side of the chair stood a table that held a timer, a box of tissues, toys, books, and art supplies. On the other side of the chair was a new machine we had started to use in the hospital called an intrapulmonary percussive ventilator (IPPV). It was noisy and bulky with multiple tubes and complex plastic contraptions attached to a mouthpiece. Mama had set out a large tub of vinegar and a clean tray where our nebulizer parts were to be sterilized. The pantry led into a tiny bathroom, which would be ours.

We thanked our parents, deeply appreciative that they had created this special space for us.

Later I looked around and saw that all our medicines and machines had been taken from the dining table, the kitchen counter and the living room floor and placed in our new, hidden, therapy room. Now no one who visited our house would know we had CF unless they came to our therapy room.

> I missed school because of a doctor appointment. He checked me and my sister. We were looking very good. We had a shot but it did not hert [sic] a bit. After the doctor we went to buy shoes for my mom.
>
> —Ana, age eight

For years, we visited Dr. Robbie twice a month for checkups. The drive to Kaiser became so familiar that if I closed my eyes I would know when we arrived just from the feel of the roads. We passed bustling Mexican stores with piñatas hanging in the windows, a sprouting Koreatown, homeless people, and day laborers hanging out on the streets waiting for a chance to work. Sometimes, if there was an accident on the freeway, we took the roundabout route along Sunset Boulevard, passing the opulent mansions of Bel Air and the lively hangouts of movie stars in Hollywood, where the Capitol Records sign flashed brightly and billboards promoting the latest blockbuster rose high enough to touch the sky.

The mornings were always long. On one particular visit, we sat in the waiting room for over an hour. Mama looked tired already. I examined the wrinkles that made her face look like cracked glass. Her eyes were glazed, and she seemed to be daydreaming of being somewhere else. Sometimes her expression became blank, turning so zombie-like that it scared me.

Our visit with Dr. Robbie came and went, ironically brief despite the long anticipation, and culminating in nothing more than another order for antibiotics scribbled illegibly on a prescription for each of us, which he handed to my mother. "Try this, and we'll see them back in two weeks."

"Stay out of trouble, you rascals," Dr. Robbie said as he gave us his characteristic bear hug. With a twinkle in his eye, he was the most caring doctor I could imagine.

We thanked him and then headed to the laboratory across the street. There, we had another long wait, amid the screams of babies and the groans of old men getting their blood drawn. Finally, it was my turn. At seven, I had no hesitation about getting stuck with a needle. I winced a little, but Mama always told me that I had to show *gaman,* Japanese for "endurance." I wasn't going to scream frantically like the other kids and cause a scene. It was no big deal.

Next we headed back across the smoggy street to the pharmacy to wait in another long line to put in the prescriptions that Dr. Robbie had ordered. We stood silently, waiting our turn. Mama's face tensed with worry. It was already past noon, and my stomach grumbled with hunger.

At last, our number was called. The clerk greeted Mama with a dreary frown that seemed to say, *I'm tired, and I hate my job.* She was a large, middle-aged, Caucasian lady, with glasses that perched on the end of her nose, and she smelled of potpourri.

The clerk looked up as Mama dug through her papers to find the two prescriptions.

Mama told her she needed an antibiotic and struggled with the complex pronunciation of the medication, *amoxicillin.* "I would like to have the syrup." The last word sounded more like "shee-lup."

The clerk looked at my mother and asked her to repeat what she had said.

Mama looked dismayed. Her posture shifted. "I would like amoxicillin syrup." She handed over the prescriptions. She spoke slowly, repeating, ". . . a-mox-i-cillin *shee-lup.*"

The lady repeated that she couldn't understand her.

"The liquid, for my girls to drink."

"Oh." The clerk grabbed the prescriptions and began writing down the order. She then casually glanced at my mother and said, "I can't understand your accent. You need to learn to speak English."

Holding onto the counter with my small hands, I looked up at the two of them. Mama sounded fine to me. I could tell she was humiliated, but her brow bent with resentful fury.

This had happened before, and Mama responded with her usual retort, saying that she did speak English and that most people understood her just fine. She told the clerk that this was Los Angeles and that there were many foreign people here. She ended her defense with "Perhaps you need to learn to understand foreign accents."

The woman huffed. She turned to place the prescription on the counter behind her, ignoring Mama's rebuttal. She handed my mother her receipt, gave her a number, and nonchalantly told her to wait twenty minutes.

"I hope you are not so rude to other people," my mother stated, stepping away from the counter. She turned to Ana and me as we walked away. "Isn't she awful?"

Mama's accent caused her much stress over the years. She struggled with "v," "th," "r" and "l." Dad even made fun of having "flied lice" for dinner. We unconsciously adopted some of Mama's pronunciations. An astute third-grade teacher referred Ana and me to speech therapy when she noticed that we said "wabbit" for rabbit and "ca-wa" for car. For a good half of the school year, every week, Ana and I were excused from class to sit in front of a nice lady who used tongue depressors to teach us how to roll our tongues under the roofs of our mouths to use "r" correctly.

The day at the clinic had been long, and we were tired and hungry. These bimonthly visits took a toll, and to confront such ignorance added one more layer of frustration for Mama.

We crossed the street yet again to a small restaurant that sold freshly made egg rolls. "We should be proud to be Asians in Los Angeles," she stated as we devoured the steaming treats. Oil dripped from the egg rolls. I knew my tummy would ache, but the scrumptious taste made me ignore the consequences.

"Mama," I said, "*Kusuri.*" I asked for my medicine.

Mama reached for her purse and handed each of us little tea-bag-sized packets of Cotazym powder. I grabbed a packet, shook it, and poured its contents into my Coke. I watched as the enzymes started to bubble and digest the very liquid in which it was meant to dissolve. It fizzled for a moment and grew like magic, forming a layer of brown foam. In a big gulp, I drank it down, knowing that I might be spared a tummy ache because I took my medicine. After lunch we returned to the pharmacy to pick up our prescription. The rude clerk was nowhere in sight. By two o'clock we were headed back to the car.

Although I was tired, I eagerly looked forward to the best part of our day, a special outing to *Nihonjin-machi,* or Little Tokyo, in downtown Los Angeles, where we stocked up on goodies like *miso* paste, *azuki,* dried fish, and *sashimi.* We stopped at the Sanrio store to gaze at the colorful cartoons of Hello Kitty and Little Twin Stars, and at Ikeda Bakery, where our mouths watered as we eyed the meticulously decorated pastries. Mama always bought us *anpan* or *creampan,* our favorite bread roll with sweet beans or light custard oozing out with the first delicious bite.

We carried our grocery bags filled with Japanese comfort foods back to our station wagon and climbed into the backseat. Mama drove west toward the beach, away from the smog of downtown, toward home.

Chapter 4

Culture Clash

Ana

I went to school. After school I did my therapy. My sister said when we did chest percussion she said I had to do her so I did. After that I went to play handball with my friend and we played fine.

—Ana, age eight

After our first hospitalizations, Isa and I enjoyed several years of stable health. Mama and Dad were determined to make our childhood as normal as possible, despite our daily ritual of therapies, bimonthly doctors' visits, and occasional hospital stays. Dr. Robbie's words greatly influenced my parents: "Give them as much normalcy as possible. Enjoy them while you can. Give them a happy childhood." He also instructed, "Exercise will help clear their lungs and keep them strong." So Mama and Dad encouraged us to be as active as any other kids.

On the surface, we looked like an all-American middle-class family. We got a dog (a black-and-white husky mix named Moui), pet hamsters, a turtle, and some birds. Between playing with the neighborhood kids, Isa and I took art classes, went to Indian Princesses, Girl Scouts, and YMCA day camp, where we blended in among our healthy peers. Ryuta was active in Boy Scouts, flag football, mountain biking, junior lifeguarding in the summer, and eventually surfing. Our weekend family outings always included hiking in the local mountains.

Every Saturday morning, while Mama went to her own art class, Dad took Ryuta, Isa, and me to Japanese school. Getting ready was always an ordeal, more because of my brother's protests than our long morning therapies. He hated going to school on Saturday mornings and would make every excuse not to go: "I lost my Japanese book"; or "I'm watching a good show" (usually a Super Friends rerun); or at worst, curl up under his blankets in bed and shout, "I don't wanna go!" Dad insisted it was important that we learn our mother's tongue as we prepared for school. He hissed at my brother's protesting and raised his voice until Ryuta, pouting, reluctantly headed toward the car. I envied Ryuta for his lack of concern about whether Mama or Dad would get mad at him. He said anything he wanted to them, while I always wanted to please my parents.

The Japanese classes we attended were filled with dozens of half-Japanese children, many of whom, like us, couldn't quite fit in with their pure-Japanese peers at the school. The teacher flipped flashcards of cartoon images as we memorized vocabulary words like *rosoku* (candle), *saru* (monkey), *kirin* (giraffe), or *reizoko* (refrigerator). We learned basic conversation and how to write Japanese characters, or *kanji*. I never took Japanese school seriously, rarely studied, and never opened my book until the following Saturday morning.

Our best Japanese teachers were our friends Akemi and Naomi, two outgoing neighborhood girls a few years younger than Isa and me. Mama befriended their mother, Akie, who only spoke Japanese. While they gabbed and chuckled over tea, the four of us would roller-skate, play with our pets, or gather in our tree house. We scrambled effortlessly up to the little house that Dad had constructed in our towering eucalyptus tree, finding solace there. The leaves rustled in the wind as we made up adventures of our childhood heroes like Pippi Longstocking, Laura Ingalls, and the Bionic Woman. Sunlight seeped through the canopy, forming sparkling shadows on our faces.

During one playdate, Akemi and Naomi sat on our bedroom floor while we played doctor. I pulled out a real syringe, which Isa and I used to draw up antibiotics for inhalation from small vials. I pretended to draw blood, carefully removing the syringe cap and pushing the needle into the soft fur of my teddy bear. We played for hours, poking our teddy bears as if they were voodoo dolls, pretending to tie tourniquets around their paws, and wiping their fur with cotton swabs soaked in alcohol, just like in the real hospital. We placed nebulizer masks on the teddy bears' faces to help them breathe and patted their chests like our own chest percussion. Finally, Mama walked in and saw us playing with open needles. She screamed at us in Japanese, horrified that we were using our medical equipment for play, and confiscated our needles.

Mama enrolled us in gymnastics class with Akemi and Naomi. Their flexible limbs and short stature made them skilled tumblers. Isa and I struggled to keep up, and every tough routine would make us cough. Akemi or Naomi would approach us and ask if we were okay while patting our backs gently.

Mama told us that other parents would often tell her not to bring her sick daughters to practice. She had to explain that we had a chronic illness and that it was not contagious. Some people reacted sympathetically, while others were unmoved or unconvinced. Mama rarely told people that we had cystic fibrosis because most people didn't know what that was and the complicated word just scared them. I think she also hated having to explain our situation to complete strangers, and I was always embarrassed when she did.

After gymnastics, we usually went over to Akemi and Naomi's house for *oyatsu,* or snacks. Akie always prepared the most expensive and delicate Japanese pastries for us. Often we would spend the night at Akemi and Naomi's house. It was an ordeal for Mama to pack our medications and treatment machines, but the thrill of spending the night with our best friends made it worthwhile for us. As Mama departed, a long apologetic exchange with Akie ensued about the imposition of taking care of us for one night. Akie graciously helped us with our treatments, clapping our backs following Mama's earlier instructions. When she percussed me, her gentle hands were devoid of the slapping of my mother's touch, but her pats were timid. Maybe she was afraid of hurting me.

"Am I doing *pan-paka-pan* the right way?" Akie asked. She had used the word Mama made up for our therapy, a word that mimicked the sound of our chest percussion. I answered in Japanese that she was doing a good job, even though she was actually hitting me on the spine. I swallowed the discomfort.

I glanced at Naomi and Akemi across the room as they danced to a record of *Annie,* the musical. Like many little girls growing up in the seventies and early eighties, we were obsessed with *Annie.* The four of us had written an original script adapted from the musical. I always played Miss Hannigan, the overbearing and often cruel head of the orphanage, because of my strong, bossy personality. Akemi would play Annie, while Naomi and Isa played the younger orphans, Molly and Pepper.

Akemi and Naomi epitomized health. I watched as they danced; they had such strong muscles and energetic movements. I wished I could dance like them. Isa watched them, too, as she sat inhaling through her nebulizer. Behind her green mask she joined Akemi and Naomi as they sang "The sun'll come out, / Tomorrow, / Bet your bottom dollar / That tomorrow /

There'll be sun." At the time, we could not fully appreciate how much hope that song gave us for our own tomorrows.

It was a warm June afternoon in 1979, and the Southern California sun shone in a cloudless blue sky. Dad had just picked Isa and me up from swim team. My hair was still wet, and my lungs felt clear. Isa, Ryuta, and I were riding in the backseat of our Plymouth Volare, watching the others cars speed past us along Sunset Boulevard.

Ryuta grew restless. He grabbed my cheek and with his fat finger pushed against the scar below my nose, a reminder of a bad fall from my bunk bed years earlier.

"Scar face!" He squealed. "You are so ugly. Ah-ha! You look like Medusa! I better not look at you or I'll turn to stone!" He pulled my hair and held his arms above his face to shield his eyes from the view. I yelled for him to stop, but my pleas just fueled Ryuta's amusement.

Isa laughed, glad she was being spared. Just then, Ryuta let go of me and grabbed her arms, pulling the sleeves of her rainbow-striped sweater. He giggled as he tugged them and then tied them into a tight knot. Isa flailed her frail arms, but he was too strong. "Let go! Quit!" she yelled. "Daadddd! Make him stop!" Now only an orangutan could fit into her favorite sweater.

Dad looked in the rearview mirror. "Ryu-chan! It's enough, now!"

Ryuta stopped momentarily, but within minutes he had quietly resumed his harassment, this time pinching my cheeks. His backseat torture sessions were routine, and I dreaded these car rides.

The car swerved through narrow, winding streets, passing Dead Man's Curve and the Palisades Country Club and heading toward the UCLA campus. It was the annual Father's Day Father and Son Faculty Baseball Game, and Mama had insisted that Dad attend with Ryuta. Dad had absolutely no interest in sports, but Mama wanted to make sure Ryuta wasn't feeling left out.

That day, Mama joined her Japanese friends for an art lesson in Little Tokyo. So Isa and I joined Dad and Ryuta, designated cheerleaders for Dad's first-ever baseball game.

But first, there would be a pit stop. As we drove along the sycamore-lined streets of the campus, Dad suddenly swerved to the side of the road. We all looked up, startled, as he unbuckled his seatbelt, flung his door open, and sprang to the curb. A large oak desk rested on the curb, next to two full trash bins.

Dad examined the old desk, tenderly caressing its smooth surface. He commented on what a waste it was to throw such a magnificent piece of furniture away.

Neither Dad nor Mama could shed their wartime habit of hoarding. Our overflowing closets and garage could hardly be trespassed. Looking for an umbrella on a rainy day involved hunting through piles of Dad's old hiking boots, with their worn, wrinkled leather that reeked of mildew and mothballs. To him, there was nothing wrong with saving old things. He often complained that the problem with Americans was that they just consumed and threw everything away.

He turned around and faced three pairs of eyes staring at him blankly. *"Masch* out, *kinder."* We got out of the car as he opened the back and pulled down the seat. He asked Ryuta to help him lift the desk.

I remarked that we were going to be late to the game, but Dad ignored me as he lifted the front of the desk into the back of the station wagon.

Ryuta looked around and muttered, "I hope no one sees us." Dad countered his embarrassment by showing off with an American proverb: "Finders keepers, losers weepers."

Dad lifted the bulky desk as Ryuta struggled with the weight of a corner. Isa ran up to another corner and tried to help, and I joined her. With all of us pushing and pulling while Dad barked orders, we finally slid the desk into the back. Dad tied down the hatch with a rope, and the four of us crammed into the front seat. We inhaled the stench of exhaust as Dad drove off to the game.

We arrived just as the game was starting. Dad shook hands with a few colleagues, people I didn't recognize. This was the first time he had taken us to an event at his work, and some of the faculty seemed surprised to discover that Professor Stenzel even had children. Twenty pairs of fathers and sons stood before what seemed to be an umpire, who had just finished dividing the participants into teams. The snack and drink tables had been ransacked.

Dad motioned to us to sit on the bleachers with the girls. One girl, a little older than me, sat down beside us. She pointed to Dad and asked if he was my father. I nodded.

She examined my tall, sinewy father with his thin features and sandy brown hair. She turned back to me and asked if I was adopted. I said no. Then I had a moment of doubt: *Was I?*

She said I didn't look like my dad so I told her my mom was Japanese. She paused and then asked if I ate *sushi* and liked Hello Kitty. I smiled and nodded.

We were interrupted when the loudspeaker boomed. A voice welcomed everybody to the sixteenth annual Father's Day Father and Son Faculty Baseball Game. The national anthem blared from the loudspeaker, and the crowd rose in unison. Hats were removed, hands placed on hearts, heads tilted toward the sky. In a buzz, the words of the American anthem began. *O say, can you see, by the dawn's early light . . .*

I stopped there; I could go no further. I didn't know the words. I looked over at Dad and Ryuta. Their lips, too, were unmoving. The crowd sang with determination, and we stood there, silent.

When the game began, Dad was up. He grabbed the bat and positioned himself at home plate, ready for the pitch. I had never seen him play baseball. In fact, I wondered how he even knew how to play. He had never watched sports on TV or even been to a baseball game. Dad viewed sport as exercise, not entertainment.

The pitch was cast, and Dad swung the bat with vigor. *Whack!*

Isa and I stood up, cheering. We saw Ryuta jumping up, clapping. As the ball flew into the field, Dad dropped the bat and ran as fast as his hiking legs could go. Fueled by a jolt of adrenaline, he headed for third base.

I gasped. There was laughter from the crowd.

I heard voices in the crowd say, "I'll be darned. He's going the wrong way," and then, "I can't believe Professor Stenzel doesn't know how to play the game."

The girl sitting next to me rolled in her seat, snickering. I glared at her.

Dad made it to third base with a look of satisfaction. Then he looked at the crowd and his features sank as he realized his mistake. His legs dashed away from the base and then back toward it again, unsettled, until he took off again, running across the field, through the pitcher's mound, toward first base. The ball followed him, thrown from an outfielder to the first baseman, who struck Dad's back with his mitt.

"Ooutt!!" the umpire screamed. Dad's pace slowed. His hair hung over his eyes as he lowered his face in disappointment, embarrassment, or both.

When Dad returned to the bench, Ryuta kicked up dust with his feet and groaned, "Gawd, Dad! If you didn't know how to play, why didn't you just say so?"

We left the game later that afternoon, dejected. Dad and Ryuta's team had lost. In the car, there was silence. Ryuta sulked, looking out the window, not even interested in teasing us. I was embarrassed for Dad and for Ryuta. Our family seemed totally un-American, and all of the UCLA faculty knew it. The Stenzels were from a very different world.

"Mama, why do I have to wear this?"

Mama tugged hard on my *obi*, a silk belt, so that it was snug around my waist, holding shut the *kimono* that she had sewn just weeks ago. The floral polyester fabric was smooth against my bronze skin. I began to itch as my eczema flared, reacting to the combination of polyester with my salty perspiration.

Mama explained that Isa-chan was wearing the same and that we'd look cute together. She began working on my hair, affixing a gaudy ornament to my head: a large ribbon piece with fake miniature flowers and metallic chimes dangling from it; the chimes bounced, jingled, and threw back reflections with each move I made. It was a cross between something hung on the rearview mirror of a car and a pet's toy. My hairpiece was blue, and Isa's was pink.

We were dressing for our eighth birthday party. Mama beamed with pride as her sewing artistry came alive. Standing side by side, Isa and I stared at our reflections in the large mirror that covered an entire wall of my parents' bedroom. Our dark hair was limp under the hair ornaments, our almond-shaped eyes brown and timid, our noses small and rounded. We were identical, absolutely identical, except for the scar under my nose from my bunk bed accident. I frowned in the mirror, watching as my scar buckled under my nose. I hated that difference between us. I grabbed Isa's hand. We intertwined our fingers and examined our hands closely, as we often did, giggling at our likeness. We couldn't even tell whose fingers were whose. Our play was disrupted by Mama's voice.

Mama squealed with delight and told us how wonderful we looked. She ordered us to put on special socks sent from Japan with our new *geta*. *Geta* are wooden shoes that are raised by two wooden bars perpendicular to the sole of the shoe. When I slipped mine on, my toes ached as the velvet strap dug into the space between them. I wobbled about unsteadily, trying not to slip on the hardwood floor of our hallway. The shoes made a clamoring noise as I walked, like sticks hitting each other. I could only take small steps, as the *kimono* wrapped tightly around my waist and fell straight down my legs. I felt funny in this peculiar costume but was pleased that it made us unique on our special day. Clearly, we'd be the only ones dressed up in these exotic outfits.

My mother's shrill voice rang out again, calling for Dad to look at us. After a few moments, Dad emerged from the garage, where he was building a solar water heater. On weekends, he spent hours in the garage working on personal projects that combined his love of physics and engineering. We'd find him there, plugging away with the soldering iron, pliers, and wires.

He grinned when he saw us. His head tilted slightly, and his wide smile showed off his perfectly straight teeth. He remarked on how cute we looked in our kimonos and how we really looked like twins. He turned to my brother's room and called for Ryuta to come see us. My brother emerged from his room, where he had been playing with his Legos. "How cuuute . . . Twiiinns . . . tch . . . ," he smirked, before retreating back to the room.

An hour later, our friends started to arrive, mostly kids from school and the neighborhood.

Our next-door neighbor Sue admired our outfits, touching the *kimonos'* fabric. She asked which of us was Ana and which Isa. I told her which twin I was as Isa explained that I wore blue and she wore pink and pointed to our hair ornaments.

Then Akemi and Naomi arrived, bringing *onigiri*, or rice dumplings, and red bean cakes made by their mother.

I could see the frowns of my American friends when the Japanese food was spread out on the table. Yet my mouth watered as I admired the feast: rice balls, red bean cakes, *gyoza*, rice crackers, German pretzels, Nutella sandwiches, and, on the side, Kentucky Fried Chicken and potato chips for the American guests.

One of my American friends, Rachel, said that this was the weirdest party she had ever been to. But Sue encouraged her to try new things, and by the end of the meal, Rachel was devouring the Nutella sandwiches, chocolate smeared across her teeth as she grinned happily.

Later, we sat in a circle to open gifts. I grabbed the parcels sent from Japan and Germany first. As I tore open the package from Germany, I could smell the magical aroma of that faraway place—pine with a hint of my grandmother's cigarette smoke. Inside were *lebkuchen* (German spice cookies), *Mozartkugeln* (marzipan), and *milka* chocolate in purple wrappers. There were two Steiff stuffed animals and a German board game called Mühle. There was even a gift for Ryuta—Playmobile figurines. Even when it wasn't his birthday, our German grandmother, whom we called Oma, always remembered him.

My Japanese relatives sent hard candies shaped like cherry blossoms, origami, and stationary depicting one of Japan's most famous cartoon characters, *Doraemon*.

Later, we celebrated our birthday around a cake adorned with sixteen candles, eight for each of us.

"Don't you forget your medicine." Mama interrupted, standing over the dining table in front of my friends. She tossed two packets of enzymes by our drinks. I grabbed mine and opened the envelope, and poured the contents into my milk. I explained to my friends that I was mixing my medicine so that I could digest my food. The milk turned yellow, and its consistency became creamy like buttermilk as the enzymes fizzed. Dad jumped in, explaining to our friends that we both had a sickness, that we shared it, and that as long as we shared the sickness, we would both be strong. I looked down at the table in embarrassment when he told everyone about my disease.

At every birthday party, we shared everything—gifts, birthday cake, even medicine. It made being different from my American friends easier, knowing that Isa and I were different together.

My stomach churned, and I could feel an eruption starting to boil. The day before, I had feasted on too many pieces of Kentucky Fried Chicken, the oil and salt of the meat melting delightfully in my mouth. I knew that the packet of powdered enzymes I had mixed into my milk at my birthday party wouldn't be enough to dissolve the fat. My dysfunctional pancreas scoffed at me, calling me a fool for testing it. The pain was an intense combination of fire and numbness, stabbing and knotting. I doubled over, my muscles weakening and making my legs wobble as if they would buckle at any moment. Even after eight years of living with CF, I had not developed the willpower to avoid eating what I liked.

I yearned for Isa's presence. I fantasized that when she was nearby, my pain would magically leap to her. Sometimes my stomachache would suddenly disappear and moments later, Isa's face would scrunch up as she started to writhe in pain. I secretly cackled like an evil magician when I found relief in her discomfort.

After a long visit to the bathroom, I approached Mama. "Mama, *pon pon itai*" (my tummy hurts), I complained.

"Oh, Ana-chan, not again. Mama will prepare a hot bottle for you and you go lie down in Mama's bed." She never lost her Japanese habit of referring to herself in the third person, and it was natural to my ears.

I secretly enjoyed the privilege of hiding away in my parents' bed, avoiding the late-afternoon chores and, especially, my homework. As I lay on the cool bed made soft by our playtime jumping, I smelled Mama's flattened pillow. The scent of her pleased me, like her embrace, and I examined the strands of her hair left on the pillow.

Mama brought me the glass jar filled with hot water. She laid Dad's old bathrobe over me, and it engulfed me. Telling me to rest, she closed the door and left me in my private space of pain mixed with delight. I pulled up my shirt and placed the warm bottle on my belly. It felt good. The heat spread through my insides, soothing the pain.

I peered at the fabric of Dad's terry cloth bathrobe and saw the breaks in the pattern that we kids had inflicted over many naps and timeouts in my parents' bedroom. Choosing carefully, I pinched a loop between delicate fingers and pulled. With delight, I watched an entire row of loops disappear, leaving a barren line in its place, as the thread between my fingers lengthened. I chose another loop, my eyes straining with concentration. I pulled and pulled, breaking off the pieces of thread and balling them up in my palm. My intense focus on this destructive project made my tummy ache disappear.

Just then, I heard loud footsteps running down the hallway, and a door closing. A moment later, I heard Ryuta's shriek: "Whhheeew! Ana's done it again! Stunk up the bathroom with toxic fumes!" Just then he barged into Mama's bedroom, jumping on the bed. His navy corduroys squeaked. The jarring motions made my stomach pain return. "You reek! You reek! CF stands for cruel farts!"

"You're *ya*! Rude!" I shouted. I swung at him and pushed him away. "I can't help it!" From the kitchen I could hear Mama's faint voice, "Ryu-chan, *yamenasai*! Stop!"

"I need a gas mask! Mom! Get me a gas mask!" he continued as he jumped off the bed and darted out. Ryuta's insults left me seething.

Ryuta's presence always filled me simultaneously with dread (of his cruelty) and delight (at his attention). He coped with having sick twin sisters by being the family clown and tyrant and embarking on a lifelong habit of teasing and harassment. His wiry brown hair styled in a bowl cut encircled a mischievous smile and plotting eyes. Once, Ryuta wrestled me down, held my head against the carpet, and shoved a large kernel of corn into my nose. I screamed as it became wedged in my nostril. Dad had to use his fine tweezers to remove the kernel as I struggled to breathe through one nostril. As Dad worked on me, Ryuta's hysterical laugh rang out. Sometimes my parents tried to intervene, but ultimately they seemed to laugh off his terrorizing of Isa and me, brushing his behavior aside as innocent and brotherly. "He doesn't know how else to show his love," Mama would say.

Later that evening, after Ryuta had been riding his bike outside in the cool air, he started to wheeze. Ryuta always complained about body aches, and I thought he just wanted the attention. But his asthma attacks were real. He wheezed like an out-of-tune accordion and coughed with roaring dry explosions; it was a cough totally different from my CF cough.

"Oh, my goodness, Ryu-chan, your breathing is just awful," Mama said during dinner. Mama told him he had overdone it by playing outside. Dad complained unsympathetically that Ryuta should be stronger, that exercise was supposed to toughen him up.

Ryuta coughed as he gulped down curry rice. I stirred my *ojiya*, a mild rice-and-egg porridge that Mama made just for me to soothe my irritated gut. The eggs were half done so that the wet yolks split apart like I was painting with my spoon on a white canvas.

After dinner, Mama made Ryuta try our breathing machines. He sat down in our therapy room and placed the mask from our nebulizer over his face. He looked pathetic, his face contorted and sickly. I never looked like that. He was really milking it.

"I hope this will help your breathing," Mama said.

Isa and I stood by him. "Take deep breaths, Ryuta," Isa said, patting him on the shoulder. He coughed into the mask and pulled it away from his face.

"Leave it on! Don't mess with it," I instructed.

After a few minutes, Ryuta said, "Mom, I don't feel so good." His face turned gray as a stone.

Mama insisted that Ryuta keep the mask on, hoping it would open up his lungs. She looked worried and threatened to take him to Kaiser if his wheezing didn't subside.

Just then, Ryuta let out a loud, ferocious cough, threw his body forward, and vomited all over the therapy mask, tubing, and recliner. Isa and I jumped back as he spewed half-digested curry rice.

We shrieked and started laughing. "Ah, ha! It's just therapy! It's no big deal to us, and you can't even handle it!" I pointed at him, delighting in the revenge that he deserved for teasing me about my stomachache earlier that day. "You got the gas mask you wanted, and it made you throw up!"

Isa plugged her nose, "Man, curry vomit stinks!"

Chapter 5

Becoming Japanese

Ana

Going to Japan was the best summer of my life.

—Isa, age ten

In 1980, Dad became a tenured professor. He was invited for a sabbatical by Tokyo University, and Mama persuaded him to take the family. Dr. Robbie approved our going as long as we took along our nebulizers and monitored our health carefully. "You need to live your lives as a family," he told Mama. "Take them to Japan. Enrich their lives while they are healthy."

Isa and I were excused from school, and in March, we all arrived in the crowded city of Tokyo. We rented a large home in a suburb called Shimorenjaku. The early spring left frost on the grass in the garden of the home, and the air chilled our rosy cheeks unlike any cold we had experienced in Los Angeles. Isa and I were placed in the same second-grade classroom at the local elementary school.

Mama came with us on our first day of school. Before class started, Mama confided to our teacher that we had a health problem and that we coughed. She apologized that our coughing would disrupt the classroom but reassured our teacher that it wasn't contagious.

I watched Mama. Instead of her usual tired look, she had the charming smile and overly polite nature of the stereotypical Japanese mother. Her soprano voice remained high-pitched as she spoke her native language.

The teacher bowed politely, insisting that she would take good care of us and for Mama not to worry. After Mama left, our teacher announced to the class that we were new students from America, and she introduced us by our Japanese names, Mariko (me) and Yuriko (Isa) Stenzel.

I stood before the crowd of restless second graders. They all looked alike—dark black hair, narrow eyes; even their backpacks were the same. Our chestnut hair stood out in a sea of darkness. I could feel their steady gaze. A few smiled, but most stared at us with curiosity.

My teacher instructed me to sit next to a kid named Morita-san. In Japan, even children were referred to by their last names, followed by "san," a formal suffix. Now Isa and I even had the same name. As I sat down, Morita-san turned to me and snapped, "Gaijin." I didn't know what that meant.

Later that day, there was an assembly during recess. The principal, dressed in a dark business suit and white gloves, stood on a podium in the school courtyard and made an announcement that I couldn't understand. As he spoke, the children lined up like dominos and began to march in a circle. Isa and I mindlessly merged into the flow of traffic. Pressed against Isa in the crowd, I whispered to her, asking what we were doing. I felt like a silly soldier. She shrugged. We held hands and kept marching.

After the marching rally was over, we were free to roam the schoolyard. Ryuta's large build and light brown hair caught my eye in the distance. He was kicking a ball among a group of older boys. At the end of the schoolyard was a pool, a garden of vegetables and sunflowers, and a line of bicycles. As Isa and I explored, a crowd of Japanese boys walked toward us.

"Gaijin! Gaijin!" one of them taunted. There was that word again.

Our classroom was located on the second floor, overlooking the yard where we marched. The children in the class were divided into small teams. Every lunchtime one team was in charge of going to the cafeteria and bringing back a large silver cart loaded with scrumptious foods—enough, it seemed to us, for a feast. These children decked themselves out in white gowns, gloves, and shower caps and proceeded to serve all the other kids systematically. There was no complaining; this was just how it was done. Once a week, after school, the team on duty would stay late to move all the furniture to one side of the room. Then, after dipping rags in soapy water, the children lined up along the end of the room. Each child got down on his or her knees in front of a row of floor tiles. The chanting began when the teacher said "Isse, no, se!" (Ready, set, go!). In unison, all of us kids would start counting, "Ichi, ni, san, shi..." counting up to ten as we scrubbed hard on one tile. After we reached ten, we backed up all together and continued the scrubbing. I had never thought cleaning could be fun, but with this routine and teamwork, no one complained. Even at eight, I knew this could never happen in America.

After school, as Mama was preparing dinner, I asked her what the word "*gaijin*" meant.

She looked up, still holding the knife as she sliced green onions. I could hear the fish sizzle in the pan. "It means foreigner. Why do you ask?"

"Kids at school called me that. I didn't know that word."

"Well, don't you let it bother you. They are just teasing you because you are different. There is a Japanese proverb that says, 'The nail that sticks out will be hammered down.' Japanese don't like anyone who is different."

I told Mama about the cleaning we had to do after school.

Mama insisted that cleaning was not good for us, that the dust would bother our lungs. She wanted to talk to our teacher and have us excused from the cleaning practice. Her back was turned away from me as she put the washed rice in the rice cooker.

I pleaded with her not to, explaining that it wasn't that dusty and that it had been fun. I didn't want anyone to know about my sickness. I dreaded being that nail that would be hammered down.

Foreigner. So that's what *gaijin* meant. It sounded like *ninjin,* which I had learned in Japanese school in America. *Ninjin* meant "carrot."

A few days later was "Health Day." We had to strip down to our underwear in the classroom, among boys and girls, and march downstairs, cold and exposed, toward the nurse's office, where we would each have an X-ray and an EKG. I retreated in embarrassment as kids stared and asked about the vicious scar on my belly; I had never let any of my friends back home see my scar.

As we lined up, the naughty boys pulled their underpants down and danced naked in front of us shrieking girls. Morita-san came up to me in his underwear, decorated with robot cartoons. He shouted, "*Gaijin! Gaijin!*" I grabbed his arm and shouted in his face, "*Ninjin! Ninjin!*" as I socked him on the cheek.

He froze. His jaw dropped, his face wrinkled, and he quickly walked away.

Despite Morita-san's taunting, Isa and I made friends with other classmates. After school, Ryuta, Isa, and I would walk to *Inokashirakoen,* a nearby park, to meet our new friends. We'd wander there for hours, hunting for crawfish in the streams and beetles in the trees. In the spring months, we bought *osembei* (rice crackers), and ate them under a canopy of cherry blossoms as petals fell like snow around us. Other days, Isa, Ryuta, and I would take a paddleboat out on the lake, feeding the *koi* in the water and watching the tree snakes squirm. The park, like most of Japan, was a safe place for children; only the setting sun and the evening cries of vendors on bicycles calling out, "Tofu! Yams! For sale!" signaled that it was time to head home for dinner.

Several months into our visit, Mama announced that she was taking us out of school for a week to see Japan. Our health was stable enough to allow us to travel. In fact, we visited doctors more for Ryuta's asthma than for our CF. It was time to explore Mama's country.

Within a few days, our family was hiking on the hillsides of Mount Fuji with Obachan, my uncles, and my cousins. Lava gravel crunched under my feet as I hiked up the foggy mountainside. In the distance, I saw a patch of white snow against the black lava. Although it was July, the cool mountain air raised goose bumps on my skin.

Mama and Obachan straggled behind the rest of us. Even at sixty-four, Obachan marched forward on the path, her back curved as she leaned slightly forward on a wooden walking stick. We stopped and waited for them to catch up. Obachan smiled when she reached us, her gold tooth gleaming at me, her gray curls moist against her forehead.

Later, our entire family drove to a nearby military cemetery, where my grandfather was buried. The cemetery was compact with large granite gravestones lined up side by side like dominos. *Kanji* characters decorated the tombstones. Some had Buddhist statues around them. We walked around the cemetery, solemn. At last, Obachan pointed out our grandfather's, Ojisan's, grave.

She crouched down, groaning at the pain from her stiff legs, and began to remove the leaves that covered the tombstone. The gray stone was inscribed with *kanji* characters of his name, Sukehisa Arima. My uncle brought a bucket of water and began to wash the gravesite. When it was cleared of dirt and leaves, Obachan laid down a bottle of *sake*, an orange, and a candle.

After the visit to Mount Fuji, we continued south on the *Shinkansen* (bullet train) to the ancient capitals of Kyoto and Nara, where we toured old temples among free-roaming deer. In Kyoto, a crowd of giggling schoolgirls dressed in blue-and-white uniforms and carrying Hello Kitty notebooks surrounded Dad. Some clicked away with their cameras, shouting in their pitiful accents, "American! American!" Several held out their notebooks, asking Dad for his autograph. Dad kindly signed their books, smiling at all the attention.

During our six-month stay in Japan, Mama and Dad frequently took us out of school to enjoy the countryside. We soaked in the scalding waters of

Izu-kogen, Japan's most famous hot springs, where we stayed in a quaint Japanese inn that served hermit crab and marinated grasshoppers for dinner. We even visited Hiroshima and were horrified by the atomic bomb museum and its graphic images of death and destruction.

Just before we returned to America, Mama organized a family reunion, mainly so we could meet our grandfather's side of the family. For Mama, the rare chance to see the Arimas brought back the only connection she still had with her father.

The day before the big event, Mama spent hours in the kitchen. She scurried around, a bit frantic, feeling the pressure to impress her relatives with an extraordinary Japanese banquet. A perfectionist by nature, she was determined that everything be just right.

When the day came, relatives arrived in droves, and the house was filled with complicated Japanese words I struggled to understand. Mama seemed happy, laughing with ease among those who were strangers to us.

Mama's relatives talked in Japanese about how prestigious it was that Dad was a distinguished professor who could provide our family with the chance to live in Japan. They hovered around Dad, who was standing at Mama's side, smiling politely while trying to understand the conversation. Mama covered her mouth as she smiled bashfully. To her relatives, Mama was the symbol of a dutiful wife, a *soukou no tsuma*, which translates to "a wife who makes pickles for her husband."

The faces of dinner guests lit up when they saw the six-course meal of ginger pork, *sushi, nabe* soup, noodle salad, *chirashi* rice, and *dango* cakes that Mama had prepared. The table was adorned with over thirty small matching Japanese dishes, all artistically displayed on woven placemats next to the finest chopsticks and their holders. *Sake* was poured, and everyone had a festive time. When all was done, Mama beamed with pride, her face red as a beet from too much *sake*. After the last guest departed, she quickly retreated upstairs, where she passed out from exhaustion.

We returned to America in the late summer, in time to start third grade. Some things had changed while we were away; others had not. Our house was the same. Akemi and Naomi still came over to play. Dad talked about a Californian named Ronald Reagan who was running for president. We took an interest in new pets because of the *kabutomushi* (large beetles) and water turtles that Ryuta had smuggled home in his pockets from Japan.

But we were different. We had become culturally Japanese.

When we returned from Japan, Mama had changed too. For her, leaving Japan symbolized a final good-bye to her homeland. Being in Japan had been good for her. She felt a strong sense of nostalgia for the Japan she missed. Things were familiar, and she was comfortable. But staying in Japan was out of the question—the healthcare system would not be good for us, and life would be difficult for Dad. America was her home now. She wanted to be more than a homemaker and began to explore a new purpose for the next phase of her life.

After a few months back in Pacific Palisades, Mama announced that she wanted to become a respiratory therapist. Although we had just enjoyed several healthy years, our lung disease was beginning to rear its ugly head. We coughed regularly; our lungs were congested; and we had difficulty gaining weight. She chose to study respiratory therapy so she could learn more about managing our disease. She also wanted more financial independence and self-sufficiency. Studying in English was tremendously challenging, but her determination overcame her limitations.

One day during her respiratory care class, a guest speaker spoke of the advances in cardiopulmonary transplantation. It was 1983, and the first lung lobe transplant had been performed by Dr. Joel Cooper at Toronto General Hospital, following the first heart-lung transplant, which had been performed in 1981 by Dr. Bruce Reitz at Stanford Hospital. The speaker indicated that CF patients could be excellent candidates for lung transplantation. It was the first time my mother had ever heard about lung transplants, and she eagerly broached the subject to Dr. Robbie.

She asked him if we could benefit from such a surgery. Dr. Robbie said he could sense Mama's eagerness. He had seen it many times before. But then he explained that the science of lung transplantation was in its infancy and that the surgery was extremely experimental. There were countless risks. He said that in order for this to be an option for us, Mama and Dad had to do their best to keep us as healthy as possible until there were more improvements in the success rates. He warned, "Getting a transplant is often like trading one disease for another."

Mama's spirits sank, her immediate hopes dashed; she understood, but she was not prepared to give up. She replied, "I still hope that someday my daughters will be saved by lung transplants."

During our nebulizer treatments, Mama would shout at us, "Take deep breaths!" When she did our chest percussion, she was passionate about the new techniques she had learned in school. She would say, "Now blow out as much air as you can! Cough! Cough! Don't you hold in your cough! You must clear your lungs constantly because bacteria multiply every twenty minutes!"

Isa and I cooperated, eager to please.

"And squeeze *aaalllll* the air out until you are all empty!" Mama pushed her hands against our chests, shaking them with vibrations. Immediately, we coughed violently and brought up mouthfuls of mucus.

"*Yokatta!*" She clapped her hands, laughing, thrilled that her new techniques worked so well to clear our lungs. She explained that this new airway clearance technique was called forced expiratory breathing.

We were less than comfortable with this self-induced coughing fit, but with practice we each learned how to squeeze our own lungs like sponges, forcing the thick mucus to pour out of our large airways. This new technique of aggressive coughing fit my parents' mantra, "The harder it is, the better it is for you." The temporary discomfort was followed by longer periods of feeling clear and open. In the long run, these violent coughing methods saved our lives.

After Mama graduated from respiratory therapy school, she went to work for Santa Monica Hospital. Our sweet mother evolved into an overwhelmed, stressed-out, demanding woman who insisted that we assume the burden of household chores. If we protested, she would scowl, and she would raise her voice in crescendo, "*Ikemasen!*" (Don't do that!)

She was particularly strict with Isa and me. We had to mop, vacuum, clean our rooms, do laundry, and cook meals. We sulked when she'd ask us to do something, saying, "Yes, Miss Hannigan," under our breath and humming, "It's the Hard Knock Life," the orphan work song from *Annie.*

Mama forced us to do chores even if we felt sick. Her demands were relentless: "Peel the potatoes while you are sitting and doing your nebulizers. Then put the chicken in the oven, set the timer, and take a nap for one hour. After your nap I want you to vacuum."

Mama's work and family responsibilities gradually consumed her. One evening, she entered the front door after working all day. I looked up from the piano, where I was practicing for my recital. She looked awful. Her hair was messy, and I noticed a thread of gray above her forehead. Her face was red and her eyes sunken in with dark circles below them. Without a word, she removed her white coat and tossed it on the sofa. She kicked off her shoes and headed for her bedroom.

I greeted her but she walked past me. "Mama is going to sleep. You girls take care of dinner, okay?"

I asked her what there was to cook, and she snapped, "You figure it out. I cannot do everything here." She slammed her bedroom door.

I got up from the piano and headed for the kitchen. Searching the cabinets, I found a box of Hamburger Helper.

Isa walked into the kitchen. I told her that Mama was in a bad mood and was making us cook. Confidently, Isa stated that she would make salad and I should make the main course. It would be a team effort. Ryuta and Dad were at a Scout meeting, so we only needed to cook for ourselves.

Within an hour, dinner was ready. The aroma of ground beef permeated the kitchen.

I walked toward Mama's bedroom and opened her door. I could see the mound that made up her body under the covers in the semidarkness. She always slept with the covers over her head, which perplexed me because it seemed so stuffy.

I stood over her bed, watching her chest move up and down. In the dim light I could see *The Marriage Handbook* on her bedside table.

"Mama," I said, gently pushing on her body. "Dinner time. Get up."

She stirred and then cried out for help: "*Tatsukete!*" It startled me. I thought she was dreaming.

I sat on the bed, leaning against her.

"Mama, are you okay? Dinner's ready. Can you get up?"

Mama lifted the covers from her head. Her eyes were open.

"Ana-chan, it is too much . . . I do not want dinner." She pushed me away. "Go on. Mama is going to die now."

Her words scared me.

"No, Mama, don't say that. We need you. Why do you say that?"

"Mama just wants to be alone. Never mind. I am so tired. Leave me alone." She turned on her side and exhaled. "The worst mistake I ever made in my life was marrying your father and coming to America."

Her words stung. I wanted to cry, to help her, to make her happier. But I just felt in the way and silently tiptoed out of the room. What about therapy? We'd have to wait until Dad got home, and it would be a late night.

It was summertime when Mama's spirits began to lift, probably because Obachan was coming to visit. Ever since that first phone call Mama had made to her mother after our diagnosis, Obachan visited Los Angeles every summer.

When Obachan arrived, I embraced her, and nostalgia for Japan flooded my mind as I inhaled her familiar scent. Obachan's short peppered hair curled properly. Her narrow eyes sparkled. Her cheeks drooped but were silky to the touch, like *mochi* rice cake.

She looked into my eyes and said in Japanese how happy she was to see me again. I smiled up at her. Her wrinkled hands stroked my hair. She stopped suddenly, her hand grasping the back of my head. "What's this?" She held firmly to a knot in my hair that had formed months ago. Even my teacher at school had noticed it and questioned Mama about it. I explained to Obachan that it was a knot that I couldn't get out.

Obachan scolded Mama, asking her what kind of mother she was to have children with uncombed hair. Mama glared at her. "Mama is too busy working to notice such things."

The next day, Obachan sat with me for over an hour, tugging and pulling through the bundled mess until the comb slid cleanly through my long hair. As she tugged, she muttered about what a shame it was to be neglected like this.

Later that week, while Mama was working, Obachan, Isa, and I sat around the floor in our bedroom folding laundry. We struggled to speak to her in our broken Japanese. I was eager to learn about her past so I asked her why she had never remarried.

She giggled. "Because no one ever asked me."

I told her how Mama said she was so beautiful and such a successful businesswoman. Obachan smiled while her eyes focused on a plaid shirt of Dad's that she was folding. She explained that after the war, some widows gave their children up for adoption, and some even killed their own children, so they would be eligible to remarry. In traditional Japan, no man would ever marry a woman with another man's children. But to Obachan, her children were her world. She had been determined to raise them herself. It was her responsibility, and she worked hard to bring them up. She explained that our maternal great-grandfather died young of an ear infection and our paternal great-grandfather died young of syphilis. So Arima and Honda women were used to raising children alone.

Suddenly, Obachan held her wrinkled hand over her mouth, throwing her head back with her sweet 'A-he he he' laugh. "I raised four children alone and I worked in the inn . . . and none of them ever had a knot in their hair!"

I stretched out my legs. I was not used to sitting on the floor, Japanese-style, for hours. She noticed my socks and remarked how dirty they were. She sighed and muttered something about how our mother wasn't treating her children well and that she would have to buy us new socks.

The effort required to communicate only strengthened our resolve to share the details of our lives with her: our school, friends, and travel adventures. Even when we struggled with translations, she'd say, "I don't understand what you mean!" and we would all laugh at our own language barriers. During these moments of conversation, I felt connected with my grandmother. She was the tie to our culture and our past, and her love for us shone in each affectionate smile.

Chapter 6

Our German Roots

Ana

Japanese food. Japanese friends. Japanese school. Dad must have felt our connection to our German heritage was lacking because when I was ten he decided to take Isa and me to Germany to visit our grandfather, Opa, and our grandmother, Oma, for the first time. Dad had once tried to get us to learn German, but we quickly lost interest, mainly because the German relatives spoke such excellent English.

Isa and I stayed with Oma and Opa for two weeks while Dad attended a European physics conference. Our grandparents lived in a small loft in Bremen on Heinrich-Hertz-Strasse, where Dad and his brother, our Uncle Jürgen, had spent their teenage years.

Oma and Opa were strangers to me. Georg Stenzel, our Opa, now seventy-five, had survived a stroke and walked slowly, shuffling his feet and panting heavily while climbing the stairs to his loft. During the day, he wore a neck brace to keep his droopy head upright. He smelled of fresh Nivea cream in the mornings, faint cigarette smoke and Schnapps by the afternoon. Opa still spoke English well, even though five decades had passed since he had lived in London in the 1930s. He spoke slowly and with a slur because his left side was partially paralyzed. During our first meal together I studied his face in disbelief. We were related? He had a wide round forehead and bleached, wispy hair. Opa's blue eyes met my dark oriental ones, and his needle-tip pupils focused on me. After a moment, he bugged out his eyes, and we both laughed.

Ada Stenzel, our Oma, was a lively sixty-six-year-old. Isa and I had inherited her hair: dark brown that didn't gray, noodle-straight, thin and limp, which she always wore in a bun. There was a lot of her to hug, and she waddled because of her weight. She smoked heavily and had breathing difficulties of her own. Once during our visit she laughed so hard she began to cough, wheezing and hissing like a hot kettle. She settled down, holding her chest, and said, "Now I know what you girls go through." But she was full of energy, on a mission to care for her ailing husband of nearly fifty years. She was the perfect grandmother to her young guests from America.

Oma was proficient in English and rather verbose; the more excited she became, the faster she spoke. She was a jokester at heart. Once she threw a glass cup from the kitchen across the living room, yelling, "Watch out!" We winced, waiting for the glass to shatter. Instead, it landed and bounced; it was special nonbreakable glass. Oma chuckled from the kitchen.

Mama had written a long letter to Oma about CF, with detailed instructions to feed us high-calorie foods and to make sure we took our medicines and got exercise, and she had included the phone number of a cystic fibrosis specialist in Hamburg.

On the day of our arrival, I plugged in our ultrasonic nebulizer machine, connected to an electricity converter that Dad had built. The nebulizer cup vibrated, but no mist flowed through the tubing.

I jiggled the machine and pulled the cup from its base. Below the cup, we could see that the sensitive crystal, the one that created the ultrasonic wave to make the salty mist, had cracked into a dozen pieces. The 220-volt current had blown it. "Too bad," Isa said, lying back on the couch. "Can't do therapy!"

I was overjoyed. The freedom was tantalizing. For the next two weeks, we skipped our breathing treatments. This precious respite was the one and only time we ever missed our treatments, and we didn't even get sick.

When Dad called later that week to check on us, he insisted we still had to do our chest percussion. Still, not using the machine shortened our therapies considerably.

After dinner, in the corner of the room, Isa laid on a pile of pillows on the red sofa that reclined. I sat next to her, and like Mama and Dad had taught us, I smoothed out her pink Izod shirt and began to pound her back. Isa coughed and spit out into tissue. Opa sat across the room reading an issue of *Der Spiegel*. Oma stepped out onto the balcony that was sheltered from the warm afternoon rain. She turned her back to us and fiddled with her fingers. Within seconds, I could see a ribbon of smoke rising over her head.

We glared at our grandmother. Dad said she had been smoking for forty

years and that she couldn't help it, but I still felt resentful. Our Japanese relatives were also smokers. And we were the ones with lung disease!

Just then the phone rang. Oma turned quickly and put out her cigarette,
slid open the glass door, and ran to the phone.

"Hallo? Hier ist Frau Stenzel."

In a few moments, she was rambling in German in her animated way.
She seemed to be consoling the person on the other end. Then she hung up
the phone.

It was Mrs. Schilling, Oma's neighbor from the loft next door. She was
worried about the hitting and choking sounds she could hear and wanted
to know if everything was okay. Oma explained everything to Mrs. Schilling. "Ah, you girls have to go through so much, such discipline," Oma said
to us, as she nodded her head.

I apologized to Oma for making so much noise and embarrassing her,
wishing that we could skip our chest percussion, too.

Oma then suggested a practical solution—music. She switched on an old
radio and fiddled with the dial until rock and roll blared. She turned up the
volume. It was the Go-Go's "We Got the Beat."

"Hey, I know this song!" I stated as I began to hum along and pound Isa's
back to the rhythm of the music. Soon the music drowned out the sound
of therapy.

Time passed slowly during our visit. A warm sticky German summer rain
kept us indoors on most days. One afternoon, Opa and Oma took Isa and
me upstairs to the attic and, with only the weak sunlight coming through
a small square window, meticulously poured over old photographs. It was
all very fascinating to us, even as kids, to know we were related to these
people—historic, attractive, and white.

Oma stroked a dusty black-and-white photo of a middle-aged man with
dark eyes and said that the man in the photo was her father, Max Koenig,
who had been killed on the first day of World War I, just days before she
was born. Oma's mother was so saddened that she didn't care about her
newborn daughter's name. She chose the first girl's name in the baby book,
Ada. Oma's eyes looked sad. There was so much death back then; it was
just a part of life. I felt so lucky that none of my immediate family had died.

Oma and Opa showed us pictures from their wedding. They were married on June 27, just days before the 1936 Berlin Olympics, in Breslau, Germany. Dad was born there, too, but after the war, it became part of Poland.

I pulled out a photo of a handsome soldier bundled up in a heavy coat
and fur cap. On the arm of his coat was a swastika. With his slurred speech,
Opa talked about his military service in Norway and nights spent watching for the British, sometimes standing in snow up to his waist and at tem-

peratures down to fifty below zero. He reminisced about the beauty of the northern lights in the endless Arctic darkness. We saw pictures of Dad and his brother, Jürgen, as kids, wearing lederhosen. Dad's stringy hair was parted on the side in the same style he still wore many decades later. His expression seemed distant and serious. Opa told us how, when he came home from the French prisoner-of-war camp in 1948, Dad didn't know who he was when he showed up at the doorstep. Opa had been drafted before Dad was born, and Dad was eight when they met for the first time.

Isa asked Opa if he was a Nazi, and I quickly nudged her for asking such a rude question. Opa told us that he had been drafted to serve his country, that he had had no choice. He talked about how the war was such a waste, with so much death and destruction for Germany. He firmly believed there was no way Germany could have won the war. We peppered him with questions, like if he had ever killed anybody, when he had been the most scared, or what he had thought about Hitler. He smiled awkwardly and told us there was no point in discussing those terrible years.

Dad hated to talk about his feelings, and Opa was the same way. As a frail old man, Opa seemed so innocent, so vulnerable. I made up my mind, right then and there, that my grandfather was a decent person, not an evil German soldier like those so often depicted in the movies. He valued life and abhorred war.

Years later, I would regret not asking him more about his youth and the war. Did Opa agree with Germany's attempt to conquer Europe? What did he think about the Holocaust? Dad always said racism as a philosophy was as accepted then as multiculturalism is now by my generation. Did Opa just accept the social values of the time, or did he question and resist them? There was so much more I wanted to know.

The stories Oma and Opa shared about the war made it seem like our lives were so easy. They must have had good genes to survive such physical hardship. If they could live through the war, I could live with CF. But if I had had to endure what they did with a disease like CF, I would have died for sure. No hospital stays, no antibiotics, no nebulizers. Isa and I would just have withered away.

The following day, Oma took us shopping in downtown Bremen. The heels of Oma's sturdy pumps made a *rat-tat-tat* clicking sound as she led us through the cobblestone alleyways and plazas of downtown Bremen at a deliberate pace. She took us to the glass-blowing shop, where we watched the artisan create animal shapes from blobs of fiery glass. We peered up at the Gothic steeples of the town's central church from the Middle Ages. We took pictures in front of the Bremen Town Musicians statue, and ate bratwurst with mustard in buns from a street vendor in the town square. Oma bought us white leather clogs so we, too, could click on the cobblestones. We visited Karstadt, a German department store, and admired its abundant selection of perfumes and chocolates.

One day, when Oma was preparing dinner, Opa took Isa and me outside to play with a ball. He shuffled slowly across the street as Isa and I scampered ahead to a grassy field. As I watched him, I muttered to Isa how slow he was. She scolded me, saying that I was being mean. But it was true; I was impatient with our slow grandfather. Everything about him was defined by his declining body: his failing hearing, his slurred speech, his struggle to move. I would hate to be so tied down by frailty.

It was a sunny day, and it felt good to run around. Soon we were playing soccer, kicking the ball back and forth. We wore new knickers that Oma had bought us and matching tops from Obachan with Japanese cartoons on them. Opa paused often to take pictures of us.

At one point, I kicked the ball poorly, and it flew across the field and rolled into a ditch. As we ran over to climb down into the ditch, Opa yelled in his thick guttural accent that he would get the ball. Suddenly, he picked up his pace to a faster hobble.

I tried to stop him by telling him I'd get the ball, since I was the one who had kicked it into the ditch. But Opa would not listen. He was already descending into the ditch, red-faced and panting, planting one shaking foot over the other to get down the ditch. He knelt down and struggled so desperately I thought he would die right then and there. I thought about how upset Oma would be if she knew what Opa was doing. From above the ditch, I yelled to Opa, asking him if he needed help. He ignored me.

He finally managed to fetch the ball and throw it back, then start his slow and painful ascent back up the slope. I was gasping myself by the time he reached the top, but I was also deeply proud of Opa's determination. He wouldn't let his weak body get in the way of his goals. Now I wanted to be like him.

Our visit with Oma and Opa ended when Dad returned from his conference. Dad took us on a train to visit our Uncle Jürgen and our aunt and cousins for the first time, near Heidelberg. Before we left, Oma had given us some toys for the long train ride, and we had embraced Opa and Oma at the train station. They smelled of coffee and cigarette smoke, and those scents imprinted themselves on my memory. Isa and I felt grateful for the time we had with our grandparents, but it was the last time we saw them together. Opa died in his sleep three years later. To this day, I wish I had known Oma and Opa better. They could've made me feel more German.

Chapter 7

The Flamingos

Isa

Cystic Fibrosis Summer Camp is the best place in the world where you meet new friends, no one stares, and you get all the food you want, plus, a t-shirt, bag and arts and crafts.

—Isa, age fourteen

Flipping through a magazine at the grocery store, Mama perked and froze, reading. She said in amazement, "*Heii . . .* There is a summer camp for children with cystic fibrosis."

Ana grabbed the magazine, and I peered over her shoulder. We were floored. We had never known more than a handful of CF patients at our hospital, and most had died. Now, we had to digest the fact that there were many more children living with CF out there, and better yet, there was a real summer camp just for us!

We sent away for information, and when we finally received the camp application, I read it over and over again. Its cover showed a girl, pale and skinny, holding a nebulizer. *Wow, that's me!* I thought. The application asked about many things I knew well—enzymes, treatment schedules, salt tablets. At eleven, I had never been to a summer camp, because it was too embarrassing to have to do therapy in front of normal kids. This would be different.

The night before camp, I was so excited I couldn't sleep. I was finally going to fit in. The next morning, families gathered in the parking lot of the Cystic Fibrosis Foundation's office in Anaheim. Ana and I eagerly boarded the camp bus, which bustled with other children with CF. We waved good-bye to Mama, Dad, and Ryuta through the open window.

"One whole week without therapy! What will we do with ourselves, Reiner?" we heard Mama joke to Dad.

"Have fun with your own kind," Ryuta hollered, waving.

Behind Ana and I sat a noisy girl. She was about our age, and for the entire bus ride she laughed and harassed her little brother and sister who sat next to her. The three of them looked chubby and totally normal. The girl wore a pair of dolphin shorts and a peach-colored sleeveless T-shirt, matching her sister's outfit. I scanned the bus. Some kids looked really emaciated. Some sucked on oxygen through tubes that ran under their noses and were connected to green tanks. Others ran up and down the aisle playing tag. Over the roar of the bus engine, I could hear thunderous coughing. It was music to my ears.

When we arrived at the camp, nestled in the mountains of San Juan Capistrano, several frazzled counselors—volunteer high school and college kids—scurried about looking for their assigned campers, nervous about whether the chest physical-therapy training they had received was adequate for the sick kids that would depend on their care. Kids dragged their dusty therapy machines and sleeping bags to their cabins. The kids with feeding tubes lugged their pumps and crates of formula, in search of strong adults who could help them carry their load.

We found our counselors: Denise, a calm, sweet, maternal woman with dense, curly, long black hair, was in stark contrast to Idel, a short, round rambunctious woman who was looking forward to a week of wild antics. We immediately trusted them, and we knew we'd be in good hands. They gathered a flock of other preteen girls and headed to our hilltop cabin. Towering oaks, juniper pines, and sycamores provided shade from the hot Southern California heat. Dust clouds flew as we dragged our heavy bags, and the prissy girls shooed away the flies that sought the moisture of their nostrils. Our cabin was rustic, with wooden bunk beds and beamed ceilings decorated with cobwebs. It smelled of summertime.

The noisy girl from the bus was in our cabin. She introduced herself as Karen as she unrolled an old blanket instead of a sleeping bag on her bunk. After we introduced ourselves, she asked if we were twins. "That's so cool! Isn't it great having a sister with CF?" As we unpacked, Karen asked why our nebulizer machine looked different from hers. She told us how she didn't have to do treatments at camp because her doctor had said she was healthy enough to skip for a week. Karen was so lucky. I remembered how we had had that pleasure in Germany.

Karen Godfrey was a stunningly beautiful auburn-haired girl whose fair skin glistened with light freckles. Her sturdy build suggested a strong character. In no time, we had met the other girls in the cabins, for whom we immediately thought up private nicknames. Katie, "The Good Girl," was another new camper, a reserved blond with meticulously feathered hair. She wore fashionable Jordache jeans and a striped neon blouse that still showed pressed lines from being ironed. Michelle, "The Model," was twelve but looked older with her perfectly polished nails, styled hair, and shiny lip gloss. She had more bottles of makeup and hair-care products than she did pills. Renee, "The Hypochondriac," was a freckled redhead, slouched and whiney with weakness from the moment we met. She looked sturdy to us and had bursts of energy when she wanted to. We named our cabin "The Flamingos," symbolically delicate, balanced, and very pink. After we unpacked, Karen became the self-appointed leader of the cabin and directed us to explore the camp. Ana and I followed dutifully.

We soon found the boys' cabins on the other side of the camp. "The Skanks" housed the predictably vulgar and energetic preteen boys who immediately became the targets of our camp pranks. The guys surrounded Ana and me, intrigued by seeing twins.

"You guys have CF?" said George, a lanky Hispanic preteen wearing a Van Halen T-shirt. "I thought Chinese people don't get CF."

"Excuse me," Ana said in a singsong rhythm, crossing her arms. "We're not Chinese."

I told him we were half-Japanese, and another guy told us we were like Sonya. We met Sonya later: a scrawny six-year-old half-Korean girl with doll-like cuteness who searched for sympathetic adults to carry her piggyback around camp. To this day, she remains the only other Asian person I have ever met with CF.

This was Karen's second year at camp, and she led us to the mess hall to meet the camp staff. These men were warm, fun-loving Bohemians who, for one week a year, became our surrogate father figures and encouraged us to have fun, experiment with our identities, and grow up confidently. Bob Crabb, the camp director, was a bald English teacher with a Cheshire-cat grin, a romantic idealist with a fondness for storytelling and Bob Dylan songs. Rocky, another balding artist, was easygoing and philosophical, a talented guitarist who loved to tickle and tease adoring kids. Mike was a mean-looking, tattoo-covered truck driver; he scared me until I discovered that he had the soft side of an angel. Thirty-year-old Bob Flanagan had spiked black hair, a pale face, and a mischievous grin, and he was the oldest person with CF we had ever met. I was mesmerized as I stared at him.

Flanagan greeted us and welcomed us to camp. He proceeded to make silly jokes about CF, like how it stands for coughing fit, clubbed fingers, constantly farting. He had the same witty humor as Ryuta. We giggled. I immediately trusted this group of men, and I felt safe with them. I felt that I could tell them anything.

That week, we played cabin competitions and games, went swimming every day, performed in a talent show, and sang around the campfire. We went on a nature walk, had a tug-of-war contest over a pool of mud, and attended a carnival. We wore outrageous and creative costumes every night for dinner that matched that year's camp theme of the "Rocking Fifties." "Ranger" Gordon, a biology teacher with a twinkle in his eyes who drove to camp in his rickety '67 Volkswagen van adorned with Grateful Dead stickers, brought his 200-pound python, Mingus, to camp, and we wide-eyed kids reached out with trembling hands to pet the smooth, muscular beast.

One day, Karen rallied us all to go on the hike that was scheduled for that afternoon. Ana said she couldn't go because she had a fever that kept spiking, but I insisted I was up to it.

The next day, while Ana and Katie rested, Karen and I marched ahead past the crowds of little kids and counselors, up the steep sandy path to a large white cross that sat on the top of the mountain. We didn't just hike, we ran. *We ran.* I coughed and panted but stayed right behind Karen. In the harsh sun, white specks of salt crystals covered our arms and foreheads.

Karen encouraged me to keep up. I didn't know what the hurry was, but we were on a mission to prove that we could run up and down the mountain faster than everyone else. It felt great to be the healthy ones in the cabin.

"So, girls, what'd ya wanna do for our skit?" asked Karen at dinner on Tuesday. Every cabin was signed up for a skit for the talent show, held on Thursday night.

"Skit?" I asked, with a plummeting gasp. "Oh, no. I can't be in a skit." Being the center of attention would be torture.

"Oh, it's not a big deal. What's there to be afraid of?" she said.

I told her I hated being in front of an audience because I'd look stupid. She told me everyone at camp was self-conscious about something, but it didn't matter since we all understood one another. In no time, Karen was coaching me to lip-sync and dance along to Cyndi Lauper's "Girls Just Wanna Have Fun." Ana took charge with Karen, telling all of us to line up and kick our legs together in one of her favorite dance moves.

As we practiced, Karen yelled to me, "That's it! Let go! Shed your shell!

Be free! Go crazy!" The more she encouraged, the more I danced. With her
help, I acted silly and stopped worrying about drawing attention to myself.

There was a dance in the middle of the week, and we spent hours anxiously wondering and plotting who would take whom to the dance. We
feathered our hair and stabilized the high puffs with a third of a can of hair-
spray. We shared clothes, applied each others' makeup, and gave fashion
tips on how to dress like Madonna or the Go-Go's.

Music was a strong component of the camp. The first evening, Bob Flanagan and the leaders of the camp went from cabin to cabin with their guitars to serenade the new campers. Rocky plucked his acoustic guitar and
sang with the fervor of a professional musician. Bob Crabb strummed his
guitar, and his gray mustache quivered with each note. Doc Harwood, the
camp physician, plucked a towering bass cello that let out mellow vibrations. Bob Crabb and Rocky would harmonize as they faced each other,
communicating through guitar strums and vocal tones. At our cabin, as the
guitar chords merged sweetly, Bob Flanagan's deep, resonant voice pulled
us smoothly into the lyrics of the "Brand New Tennessee Waltz": . . .
"Cause love is mainly just memories / And everyone's got him a few, / So
when I'm gone I'll be glad to love you." His romantic voice melted us, and
we were forever entranced by him.

Each night we gathered around a campfire, with the camp leaders strumming their guitars and banjos. Under a warm sky, wild bats flying overhead, we sang traditional campfire songs as well as other songs that poked
fun at our common disease. Bob Flanagan stood center stage with an en-
ticing smirk, held up his finger and sang:

Old Ben Lucas, had a lot of mucus, running right out of his nose.
When it's cotton picking time in Texas, it's booger picking time for Ben!
He rose his finger, mean and hostile,
stuck it up his big ol' nostril,
out came a green one once again!

The kids groaned in disgust, pantomiming nose picking to match the lyrics.
The little boys fell out of their seats with gleeful laughter, until coughing
fits resonated to the music.

One night, as I dozed off in my sleeping bag, I realized that my fingers
felt wet. I opened my eyes and made out Karen's silhouette. She was holding a cup of warm water under my hand. A loud cackling hyenalike shrill
jolted me awake, and Karen roared, "I'm trying to make you wet the bed!"

I sat up and laughed as she ran from bunk to bunk in the dim light, giggling and tickling all the other half-asleep girls. Then, in a wild burst of energy, she threw open the door and at the top of her lungs shouted, "Bob Crabb, Bob Flanagan, and the rest of those assholes wet the bed every night . . . and they hump!" Ana and I burst out laughing so hard our stomachs hurt, and we coughed our brains out.

"Thank God the counselors are still at their meeting! You'd be in big trouble!" Katie yelled to Karen.

The week at camp seemed to pass slowly. My skin bronzed under the sun, while the other kids complained of sunburns on their fair skin. The girls from my cabin hung out with the Skanks, sitting in lawn chairs that had been pulled into a circle in the middle of the cabin or leaning on the bunks. Van Halen blared from a run-down cassette player as we munched on junk food and drank Cokes.

We were all experts on life with CF. We compared hospitals, what treatments we had to do, and what surgeries we had had. Many of the other kids had had sinus surgery to clean out the same infection that plagued the lungs. I had never heard about that before. Everyone complained about looking much younger than their age. The guys talked about the nurses they had crushes on. We all joked about morbid stuff, like what it was like to have rigor mortis or what we wanted at our funerals.

At dinner one night, Bob Flanagan asked if he could sit with us. We were ecstatic, as if a celebrity had sought out our company. He proceeded to take his enzymes and shove them up his nose. The entire table of preteen girls shrieked with laughter at this giant clown. As he laughed I noticed something silver in his mouth. His tongue was pierced.

Beneath his silliness, Bob was a gentle man. He told us he was an artist and a writer. He asked about my family and school, and we were surprised to learn we were neighbors; he lived near UCLA. He was impressed that Dad was a professor there. "Straight and narrow. Must be a proper family." He winked and exposed a sly smile. "But I know what you're really like," he teased. "I know you're just two good girls on the outside, but really you're just dying to be naughty."

Later during the meal, he asked Denise, our counselor, how her year had been. She said it was a rough year, that her husband had lost his job and her mother was sick.

Suddenly Bob broke into song. He sang a verse from Hoyt Axton's "Boney Fingers," a song about having hope during difficult times.

On cue with the chorus of the song about boney fingers, he raised his long clubbed fingers, then jerked forward his middle finger and waved his hands around. Ana and I widened our eyes, laughing at his naughtiness.

"Girls, when life gets hard, just fuck it. Just say fuck it. That's what you gotta do."

"Yeah, fuck it," Karen repeated.

"Fuck it!" we all hollered, giggling with liberation.

All that week and for years to come at camp, Bob taught us how to rebel. I had yet to learn how to express anger, and he taught me that profanity was a healthy form of self-expression. In the years ahead, Ana, Karen, and I earned the reputation of having truck drivers' mouths. Our cussing and rebellious jokes seemed to provoke the other kids, and we became targets of harsh pranks. Once, in the middle of the night, an older girl dressed in a frightening chicken costume ran through our cabin cackling. On another night, the boys from the Skanks barged into our cabin of sleeping girls and dumped buckets of ice water over Ana, Karen, and me. Both episodes unleashed a flurry of vile, passionate profanity.

On the last evening of our first summer camp, a memorial service was held around a radiating campfire. We sang songs about loss:

> Remember me, when the candle lights are gleaming,
> Remember me at the close of a long, long day;
> It would be so sweet when all alone I'm dreamin',
> just to know you still remember me.

As the embers of the fire rose into the night air, the names of campers who had died during the year were read aloud. Friends and counselors told stories about their spirits and pranks. I looked up at the faces around the campfire, glowing in bronze light, their cheeks shiny with tears. Even the grown men cried, sharing their emotions without inhibition, something I had never seen in Dad. Illness and death stared us in the face; crying about it was okay.

Before I boarded the bus home from camp, I said good-bye to Karen, Denise, and the other Flamingos. I approached Bob Flanagan and gave him a big hug.

"You better stay fuckin' healthy, you hear?" he joked.

I giggled and then blurted, "I love you, Bob."

He squeezed me harder. "Oh, sweetie, I love you, too."

I had never said those words to anyone, not even to my parents.

CF camp soon became the most important week of our year. It was the only place Ana and I felt normal.

After that first week, Ana and I raved about CF camp to Mama and Dad for weeks on end. They were shocked to hear about the memorial service. Mama asked if it scared us. I told her that it hadn't, really; it had just made me more aware of being alive. That memorial had been a rite of passage. I needed to appreciate every day and be grateful. I decided, at age eleven, that I had been to Japan and Germany, had a great family and many friends, and if I died young, it would be okay.

"Besides," I told Mama, "I just really need to take care of myself so I don't end up being one of those names at the campfire."

Mama didn't want Ana and me to become "death obsessed" from witnessing the sicker kids and loss at camp. But we had been obsessed with death long before we stepped off the bus at camp. Chronic worry about death haunted us because we had seen what happened to Cheryl in the hospital. Each therapy was a reminder that the sickness inside of us would eventually kill us. Camp was the only place where we could deal with taboo subjects on an emotional level.

> We have nurtured our friendship through the years, as if it were flowers that bloom year in and year out. To remember happy times we've shared fills my heart with gladness. Our friendship exists not only through the good times but the bad times as well. Isabel and Anabel, you are my inspiration and joy.
>
> —Karen, age seventeen

In the years ahead, Karen became the symbol of our love for CF camp. She was a talented conversationalist with a tenderhearted maternal instinct. She nurtured younger children with CF, giving them hugs when they cried and piggybacks when they were tired. Karen's wild humor was contagious and, like that of many adolescents, sexually charged. Ana and I became her secret lovers. When our hearts were broken from unrequited crushes with boys at the dance, she exclaimed confidently with a wink, "Who needs guys!? We have each other! We can be lesbians! There's nothing sexier than a secret love affair." This set off a round of rebellious giggles.

"Karen's my best friend in the whole world!" I told Mama, dreamy-eyed, after camp one year. "She's so perfect." After years of social difficulty at school, I had finally found a true best friend. Ana and I shared her, but Karen was so special, there was enough of her to go around.

"Don't you put all of your energy into your friendship with Karen," Mama warned. "Why don't you spend more time with your other friends at school?"

She was afraid we'd be hurt if something happened to Karen. But Karen was healthy; she didn't let CF stop her. We envied her for her health and athletic build. In high school, she played on her school basketball team and excelled in the demanding academic decathlon program. But by junior high school, Ana and I were placed in adaptive physical education class because we couldn't keep up with our healthier classmates.

As she grew older, Karen's childhood jollity dissipated, and she shared the serious side of her life with us. She envied our financial stability as her single mom struggled to put food on the table. She envied our spacious home in Pacific Palisades while she lived in a cramped apartment. Her family was constantly moving, in search of lower rents. She was jealous of our supportive father and dismissed our complaints. She told us how her dad left the family when she was five. He was an alcoholic and abusive. "Just be glad you have a father," she said.

Our parents nonetheless helped nurture our bond with Karen. Karen spent many nights at our home before and after camp and during holidays. We visited her home in Las Vegas regularly. When we learned to drive, the three of us went to Disneyland, Lake Arrowhead, San Diego, and crossed the border to shop in Tijuana. On another occasion, we shopped until we dropped at the garment district in downtown Los Angeles. We were free-roaming, adventurous best friends. Together, we could be anyone and do anything we wanted.

Chapter 8

The Word Was Out

Isa

Well today I managed to go to school again. I don't want that to sound like I'm real sick cuz I'm not yet like Alex. I've learned so much from Alex Deford. I want to live a life like she did, as a heroine, and I want to be remembered after I die like her. That's why I'm writing this book.

—Isa, age thirteen

One day when I was in sixth grade, I was staying home from school with a fever. Mama was at work, and the whole house was mine. The house was quiet. Our dog Moui was curled up under the kitchen counter. The sun warmed her black coat, and the warmth soaked into my toes as I rested my feet on her back. As I ate my breakfast, I glanced at the *Los Angeles Times* that Dad had left open on the counter. My eyes were caught by an article that would change my view of CF forever.

"Will I get my wings right away?"

"Right away, . . . And we told her that even angels don't have cystic fibrosis . . ."

I was stunned. I had never seen a story about my disease printed in any newspaper. I eagerly read about Alex, a girl born just months before Ana and me, whose short life had been filled with the gamut of CF complications—lung collapses, coughing up blood, and routine hospital stays until her death at age eight. Her father, *Sports Illustrated* writer Frank Deford, had written a book documenting the gifts of her short life and the pain CF inflicted on the family. My heart flopped around like a fish out of water as I swallowed the sadness of Alex's life.

Shortly thereafter, Mama called from work, and I told her about the article. She told me not to feel sad and said that I should not have read such a depressing story.

I begged Mama to buy the book. She did and read it first, and then let Ana read it, and then me. Mama later told me that she cried all the way through the book, that her jaw hurt for days. Ana didn't cry reading it, but I could tell Alex's death spooked her. She told me we were lucky that we had not been born as sick as Alex. She explained that as twins, we shared CF, so it was half as severe as Alex's.

I absorbed every word in the book: the details of how Alex died at home listening to Elton John's "Your Song;" how her last request was a sip of root beer; that her last words were "Which way do I go?" as her body slumped over after its last breath. I cringed when I read that the contents of Alex's lungs poured out onto her bed after her death, as the diseased lungs finally shut down. The details were morbidly fascinating; I needed to know what awaited me someday.

Alex became our sister in spirit, yet so much of Alex's life was vastly different from ours. Her parents prepared her for death, they talked openly about feelings, allowing her to talk about her disease with those around her. Maybe it was because they were totally American.

I read and reread the passages about the colonization of Alex's lungs with the bacteria *pseudomonas aeruginosa*. A year earlier, Dr. Robbie had told Ana and me that we had this same bug in our lungs and that it wouldn't go away. "For any cystic fibrosis patient, *pseudomonas* is the harbinger of death," Deford wrote.

I asked Mama what "harbinger" meant, but she told me to look it up because she didn't know such big words.

I grabbed the family dictionary from the dusty living room bookshelf and flipped through the pages until I found the word. My finger traced the definition: *Harbinger: one that announces or foreshadows what is coming; precursor.* The meaning hit me. Having *pseudomonas* was the beginning of dying of CF. That's what Alex's dad had said, and he was right, because she had died. The curtain began to fall on my own life: was this the beginning of Ana's and my end?

By the time we entered junior high, Alex's book had become popular and spread the word about CF to the general public. When Ana and I were hospitalized that October, kids in our class began to wonder. One day at lunchtime, a girl at school, Andrea, asked me why I had been absent for so long. I told her that I had a lung infection. I was too embarrassed to say more.

"Oh," she said, smiling meekly. She turned around and went to join a group of girls who were gathered by a bench. They were glancing at me, and it was obvious that Andrea, whose back was turned to me, had reported on my response. I wanted to disappear. Within minutes, she turned around and walked back to me.

"Are you sure it was just a lung infection? I mean, are you sure it wasn't what Alex had, like, cystic fibrosis?"

I was shocked. I had no idea that she knew about Alex, the book, or could even pronounce my disease correctly. For the rest of lunch, I opened up to Andrea with a deep sense of relief at being able to be candid about CF with someone in junior high. This honesty was the beginning of a deep, lifelong friendship.

Over time, Alex's book became both a blessing and curse. While her book thrust CF into the spotlight, making it seem less strange, it also led people to believe that anyone with CF was fragile or at death's door. People began treating us differently.

In science class one day, Jeremy, the boy who sat in front of me, abruptly turned around and asked, "Are you gonna die?"

"No!" I said. My thoughts tumbled around, and I said nothing more. *Of course, I'm going to die,* I thought. *Everybody is. So why can't I be more assertive? God, I wish I had a backbone!* But Jeremy had faced the front again, apparently content with my answer.

On another occasion, an obnoxious boy who liked to rub the backs of girls to see whether or not they were wearing bras, asked me, "Why don't you wear a bra?"

"Because I don't need one," I replied. I was emaciated at thirteen. My body was too busy struggling with chronic lung infections to bother with puberty.

"Why are you so skinny?" he continued.

"Uh . . . I don't know." I played dumb, reluctant to share my whole life story with this menace.

Suddenly, Jeremy walked up to the obnoxious kid and said, "Dude, leave her alone. She's got a disease."

"Is it AIDS?" he asked, laughing.

"No, dude, it's something else . . . something kids are born with and die from."

The bra-snapper looked at me, his eyes showing horror mixed with sympathy.

"Oh," he squeaked and walked away.

The word was out.

She's got a disease . . .
Are you dying?

The words of the kids at school haunted me. Maybe I was dying. Tears obscured my vision as I washed the nebulizer parts in soapy water in our dingy bathroom. Taking out my frustrations on my nebs, I scrubbed vigorously with the baby-bottle brush to remove the salty residue. I hated everything. It was all too much, and I couldn't stop crying. My heart raced, I was short of breath, and I could sense another hospital stay coming. At thirteen, it was hard to be responsible for taking care of my own health since Mama went back to work.

I had just finished an awkward therapy session with my exhausted mother, who had worked a twelve-hour shift that day. My lungs were tight, I felt as if I were suffocating, and laying upside down over Mama's lap wasn't helping. I started to cry, discreetly, using the tissues I coughed into to cover my blubbering face.

My evening crying sessions during therapy were becoming routine. I was having another full-blown panic attack. Finally Mama noticed and asked why I was crying.

I whimpered that I couldn't breathe. But it was more than that. It was everything—CF, therapy, not feeling well, the kids at school, being different. But I couldn't possibly tell Mama. She had enough of her own worries.

"Oh, my goodness." She didn't say anything else; she didn't caress me or comfort me. She just kept on percussing. After I collected myself and continued coughing, her pats on my back faded, weakly, until I noticed she was falling asleep. I didn't know if I should wake her but I wanted to shout, *I said I can't breathe so do my therapy longer and harder! Wake up! I need you to help me!* But instead I got up and finished my shortened therapy. The ventriloquist in me said, "Sorry, Mama, to make you so tired."

Shortly thereafter, Ana demanded that it was my turn to wash the nebulizer parts.

"I know. You don't have to remind me," I said. Then I paused. "Can you wash them this time? I don't feel well."

"I don't want to do it twice. That's not fair."

"C'mon. Gimme a break. Please." I was being selfish and stubborn, but I felt horrible.

"You're so lazy!" Ana said. "I'm not giving in this time. You always take advantage."

"You don't have to be bitchy about it."

Our argument descended into kicking and hitting; we fought, our eyes fiery with rage. So I ended up washing the nebulizers, a nightly ritual in which they had to be soaked overnight in vinegar to be disinfected. It really wasn't all that much work, but coming at the end of a difficult evening, it felt extra burdensome.

Suddenly, Ryuta appeared at the doorway and blurted, "What the hell are you crying for?"

I stopped, embarrassed that he should see me this way, but managed to say, "I . . . I . . . just hate this."

After a pause, Ryuta hissed, with a slight lisp, "Tschhhh," his hallmark dismissal, and left.

When the task was done, I headed to bed. The room was dark, and Ana was bundled under the covers. In the darkness, my sister asked if I was all right. We always forgave each other as quickly as we fought.

"Yeah," I muttered, settling into my cocoon. But I wasn't all right. I imagined an earthquake occurring, killing Mama and Dad and leaving me struggling to crawl out of tight spaces. I imagined the house burning down, as the fierce Santa Ana winds, which swayed our massive eucalyptus tree with ease, blew outside. I feared the dark; what if there was a robber outside, or a murderer, or someone who would kidnap me in the night?

I tried to calm myself by clasping my hands together and praying: *Please, dear, God, please let there be a cure for CF.* I squeezed my hands tighter and squinted extra hard when I said *please,* as if the extra emphasis would make God listen to me: *Please, please let me live a long, long time. Please bless Ana and let our CF get better or stabilize. Please let a doctor or researcher find a cure for CF soon. Amen.*

I nestled under the covers but remained tormented. A short while later, I broke the silence. "You still awake?"

Ana muttered, "Mmm."

"Can I sleep with you?"

"Sure." I crawled out of my bed and dove under her warm covers. Finally, the dreadful thoughts stopped, and I drifted into deep sleep.

Chapter 9

Interracial Woes

Isa

Our family is so broken. I am very unhappy about it. Mom and Dad fight, Ryuta and Mom fight, Ana and Mom fight and sometimes Isa and Ana fight. Can't we just be normal, rich, happy, clean and healthy?

—Isa, age twelve

The California outdoors was heaven for a German who had grown up skiing and climbing in the Alps, and the Sierra Nevada, Angeles Crest Forest, and San Bernardino mountains became the Stenzel family playground. Dad constructed a generator out of a boat battery so we could do our nebulizer treatments in the car, and we learned to love car camping and hiking. We spent our Sunday "family days" hiking in the local Santa Monica mountains.

Mama wanted Dad to spend more quality time with Ryuta and also to mix with other families. So, when Ryuta was eleven, he and Dad joined the Boy Scouts, where they met other families interested in the outdoors. Within a few years, Dad had become the assistant scout leader, dragging the boys on long hikes. He was the type of leader who would tell the boys, "We'll stop in another mile!" and then repeat this statement a number of times before actually stopping.

On one long climb in the Sierras, Ryuta told us that he and his friends became too tired to go farther. Dad got upset, and puffed ahead on the trail, accusing the boys of weakness. He was ruthless when on the trail and didn't care about how others were feeling. He demanded from Ryuta a strength to match his own. After that trip, one of Ryuta's friends fell asleep and didn't wake up for twenty-four hours. Mama consoled Ryuta after that trip. She told him that when she and Dad first dated, Dad had taken her hiking to the Sierras. Afterward, Mama was so tired she thought she would die. She never joined him in the mountains again until we kids were old enough to hike with our parents and slow Dad's pace.

Walking for miles was a deeply engrained habit for Dad. As a child, in the waning days of the war before Germany's surrender, my father walked for weeks with his mother and brother across Czechoslovakia from Breslau to Berlin, escaping the Russian army. Each time he hiked, it was like he was reliving his long journey as a refugee, somehow hiking away from something or someone.

Dad's motto was always "No pain, no gain." Ryuta joked to us that Dad should carry a big rock during his "death hikes" just to slow himself down. He said terrible things about Dad, often referring to him as "Adolf." He made fun of Dad's habit of eating mushrooms and berries from the woods, even if they were rotting or had worms on them, because "you can take the man out of the war but you can't take the war out of the man." Dad accused Ryuta of being a spoiled American.

Dad also joined the Sierra Club and became a ski mountaineer. On weekends, he often went to the mountains alone, where, unhindered by companions, he would climb thousands of feet to one of the peaks of the Sierra Nevada. Hiking became his obsession and the mountains his solace, far away from Mama's complaints, the pressures of his research, his daughters' therapies, the house and car that always seemed to need fixing. He could push his body to the brink; once he lost sixteen pounds on a three-week-long trip along the John Muir Trail and even urinated blood from overexertion.

Mama and Dad regularly argued about his mountain trips. Dad's weekend trips only fueled the fire of his rocky marriage. Mama nagged, "Reiner, you are having an affair with the mountains! Don't you escape again this weekend. You act like your trips are more important than your family."

These complaints didn't stop Dad. When he was at home, he spent hours poring over topo maps, engrossed in plotting his next trip, or turned family outings into visits to specialty stores to purchase mountaineering equipment. Sometimes Mama forced Dad to stay home for family obligations, and Dad would announce, "I'm grounded." Skipping a mountain trip meant a cloud of resentment would permeate the air. I sometimes wished he'd just go, because when he returned, he was relaxed and kinder, actual-ly showing some interest in our family. He came home with stories of snow-capped peaks, blizzards, and bear encounters. He was renewed, a smile on his face.

> After 9 weeks of the hospital, I'm now getting on with my life. We're back to the usual routine—family dinner fights, housework, complaints, home-work, etc. But I'd rather have this than be in the hospital.
>
> —Ana, age fourteen

We always knew our parents were from different worlds, but during our teen years the chasm between them just kept widening. Whether it was the time they spent apart focusing on us or the presence of their jobs, they seemed to stop relating to each other. Tension between Mama and Dad was constant and never more evident than at our dinner table, which became the family coliseum.

Dad often worked late, and Mama would try to delay dinner so we could eat as a family, hoping that Dad might once listen to her constant requests to come home earlier. But inevitably he'd arrive just after we had resigned ourselves to eating without him, usually after 8:00. Having long ago shed her stereotypical Japanese subservience, Mama would start the evening off in a sour mood with a biting comment directed at Dad. She accused him of avoiding the family by spending too much time at work—calling him a "workaholic"—and in the mountains. In her high-pitched voice, she nagged him to take initiative to bring Ana and me to the doctor, help out more often with therapy, or visit us in the hospital without her asking him to do so.

Dad usually laughed off her concerns. "You are talking nonsense," he would say dismissively. Sometimes, though, he would talk back, saying that he contributed to the family by working in the garden or fixing the house. Mama responded (and I agreed) that those were really just chores.

We kids sometimes took sides at these dinnertime fights. Once, Ryuta blurted out, "God, Dad, don't they have feelings where you come from?! Just apologize. How hard is that?" Mama beamed.

Ana and I often defended Dad, feeling sorry for him and emphasizing the fun we had when he actually *was* home. I tried to focus on the positive, having been reminded by Karen how lucky we were to have a father. The truth was, Dad was unemotional, distracted, and overworked. But I also felt sorry for Mama. She was lonely, depressed, and similarly overworked.

I wished we could just have a normal family conversation at mealtimes.

Ryuta usually sat silently, absorbed in his bitter teen angst, and when he did say something, it was usually rude, like a comment making fun of Mama's accent. Ryuta also never hesitated to insult Dad. Once, after dinner, Dad turned toward Mama, saying, "We have apples, bananas, and oranges . . . " hinting for her to get up and serve him his favorite dessert. Ryuta then snapped, "And you have legs!"

Ana and I tried to stimulate conversation by asking questions about everyone's day to bring some cheer to the table. We asked about Dad's research, how he was trying to make an energy source out of plasma rays, but we couldn't understand beyond his most basic explanations. Mama's face glazed over during these discussions; she had become conditioned over the years to stop trying to participate in these intellectual exchanges. Dad's idea of good family communication was to make us calculate math problems during dinner: "If you have five pounds of oranges and one pound makes sixteen ounces of juice, how much juice can you make?" If we protested, Dad criticized Americans as being too dependent on calculators. Dad liked to talk about politics, but mostly he shared his conservative opinions, which clashed with our views, resulting in more disagreements.

Mama blamed all of Dad's bad habits on his being German: "He cannot share his feelings because he is German." "He does not know how to communicate because he is German." "He works too much because he is German." She would conclude her tirade by pointing toward us, saying, "Interracial marriage doesn't work! Don't you date another culture." We laughed off her admonition, telling her that unless we found other half-Japanese, half-German boyfriends we *had* to date interracially. But I knew of many interracial marriages that were perfectly happy, like Yoko and John's, or those of family friends, like Kazuko and Mac's, or Fumi and Josh's. They all seemed content. Maybe it was just Mama and Dad, who were like a lock and a key that didn't go together.

It seemed that all my parents had in common was growing up in the aftermath of World War II in proud and stubborn but defeated and destitute countries. Our best family conversations were when Mama and Dad shared their childhood memories of the war. Dad told us how Opa had saved his Jewish boss from being arrested and how his excellent command of English allowed him to work in military intelligence and intercept British communications. Mama talked about her memories of the refugee camp in Korea where she had lived for two years after the war. From their war experiences, Mama and Dad agreed on how to raise us—to live simply, to reuse things and never to waste (especially food), to feel guilty for our abundance, and to bathe sparingly. Their connection to each other was rooted in their distant past, but in the present they lived parallel lives with only their teenage children providing a fragile bond between them.

Chapter 10

Life at Kaiser

Isa

Sometimes when talking to my friends, I feel so dumb! They know so much more than me about sex, gossip and music. But then again I know so much more than them in terms of medicine, health and hospitals. I just never say anything because it's not something they're interested in. . . . Kids we don't even know say, "You the ugly twins who were in the hospital?" Fuck them. Why do they care? Kids make faces at us and hit us. I think they do this because we're such small, naïve, shy twins ("How cute!"). Maybe I should be more active at school but I can't cuz usually I don't feel well enough. I don't know why we're so shy at school but talkative and wild in the hospital and at camp. I think our life totally depends on health and CF so we feel more comfortable around our own kind.

—Ana, age fifteen

Another tedious visit at Kaiser. Ana and I sat on the same exam table, our feet dangling above the linoleum floor. We scribbled with pens, drawing playful designs on the white paper that covered the table. The sterile room smelled like antiseptic and was silent except for the crinkling of the paper. Mama had stepped outside with Dr. Robbie, and after a while, Ana jumped off the table.

"This is bullshit. I'm bored." She went to the door and peeked out. I followed her. Down the hall, the door of Dr. Robbie's office was slightly ajar.

We could hear him chastising our mother, "You aren't taking good enough care of the girls! This isn't a game, Hatsuko! These are your daughters' lives!" He was just as frustrated as Mama that we just couldn't stay well. Ana and I closed the door and returned to the exam table.

I hoped that Mama would defend herself from these accusations. As she learned more about the disease from our CF camp friends and respiratory therapy school, Mama often suggested new treatments and medications to Dr. Robbie. But he stubbornly held to his ways. "I only let my wife tell me what to do."

In the days before managed care, Dr. Robbie was unhindered in the time he spent with us. Sometimes we were with him for an hour or more in the clinic room, talking about restaurants or travel adventures. As soon as we were old enough, he took the time to explain our disease, scribbling sketches of our plugged-up lung alveoli and other CF anomalies on the thin exam-table paper. We asked questions and listened to his responses. But when he and Mama stepped out for private discussions, we knew there was something going on. Mama would open up to Dr. Robbie in their private meetings, as if he were her therapist, pouring out her sadness about her husband's lack of participation, her worry about our health, and Ryuta's behavior.

A while later, Mama emerged; her eyes were red and her eyelids puffy. Dr. Robbie followed and sat back down on the round medical stool facing the small desk across from the exam table. His belly bulged over his belt. He pulled a fancy pen from his shirt pocket. Our hearts pounded. His bifocals rested on the tip of his nose as he pulled open the desk drawer and took out a sheet of pink lined paper. His round fingers wrote across the top line in capital letters, ADMIT. My spirits plummeted, knowing that my shortness of breath and rapid heartbeat signaled a raging infection and the 21,000 white blood cell count (normal was 5,000-8,000) confirmed my pneumonia. I was thirteen, and this pattern had repeated itself a dozen times now. Although I had already packed a few necessities in case I was to be admitted, the "ADMIT" that stared at me was the gavel's final blow.

My mind raced: What about my algebra test? Rachel's birthday party next week? The pet hamsters? Stuck between resistance and resignation, I knew that I needed to feel better, but I wished there was another way.

Mama sank down in her chair, her eyes glazing over.

"Can we make it a short one?" I asked.

"Isa, dear, you know it's too early to make that call," Dr. Robbie said. "We'll do the best we can."

I looked down at the floor. My eyes filled with tears. "I just don't want to go in. I hate this!" My voice shook with embarrassment.

"Sweetie, I know this is hard for you. It's hard on everyone. But we already tried everything. You've been doing four treatments a day since your last visit, your mom says you've been resting a lot and taking it easy, you've been on Ceclor and Septra for the last three weeks, but it hasn't controlled the bugs. You've got some nasty critters in those lungs, and we need to attack them with the powerful IV antibiotics. You know that, right?"

I nodded, composing myself. I rubbed my eyes with the sleeve of my pink jumper.

"You need to be strong." Dr. Robbie took a deep breath. He paused for a moment, caught in his private reflection, and put the pink slip aside. He pulled out Ana's chart. Turning to Ana, he asked, "Ana, how much blood did you say you coughed up?"

Ana looked up, her eyes filled with panic. "Only two tablespoons one time, and it hasn't happened for, like, three days. It happened when I was learning CPR in Girl Scouts. Isa was practicing on me. The other time was when I was break-dancing, I was doing the worm and hit my chest on the floor. I . . . I'm okay now."

Lung bleeding, or hemoptysis, is a common CF complication, caused by the infection irritating the blood vessels of the lungs, making them easy to burst. Each time our lungs bled, we felt a pop, followed by a strong urge to cough and a surge of hot, salty, watery secretions swelling up from our lungs. The blood flowed in copious amounts, sometimes uncontrollably, like a volcanic eruption. As we spit it out in any tissue, paper cup, or sink available, the bright red blood oozing from our mouths evoked images from a horror movie. Our heads pounded from incessant coughing and hyperventilating as we tried to catch our breath during these bleeding episodes. After a few minutes, the urge to cough would subside, and the episode would stop as suddenly as it had started.

Dr. Robbie lowered his bifocals and looked at Mama. "Ana's blood count two weeks ago was 13,300. Today it's 15,100. Not too bad, but it's not a good trend." He paused. "Hmmm . . . how would you feel if I admit them both?"

Ana exclaimed, "That's not fair! I'm feeling fine. I just got out a month ago!"

Dr. Robbie peered at her through his spectacles. "Ana, I know it seems so recent that you were in. But your numbers are just average, not so good. And I'm worried about your bleeding. The antibiotics we give you will decrease the infection that's causing your bleeds. If I put you both in now, you can be tuned up and better by the summer, and CF camp's coming up. Having you both in at the same time will let you guys keep each other company, and your mom can take a vacation from caring for you."

Ana and I both stopped protesting, because we knew there was nothing we could do. I was relieved that Ana was going to be in with me. She was my security blanket, my strong side, my protector, and my advocate. With her, I could handle anything, even IV sticks and bad food, annoying nurses and stress from missing school. But I was more annoyed with Mama's and Dr. Robbie's conspiracy. Why would he admit Ana just to give Mama a break? We were the ones who were going into the hospital, and she needed a break?

My thoughts churned, but like a good girl I thanked Dr. Robbie for his care. He sat in his round chair, opening his burly arms for a bear hug. We nestled against him as he squeezed out the little air remaining in our lungs.

"Hang in there, kiddos. You're both so brave. You have a nasty disease, and we just gotta do the best we can to deal with it."

We left the clinic and walked across Sunset Boulevard to the admitting department. As we waited to be admitted, Ana pulled out her notebook and began to scribble. "Mama, I'm making a list of things we need. Can you make sure to feed the hamsters?" She turned to me. "We need to call Rachel for the English assignments, Andrea for algebra, Jenny for history . . ." Her voice grew low. "This sucks. This is a conspiracy. I can't believe I have to go in too."

From the admitting department we headed upstairs to 7 North. My mother straggled along between us, somber and withdrawn at the intrusion of another hospitalization on her life. At the end of the hall I saw the clerk smiling at the front desk. She waved as we approached her.

"You twins back again, huh?" she said. "You were just here! You don't look too bad. I would never guess that you're sick! You just love us so much that you had to come back to see us!" I smiled, shrugging off her comment. I hated that joke.

Just then Anne, the head nurse, passed by and greeted us. "You know, Michael J. Fox is coming by on Friday . . . are you sure you didn't plan on being admitted to meet him?" We feigned smiles again, though this time we perked up at the chance to see another movie star. But being in the hospital still wasn't worth it.

We were directed to a room with three beds, but fortunately the third bed was empty. We unloaded our belongings and settled into our room. Later that evening I called Karen. "Hi, Karen, it's Isa. We're calling from the hospital. We're both in again. Ana's lungs are bleeding and I have pneumonia."

Her voice was sympathetic. "That sucks. Sorry to hear that. I just got out, too. Is Ana putting ice on her chest when she bleeds?"

Karen had taught us the little tricks of dealing with CF irks, ones that no health care provider knew. "Yeah, she is. Hopefully, this tune-up will get us well by camp."

"Hang in there, you guys. Don't forget to watch out for yourselves. You know how those nurses can screw up." Karen was our only friend who really understood. She had been hospitalized many times before.

Karen continued, "At least you two have each other in the hospital, to look out for each other. The last time I was in, I had to pee so bad, I called the nurse to unhook my IV so I could get to the bathroom." Her voice heaved a little as she caught her breath. "The nurses never came. I had to pull the trash can up to my bed and piss in it. Damn nurses."

I was shocked. I felt lucky. Karen went to a county hospital where the care was much worse than ours.

"Tell me about it," I agreed. "Last time I was in, my bed wasn't made for four days. I finally found the linen closet and got my own damn sheets."

And that was the least of my worries. I knew there would be plenty of stressful days when I would have to deal with incompetent nurses, days when I would have to ask for my meals and medications. I always made sure to memorize my medication schedule so that when eight hours had passed and no nurse had come to hang my antibiotic, I could ring for it. "It's four o'clock. Can I please have my ticarcillin now?" By watching the nurses carefully, I had learned to operate the IV pump myself and flush the IV tubing when the nurses wouldn't respond to my calls. Self-reliance was essential to survival in the hospital.

"But that's horrible," I said to Karen. "Couldn't you complain?"

"Yeah, I let 'em have it . . . but actually it was pretty funny. Me pissing with my pants down from my bed. I made a fuckin' mess." She giggled. Karen always knew how to change a serious moment into something to laugh about. She continued. "Well, I'll just have to get a care package in the mail to you guys right away." I smiled. That was Karen. Always generous. Always trying to put a smile on my face.

At that moment, the resident entered our room. "Well, I gotta go. Doc's here. I'll talk to you another time."

"Remember, question everything. It's your body they're screwing with so you have the right to know what's up."

"I know," I replied. "Ana says 'hi.' Love you, Karen. Thanks for being there." I hung up.

By the fourth or fifth day of our hospital stay, the powerful cocktail of multiple antibiotics coupled with an aggressive routine of four treatments a day usually kicked in, and we felt energized. For the remaining two or three weeks, we were restless, active teens, venturing outside of our room to roam the halls. My father's words rang in my ears, "You must walk! Keep up your strength!" Like always, we were not allowed off the floor and could only roam the oval-shaped ward, making mindless circles around the familiar halls, memorizing the details of each piece of artwork—the clown painting, the balloon murals—and counting the yellow and orange tiles on the floor. Each time I left our room, I went through a ritual. I unplugged the

IV pump, pushed my pole to the door, lowered the pole so that it could be pushed beneath the door and then increased the height again, so that the gravity would allow the drip to resume. All of this required careful maneuvering with one hand, since my other hand was usually taped to an IV board.

We stayed up late at the nurses' station, chatting and helping with their paperwork. Many of the nurses were immensely kind to us. They brought us books and homemade ethnic foods. Sally took us to Marineland when we were discharged. Linda brought us autographed "Far Side" posters from her friend Gary Larson. Many of the nurses washed, brushed, and braided our hair. They threw us a huge graduation party in the playroom when we graduated from elementary school. In our second home, our surrogate mothers were of all races and ages. Over the years, these nurses had raised us, teaching us values of diversity, compassion, and love.

Sometimes we'd even help the pharmacist label syringes with patient names. We played hide-and-seek with other patients in the empty rooms, closets, and play rooms. The staff tolerated our mischief, respecting our judgment and knowing we had to get the energy out of our systems. It was a rare treat to leave the floor to get an X-ray or buy food from the cafeteria downstairs or from the Mexican lunch truck outside.

That Friday, Michael J. Fox came to visit. With the social worker, we got to walk with him from room to room, helping to pass out signed photos and gifts to the patients on the ward. He greeted each child with a smile and chit-chatted, trying to hide any awkwardness from sick children. But after visiting the bedside of Logan, a swollen little boy with no motor control who was on a ventilator, Michael's face turned pale. "I gotta get outta here," he whispered to the social worker.

A week into our stay, a kid named Maricela moved into the third bed in our room. She has been diagnosed with a brain tumor several weeks earlier and was hospitalized for placement of a central line catheter to receive chemotherapy. As they wheeled her in on a gurney, she lay motionless, pale and ghostlike with the familiar yellow concoction dripping from an IV pole into her arm. She raised her delicate hand, bony and pale, and waved at me. Strangely, I always envied the cancer kids. They looked so sick with their balding heads and emaciated bodies that they were taken seriously. No one questioned why they were being admitted again. They required specially trained nurses to care for them, nurses who spent more time with them and seemed more compassionate than regular nurses.

I had been her roommate when she was first diagnosed, and I remembered the multitude of Hispanic relatives who had sobbed uncontrollably when the doctor announced that she had cancer. Maricela was a quiet girl, and we got along well. She kept to herself and did not ask many questions. But I resented her relatives, who visited in droves and spoke Spanish loudly, staring and pointing at me.

The day after she moved back into our room, I sat on my bed with a nebulizer mask stuck to my face, steam spewing out like a dragon's breath as I inhaled the salty mist. Maricela's cousin walked up to my bed. She was about seven, with wavy thick black hair tucked neatly behind her ears. She wore a tattered shirt with a faded Care Bears iron-on design. She stood watching me. I glared back through the mist. I felt like an animal in a zoo. In a thick accent, she said, "My grandmother wants to know what's wrong with you." I was annoyed. The family was talking about me from across the room in a language I could not understand. I turned to Ana, who was also doing a treatment.

"Nothing is *wrong* with us," Ana replied. "We have a lung problem, like asthma. It's not contagious." I could tell she was mad too. We constantly had to explain to all the curious bystanders that they would not catch what we had, even though our coughs roared day and night, especially during therapy. My roommates and their families gazed in horror as men in white coats beat on our backs while we lay upside down, coughing, red in the face.

The kid turned to Ana. "Are you dying?"

The questions stung me like alcohol in a cut. "No, I'm not dying," Ana replied, puffing through her mask. This kid was pushing our buttons. Ana and I knew very well that in the big picture we were dying; each hospitalization was a prison sentence to postpone that process.

The young girl walked back to her grandmother. *"No, no esta muriendo."*

The grandmother smiled weakly and nodded.

The day after Maricela's catheter placement, something bizarre happened. Our lunch trays arrived around noon. Maricela had been sleeping all morning. She seemed groggy as she sat up to examine her tray, her sparse chocolate-colored hair falling loosely onto her shoulders, with clumps of it remaining on her pillow. It was Tuesday—the day for macaroni and cheese, instant chicken noodle soup, and Lorna Doones shortbread cookies. The pediatric hospital menu was set for each day—tomorrow would be pizza, chicken drumsticks on Thursdays, chicken a la king on Friday. The meals were highly unappetizing and highly American. I missed the comfort of Mama's Japanese cooking. No Japanese rice for three weeks was unbearable.

We all silently picked at our trays. I stirred the contents of the chicken noodle soup package into the cup of hot water and watched the tiny chicken pieces float to the top of the cup. I glanced at Maricela. She was staring straight ahead, her eyes glazed over. Something seemed different about her.

She was gaunt-looking, and her freckles seemed to collapse into the pallor of her skin, as though they were disappearing into quicksand.

"Are you okay?" I asked from across the room.

"I hate Lorna Doones," she muttered.

"Yeah, me, too," I said, relieved that her response was so casual. "They're so dry and boring."

Suddenly, Maricela twisted about in her bed, her head thrashing back and forth, and she began to shout, "I hate Lorna Doones! I hate Lorna Doones!"

I began to worry. It was not like her. She shook violently in her bed.

"Ana," I said, "something's wrong. You better call the nurse." Ana called the nurse. The call light went unanswered as Maricela continued to thrash about, growing increasingly irate.

"Fuck Lorna Doone! Fuck these goddamn cookies!" She took the cookies and tore them out of the package. One by one, she threw them across the room.

At last a nurse arrived.

Ana turned to the nurse. "I think something's wrong with Maricela. She's acting weird."

Maricela turned to the nurse. "Fuck you! Bitch! Fuck you!"

As the nurse approached Maricela, Maricela threw another Lorna Doone cookie that smacked the nurse in the face. "Maricela . . . what's going on? Why are you yelling?"

Maricela ignored the nurse. Suddenly her head cocked and her eyes rolled back. Her body tightened, and she fell back onto the bed. The last Lorna Doone dropped from Maricela's grasp, crumbling onto the floor. The nurse rang the emergency intercom. "I need some assistance in 768. We have a patient seizing."

Within moments an entourage of nurses and physicians were in the room. The nurse pulled the curtain around Maricela's bed in a flurry, hiding the action from us, but we could hear the commotion. Voices spoke, "Eyes deviated . . . increased reflexes . . ."

Within an hour of the beginning of our boring lunch, Maricela was being wheeled out of the room on a gurney. The nurse told me later that her brain tumor had grown, causing her unusual behavior and seizures. She was being transferred to intensive care.

Maricela died later that month. All the chemotherapy and radiation couldn't save her. I thought about her cousin and how ironic it was that she had asked me if I was dying, when her very own cousin really was. And I never wanted to eat Lorna Doone cookies again.

But witnessing what Maricela went through made me feel lucky. "I'm so glad we just have CF," I told Ana. "Things could be so much worse."

After Maricela's departure, Ana and I enjoyed having the room to ourselves for two nights. Privacy, finally. On the third night, after we had settled into bed, one of the nurses, Maria, entered our room and flicked on the bright overhead light of bed C. She began to arrange the call bell and telephone on the bed. I knew what that meant. We were getting another roommate. Damn. Who would it be now? A crying baby? Another appendectomy? An asthmatic? A kid fresh out of surgery who would surely vomit in my face from the anesthesia?

"You're getting a roommate, girls," chimed Maria. "I want you to be nice to her. She's going to need your help." She left the room.

Ana sat up in bed. "What's up with that? Our help? We're patients too! Why do we have to help a roommate? We're not the nurses!"

Within minutes, an orderly entered our room, pushing a slender, frightened-looking African American girl in a wheelchair. She looked about nine years old. Her hair was in braids, and her hands were folded in her lap beneath a blanket. As she stood to get out of the wheelchair and into her bed, she pulled her arms out from under the blanket. Both arms were in casts up past her elbows. She was accompanied by an older woman, who was carrying a bag and folder. The woman was dressed in a blue business suit, and her panty hose had wrinkled at her ankles.

As the girl settled in, several nurses and physicians entered the room. I heard the woman introduce herself. "Lara Williams, social services." Once again, the curtain around the girl's was pulled shut. I lay in bed, quietly eavesdropping and wondering what had happened to her arms and where her parents were. Behind the curtain I could hear words like, ". . . custody . . . physical abuse . . . foster care . . ."

After the admission examination of our new roommate, the clamor of voices could be heard leaving the room, and the curtain around her bed swung open.

Maria stood there, holding the curtain. "Stephanie, these are your roommates, Anabel and Isabel. They're really sweet and will be your friends. You can ask them for help if you need it, okay?"

She turned to Ana, "You'll be a good friend, won't you? I know you're so nice and will help your new roommate out."

Ana smiled, silenced by the awkward position in which we were placed. I couldn't believe my ears. I was tired and just wanted to go to sleep. Why did it seem that my roommates were always admitted late at night?

After a few hours, I awoke to the sound of a child sobbing. The room was dark except for light that seeped in from the hallway window and bright light that shone beneath the bathroom door. The sobbing was coming from the bathroom.

I stirred in bed and looked over at Ana, who was sitting up. "Are you okay?" she shouted across the room.

Suddenly the bathroom door was flung open. Bright light poured out, startling me. Stephanie was sitting on the toilet. Her loose hospital gown had dropped down below her shoulders, bunching up helplessly around her casts so that her bare upper chest was visible.

She sobbed, "Help me. . . . Can you help me?" She looked down at her casts. "I can't wipe myself. I need to wipe myself."

I lay there frozen. Finally, Ana got up and pushed her IV pole toward her as I watched. She stood with her pole at the door of the bathroom, her body silhouetted by the light. Even from my bed, I could make out faint marks that looked like bruises on Stephanie's shoulders. The smell of shit oozed into my nostrils. Ana turned from the door, her face grimacing at the scent. I gagged.

"I can't get the toilet paper. Can you wipe me?" Stephanie cried.

Ana looked at her helplessly. She turned to me.

"I'm not going to do that. *Dozo.* Go ahead," I said. Ana looked horrified.

She stepped back, turning to me. "The nurse asked us to help, but this is too much. I can't wipe her butt. That's disgusting."

"No, you shouldn't," I said.

We had to stand our ground. We were patients here too. Good girls or not, helpful or not, friend or not, we were not going to wipe the ass of a roommate, a girl we didn't even know.

"Sorry," Ana finally asserted. "I can't do that. I'm going to get the nurse."

Ana pushed her IV pole back to her bed and grabbed the call bell. After the usual wait, Maria's shadow approached. Her keys dangled from a string wrapped around her neck, chiming like bells.

"Yes?" Maria sang. "Can I help you girls?"

"She needs help," Ana announced, pointing toward the bathroom.

Stephanie looked up at the nurse, her face wet with tears. "I can't wipe myself . . . I can't do anything. Help me . . . please."

"Well, dear," Maria replied, "Let's see what we can do." She entered the bathroom and shut the door. Ana and I could hear her voice as she tried to calm Stephanie. After a few minutes, the toilet flushed and the door swung open. Stephanie wobbled out, her hospital gown tied neatly closed around her neck. She got back into bed.

"Now, Anabel and Isabel," Maria scolded. "I thought you would be nice and help your roommate out. I'm so disappointed in you. Next time, why don't you help her, okay?"

"I'll help but not like that," Ana retorted. "I can't do that."

I wanted to say so much more, but I sulked in silence.

Ana glared at the nurse until she left, furious at her. As she left, Ana whispered, "What a lazy bitch . . . trying to get out of doing her own job. Now she makes us feel like we did something wrong. Fuck that."

I lay back in my bed, turning away from the bright hall light. *I hate it here and I want to go home,* I sighed. Closing my eyes, I finally drifted off, again, dreaming of being anywhere else but here.

After we'd been in the hospital for two weeks, the residents simply passed our room during rounds. "No changes for the Stenzels." We were there simply to finish the course of antibiotics, even though we felt better.

But the pediatric social worker, Alice, always made an effort to visit us. Alice was an attractive middle-aged brunette who painted her manicured nails to match her colorful dresses and ornate jewelry. She introduced us to cross-stitching, and on Tuesday nights she worked late, so she spent most of her evening in our room stitching away. While picking our thread colors and counting stitches, we developed a special relationship. Alice was open about her own struggles with diabetes and her difficulty complying with diet restrictions. Her genuine honesty made her "one of us." We talked about how we hated some of our roommates and the nurses who expected us to be "good girls." We talked about boys we liked, becoming Christian, or death, topics we didn't dare share with our parents.

Mama confided in Alice, too. Sometimes they had coffee together, and Mama poured her heart out about her frustrations. She was working long hours at Santa Monica Hospital, only to visit her daughters in another hospital after work. Mama was burned out with respiratory therapy. She treated people with end-stage lung disease and witnessed prolonged suffering and death for many patients. After treating respiratory patients all day, she came home to treat her own daughters. Working with the sick ate away at her hope for us.

Alice helped Mama think about exploring other career options and about going to graduate school. Mama told us how she had told Alice that she felt selfish for pursuing her own interests while Ana and I were struggling with our health. Alice had responded by saying that by taking care of her own needs first, Mama would have more energy to give back to her family. Alice felt Ana and I were mature and tremendously independent because we relied on each other, freeing Mama to fulfill her goals. Mama shared her guilt over the possibility that Ana and I might become critically ill while she was in school. Alice told her there were ways to adjust her schedule to make anything happen, graduating just might take longer. She also said that whatever happened to us in the future, Mama's life would still be *her* life, *her* future.

Eventually, Mama decided to pursue medical social work like Alice. Alice gladly wrote her a glowing letter of recommendation. Even Dad supported her ambitions. And so, at forty-eight, Mama enrolled in the University of Southern California master's in social work program. During the three-year-long program, we watched Mama study with her Japanese dictionary every evening, struggling to write term papers in English. Once, after an argument with Dad, Mama exclaimed, "Reiner, after you pay for my social work education, I will find my own job and get a divorce. But first, you must help me correct my English!"

Our friends from CF camp often complained about being bored in the hospital. To Ana and me, though, long days in the hospital were filled with potential. Creating projects and doing homework in our room made us feel productive and helped pass the time. If distracted, we did not dwell on the depressing truth that CF was slowly consuming our lives.

Ana and I had been hospitalized together again in the spring of our eighth-grade year, 1986. Late one evening, Mama visited us after work. Her eyelids drooped behind her thick glasses, her cheeks were reddened, and her wiry hair windblown from the drive across town. She laid her bags on the bed and pulled out two notebooks.

"Mama brought you a journal," she said. "Alice said you may like to write down your thoughts about the hospital. Someday I would like you to write a book about your experience."

We groaned at having to write but began dutifully chronicling our thoughts the next day. Ana wrote,

I am really scared sometimes when I can't stop coughing or breathe. When my breathing becomes so labored I get so sick of it. I feel like just yelling STOP! and relaxing my lungs for once. I sometimes wonder what life without coughing, doing therapy, or taking medications would be like. Imagine all the free time I would have! We'd probably go to sleep at 7 or 8 pm! I'm so sick of CF, CF, CF! I wish I can take my new bike and just ride away from it all and have just one day without a cough, weakness or the thought of dying.

In my journal, I wrote,

Sometimes I get really fed up when they have to restart my IV. Oh, I wish I didn't have these stupid IVs and these damn hospitalizations. Can't I just be like someone else—healthy? Sometimes all this pain and agony isn't worth it—but that is really, really sometimes. All the time, though, I love living and I love the whole world. Everything is so wonderful and great. Except for my health. I don't mean to brag, but God gave me a smart brain and a quite pretty face, but my health is awful.

It was hard for me to write. After a few entries, I got bored. It felt too dry, too stifled. I soon abandoned Mama's journals and resorted to artfully writing down the facts of our hospital experiences with colorful markers on plain white sheets of paper. I drew diagrams and pictures of hospital paraphernalia.

Ana joined this endeavor and made one page for all the doctors we had, while on a separate sheet I wrote down all the medications we had been prescribed. I scribbled in rainbow colors: *Nafcillin, Dicloxicillin, Tobramycin.* Over the next week, Ana and I hovered over our bedside tables consumed by creative fervor, creating a diary of our hospital experiences. We documented every detail of life at Kaiser, including the rooms we stayed in, dates and lengths of each hospitalization, and procedures we had undergone. The entries were simple, like the following:

I came into the hospital in June 1984. My doctor's clinic visit was successful so we went to a restaurant to celebrate. But then I had a terrific hemoptysis episode and blood was everywhere. I went to the emergency room and later Dr. Steinberg admitted me. I had Nafcillin and my arm was on fire all the time and it ruined all my veins. Even though I went home in only 2 weeks it wasn't worth the pain of IVs.

Ana wrote,

Ana and Isa both came in during December, 1985. Jessica [a friend with CF] also came in which made our stay fine. We had lots of fun . . . maybe that's why we stayed so long. We danced, talked and laughed. We played bowling with lotion bottles and a roll of tape. We got into the supplies cabinet and found a razor and Jessica taught us how to shave our legs.

We also included hand-drawn cartoons of how to put in an IV, how to check a pulse, and how to flush an IV line. We described favorite and nightmare roommates, a sixth-grade graduation party thrown by the nurses, and the movie stars who visited the floor.

It was past midnight, and we were still working. The lights in the hallway were dim. We heard a baby crying from a room down the hall. Our nurse was perplexed by our passion and asked why we were up so late. We told her we were writing a diary of our lives at Kaiser. The nurse skimmed our pages, complimenting us for our creativity and impressed by our vivid memories. Suddenly her face lit up. She encouraged us to make copies when we were done and to sell them to teach others about life in the hospital.

The next day, with over thirty pages written, we compiled the pages into a booklet we called "Life at Kaiser." Over the next several days, nurses and other hospital staff visited our room to glance at our finished work. We typed up the pages, made copies of the booklet, and sold them for a dollar each. We pleaded with the nurses not to place a roommate in our room so we could use the empty bed to collate pages. By the end of our hospital stay, we had sold more than three hundred copies. Later our booklet garnered significant recognition, and we were featured in the Kaiser Hospital employee magazine and on the local television news. We eventually received the Fritz Coleman Spirit of Southern California Award.

Every few days, Dr. Robbie visited our hospital room. He listened to our chests, saying, "Your lungs are crackling like Rice Krispies!" On one visit, he joked, "Are you turkeys keeping out of trouble? I heard you're getting rich in the hospital."

"I guess so," I replied, smiling awkwardly. "So many people like our booklet. I don't know why. It's pretty simple. We're donating the proceeds to help cure CF."

"It keeps us busy," Ana said. "People seem to like what we wrote."

"Well, of course," he said. "You guys have a lot to teach us. Someday you should publish it." He sat down on my bed, and his face became serious.

"Girls, you munchkins have a really tough disease. We can give you all these antibiotics and treatments, and they can help you some. But the rest is up to you. You have to be strong and do the best you can. You've got to do everything we tell you to do, and fight this disease with everything you've got. That's the only way to make it."

We believed every word. Over the past few years, as we had gotten sicker, we had gone from doing two treatments a day, to three, then four. Now we even woke up in the middle of the night to do a fifth breathing treatment. That was the only way we could remedy the shortness of breath, allowing us to sleep deeply enough to preserve the energy we needed to survive junior high. And still we found ourselves in the hospital far too often. We just couldn't do enough to stay well.

A few months later, Ana and I were hospitalized together again. CF camp was just around the corner, and I had recently bought a few puffy paints and white T-shirts to paint gifts for the "Flamingos." Determined to complete my project, I brought the shirts to the hospital and painted simple colorful designs of rainbows and flamingos on them. Some of the nurses were amazed at my freehand skills and inquired about purchasing shirts. It was another business opportunity that couldn't be ignored. Within a week, word had spread about our T-shirt–painting services; we posted flyers advertising the business, and customers just rolled in.

Nurses would stop by our room and joke about our being back in business. They admired how we made money while we were cooped up in the hospital. We asked customers to bring in their own T-shirts, and we painted them for five dollars each. We were walking advertisements, as we each wore a T-shirt painted with colorful flowers and tropical designs. During a few late nights, Ana and I obsessively created a catalog of nearly thirty colorful designs that customers could look through to choose their favorites. The images included fanciful unicorns, cheerful teddy bears, idyllic country scenes, and rainbow-colored balloons.

Orders soon piled up, and my paint supply began to run low. A few days later, I called Mama late at night.

"Mama!" I yelled into the answering machine. "Are you there? This is an emergency!"

I heard her grab the phone. "What is it? Are you all right?"

"Mama, I really, really need more red and yellow paint! Can you buy some for me and bring it by tomorrow?"

"Is that why you called?" She sighed. "My goodness. Don't you scare me like that. Mama thought something was wrong!"

"*Gomen,* Mama," I apologized. "I'm just out of paint, and I've got tons of T-shirt orders. Dr. Robbie said we can go home next week so I need to finish them before we leave."

"Don't you do too much," Mama said. "Remember you are in the hospital because you are sick. Don't you be too busy. You must rest."

She was right. We took our business so seriously it was often difficult to nap. Sometimes, we were discharged tired but with our backpacks filled with cash.

After that hospitalization, our business, the "T-Shirt Twins," was born. We obtained a business license and business cards and participated in local art shows. Friends and teachers at school ordered T-shirts, and our profits grew. We were featured in *National Geographic World* magazine's "Kids Did It!" and our self-esteem was finally rising. Every hospitalization thereafter became an opportunity to transform our artistic itch into hard-earned money.

For this hospitalization, Ryuta, now sixteen, was finally old enough to accompany my parents to the hospital. One weekend, Mama and Dad cheerfully entered our room. Dad brought a chess set and the latest issue of *National Geographic*. Mama carried a *bento* box full of our favorite *nigiri sushi*. A few minutes later, my brother slowly trailed into the room. Ryuta sat in the corner, avoiding eye contact. He wore a gray Quicksilver T-shirt and Bermuda shorts. His bulging knees were covered with scars from too many rough-and-tumble rides on his dirt bike.

"Hey, Ryuta! It's good to see you," I said.

"Eh," he replied.

"Mama brought you some things," Mama said, pulling out Norman Cousins's *Anatomy of an Illness*. "This is a wonderful story about self-healing." Ana reached for the book and flipped through it.

Mama beamed, "And Mama went shopping and found these for you. I am so happy about them." She pulled out matching pajamas for Ana and me, decorated with pink flamingos.

"*Domo arigato!*" (Thank you so much!), Ana and I chimed.

Just then, Sally, our favorite nurse, wheeled in the scale, exclaiming, "It's time for your weight!" I got up and stepped on the scale.

After adjusting, Sally muttered, "Okay, that's seventy . . . nine pounds. It looks like you're up two pounds!"

"That's great!" I said.

"How wonderful," Mama said.

"Damn, Isa. That's pathetic. You're fourteen." Ryuta pointed to an erupting pimple on my face and said, "You better not pop that zit, or you'll lose weight." He proceeded to sing the chorus to *We Are the World*, the 1984 song to raise money for the African famine victims. Ana and I burst into laughter. We enjoyed his clever, albeit, cruel insults.

"Is this your brother? I didn't know you had a brother," Sally said, as Ana got on the scale.

"Yeah, this is Ryuta."

"You guys don't look alike at all. You girls look so much more Oriental."

Ryuta had become quite handsome. His dark hair had turned golden from the California sun, and he had developed European facial features with a longer nose and broader forehead just like Opa. He was spared the flat face, narrow eyes, and rounded nose that Ana and I had inherited. He could pass as Caucasian and was spared the nosy inquiry from strangers that we often heard: "So, what are you?"

"Yeah, I know. Ryuta got lucky."

Mama interjected. "There is nothing wrong with looking Asian."

"Your mother's right." Sally turned to Ryuta. "Nice meeting you," Sally said. Ryuta waved his hand toward her. Sally glanced at the *sushi* Mama had brought. "Oh, you guys like that fishy stuff? Me, I'm a meat and potatoes kind of gal. That stuff won't help you gain weight, you know." She turned to Mama. "You gotta feed them high-calorie hamburgers." My poor mother always seemed to be blamed for not doing something right for us.

After Sally left, Ana and I chatted with Mama and Dad. Ryuta sat silently. I felt sorry for him. He stared at the TV on the wall, mesmerized.

"How's school?" I asked.

"Fine."

"What'd you do this weekend?"

"Nothing."

I looked at my abandoned lunch tray. The chocolate brownie remained unopened. I offered it to Ryuta.

I reached over to hand the brownie to him just as he got up to grab it.

"Nasty! Look at your blue-ass Q-tip fingers!" He shrieked, grabbing my fingers.

"Ryu-chan, don't you be so rude," Mama snapped.

I laughed despite being insulted. Whenever I got a lung infection, my oxygen levels dropped, and my fingers turned a purple-blue shade.

Hospitalizations became routine for Ana and me during our teen years, and Ryuta's moodiness grew like an ominous black cloud. He had become a sideshow, an understudy in our family play, as my parents slipped into survival mode, and they dashed between work, the hospital, and home. His teasing had been reduced to ignoring and avoiding Ana and me at all costs. When he did notice us, he would succinctly insult us and then disappear back into his silent world. For that reason, I soon gave up any and all attachment and devotion to pleasing my brother, instead saving all my affection and attention for my other more-deserving sibling, Ana. As my bond with my sister strengthened, Ryuta and I became more alienated. I gave up even trying to break through the barrier he had erected.

The bright light above my bed flicked on, waking me from a deep sleep.

"Your IV's no good, dear," a nurse said, as she slammed an IV tray onto my bedside table. I looked down at my arm, which was burning and swollen.

"Oh, I hate this." I squinted and sat up.

"I'm sorry, sweetheart," she said. She reached for my arm and untaped the IV. The tubing connected to my arm was white, and the bag on the pole read *intralipids:* pure fat. It was being pumped into me in another attempt to increase my weight. Its pudding-like pressure was notorious for corroding veins. I looked at the large bruises covering both of my arms, giving me tracks along the veins like those of a heroin addict. My scarred veins were fragile and resisted every invading needle. I had been poked four times the day before when they put in a new IV. Normally stoic, I broke down and whimpered like a baby. Now, it was time to get poked again.

As the nurse prepared the tape and IV line, I said, "Here's a good vein, my only one left." I prayed, *Dear God, let this be a good vein, please don't make me be a pin cushion again.*

The ritual began, and my heart pounded with anxiety. The nurse tried everything to prepare the vein: hot packs, extra tight tourniquets, having me do rapid arm movements, vigorous slapping on the skin, all to raise the potential vein to prick. This time, I got lucky. In just two sticks, the IV was in. I helped the nurse tape the needle down just the way I liked it; it was my little attempt at control during this ordeal. The nurse reconnected the intralipids to my arm and turned on the pump.

"Now you can finally get some rest, sweetie," she said, as she left.

"Thanks for your help," I said, even though she had tortured me.

I looked up and watched the fat droplets drip one by one into me. *What's the point?* I wondered. *I'm never going to gain weight.*

I flicked off the light and rolled onto my side. I could feel my hip bone jut out against the hard mattress. I rotated my prepubescent body in disgust. I hated looking like an anorexic. I shuddered at the memory of an incident at a store a few weeks earlier. Two older women stood in front of me while I was partially hidden by a shelf behind them. They were staring at Ana, who was browsing through merchandise across the aisle. "Oh, Mattie, isn't it just awful, how young girls these days starve themselves?"

I put my hand under my T-shirt and could feel my ribs and sternum forcing themselves through my skin. I envied my curvy friends at school. Andrea, whose voluptuous boobs were overflowing last year's bra, often said, "You're so lucky to be so skinny!" but I disagreed. I was cold all the time and had to sit on a pillow in class so my butt wouldn't burn from the hard wooden seats.

The next morning, Dr. Robbie came by. I told him about my midnight IV start and how much I hated intralipids.

"At CF camp the other kids use special enzymes that break down in the small intestine, where they're absorbed. We're the only ones using the powdered kind. Do you think those will help me gain weight?" I asked.

"You girls are Japanese," he stated. "You're supposed to be petite. Don't worry. You just need to eat more. Your time will come."

He didn't understand. I just wanted to get fatter. To grow. To be normal.

Sometimes I start to be careless of my life—not caring about classes. I do this because deep down inside I think, "why take the requirements for college, I don't even think I'm going!" But then I get angry at myself for being so pessimistic. When I saw the show of the CF lady who had a baby my views changed. Now I'm determined to succeed in school and go to college . . .

—Ana, age fourteen

I opened the drawer of my bedside table and heaved out my heavy algebra textbook. I picked up the phone. I had phone phobia; I hated calling people and always made Ana make the calls. But it was my turn. I dialed.

"Hello?" Andrea's sweet voice answered.

"Hi, Drea, it's Isa."

"Hey! How's it going?"

"I'm fine. Still stuck here," I said. "How's school?"

"It was all right. Ted is being really annoying." Andrea continued, going off about her latest boyfriend. I rolled my eyes toward Ana, who was sitting on her bed. We didn't have the luxury of going through puberty. Hormonally, we were shut off and our attraction to boys was nonexistent.

"I mean," Andrea went on, "he wanted me to go bike riding with him and got all mad when I said I couldn't. I was having my period, and was all bloated and cramping, you know how that is . . . I mean, why would I wanna be on a bike?"

"Yeah, tell me about it," I lied, pretending to know what she meant.

I remember Ana telling me how lucky we were not to have to waste so much time on the stress and strain of hormones and boyfriends. "They get all upset over just a guy, and we know about the really important things in life—like survival and appreciating every day! We are so much more mature than they are!" She was right, but I was strangely envious. Periods were for girls who planned on having sex, getting pregnant, raising families—those in it for the long haul.

After a while, I interrupted Andrea. I needed to get to the point of my phone call. "I'm really sorry to bother you again, because I know it's a pain to ask you every day, but would you mind giving me the homework assignment from algebra class today? Thank you so much, I really appreciate your help."

I sounded so Japanese. I hated to burden my friends, to call them every day for school work. But that was the only way to keep up.

"Don't worry; it's no problem," Andrea replied and gave me the assignment. She, and so many of my classmates, were so compassionate and helped us thrive in school.

We talked some more and made plans for her to visit the following weekend before I hung up the phone. I dove into the assignment, working vigorously on the problems and checking my answers at the back of the book.

During one of my early hospitalizations, I had kept up with my assignments, but report cards came out before I was discharged. I felt so insulted when my teacher gave me a failing grade! When I returned to school after that hospital stay, I handed a stack of completed assignments to my teacher and from that day forward, she knew I took her class seriously. After that, when returning to school from the hospital, I would get so stressed and tired from studying for the make-up tests that I would end up back in the hospital in a matter of weeks.

On another occasion, Ana and I were summoned to the special education office after returning to school from a prolonged hospitalization. We were asked to take a series of tests in basic arithmetic and grammar, which we passed with flying colors.

"I can't believe they think CF affects our brains!" Ana pouted.

"Yeah, we're not stupid," I said.

"They are concerned about your absences, that is all," Mama reassured us. After all, Ana had missed more than nine weeks of school in eighth grade. Most kids wouldn't be able to catch up, but then again most kids didn't have a dad who could tutor them in science and math. We had never heard about Individual Education Plans (IEPs), which are special education accomodations for people with health problems. Our family preferred to manage everything ourselves, without extra help from school officials. Still, Ana and I were obsessed with academic achievement, and it continued to take a toll on our health.

"Don't you take school so seriously!" Mama admonished me. "Nothing is worth such a negative impact on your health."

"Mama, I need to keep up. I like studying. It makes me normal. School's something I'm good at."

"Yes, but you are doing too much."

"That sounds funny, Mama. Most moms would nag their kids to study harder. Especially Asian moms."

"Well, we are not such an ordinary family. You have a special circumstance. You don't have to overachieve. It will tire you out."

"Ha! Look who's talking!" Mama stayed up late each night working on her social work papers. But she was naturally overprotective. Finally, my parents spoke to the school officials, and our teachers let them bring tests to the hospital so we could take them while my parents supervised.

I knew the stress and exhaustion hurt my health. But my friends at school were all so driven. They knew exactly what they wanted to do when they grew up. Andrea wanted to be a photographer, Josh a lawyer, Danielle a therapist, Sally an engineer, and Nancy a doctor. I had no idea what I wanted to be. I didn't even know how long I would live. But I wanted to fit in with my friends, so I took college-prep classes with them.

By the time we entered high school in 1988, Ana and I had each spent about thirty-six weeks of our lives in the hospital. Then, modern medicine caught up with the progression of our disease. Dr. Robbie consulted with doctors at the Cystic Fibrosis Foundation–sponsored Cystic Fibrosis Care Center at Children's Hospital of Los Angeles, who recommended that we start aerosolized tobramycin, a powerful antibiotic against *pseudomonas.* This treatment did wonders to curb the cycles of lung infections as well as keep our lung bleeds under control. By 1988, an oral quinolone antibiotic called ciprofloxacin had been released at Kaiser, and it kept *pseudomonas* in check as well. In high school, our hospital tune-ups could be scheduled during school vacations, so our attendance and school participation reached near-normal levels. Though our lack of physical strength still forced us to attend adaptive physical education class, we were able to walk and bike to school. For the first time in many years, Ana and I experienced the joys of hanging out with our friends, participating in orchestra and other extra-curricular activities, and keeping up with schoolwork like everyone else.

My friends were immensely supportive. Perhaps unconsciously, I chose compassionate friends who all had challenges of their own—a birth defect, a learning disability, a disabled parent, a dysfunctional immigrant family. I selected precocious friends with whom I could share intimate chats about our troubles; the rest were simply not worth my time. We sought solace from whatever curses affected us by delving obsessively into academia, building self-esteem with good grades, good SAT scores, and ambitious college plans.

As like attracts like, I found my clique to also be unathletic and disad-vantaged in the looks department. Most were close to five feet in height. My closest friend, Josh, had been born blind and with intrauterine growth retardation as a result of being an undiscovered fraternal twin. While he was still an infant, cataract surgery restored his sight, but he still had to wear Coke-bottle spectacles, and his bony, frail frame barely topped eighty-five pounds. His type-A personality, along with his caffeine addiction, com-pensated for his size, and he was well known in school for his energy and outspoken assertiveness. He did not fit the ideal masculine profile by any stretch, and his brave, aggressive, romantic gestures toward me were quickly dismissed because of my estrogen deprivation. So over the years we became the best of friends. When we were together, people thought we were just smart-alecky twelve-year-olds.

By our senior year of high school, we had agreed to go to the prom to-gether as friends. Prom made a mockery of the two scrawny kids trying to dress like grown-ups. After one Kaiser visit, Mama took Ana and me to downtown Los Angeles's garment district to find discount evening gowns that fit our figures. I wanted to hide as much of my body as possible, and

I bought a homey crewneck, long-sleeved red dress that would have been better suited to a golden anniversary celebration. Since I owned no bras, Mama had the nerve to buy me a red-laced teddy, and I scoffed at the assumption that I was supposed to be sexy. And I could not be sexy with Josh. When prom night arrived, a handsome Josh arrived at our home in his Bar Mitzvah tuxedo. While he anxiously paced and made small talk with my parents, I was upstairs nearly in tears, placing neatly folded squares of tissue into the cups of my teddy. Once I made it downstairs, Josh overflowed with nervous energy, and his fidgety, clumsy hands could barely tie on my corsage. Nonetheless, we had a splendid time together with a group of geeky friends, touring Los Angeles in a rented limo.

At the prom, we slow-danced to Chris de Burgh's "Lady in Red." Josh's beady eyes peered closely into my face, while I gazed awkwardly back at his face just three inches below mine. His broad smile eased my discomfort at my attempts to be a beautiful date. Unlike the drama of some classmates' prom nights, there was no romance, no loss of virginity, no wild drinking or smoking during our evening. My only rebellion that night was that I skipped therapy.

Our "healthy" high school years were a mere illusion created by the mask of heavy antibiotic use. But we thrived on the renewed sense of well-being. Our quality of life skyrocketed, and emotionally we felt a sense of accomplishment: we had overcome the challenges of CF. We had survived the turmoil of our early adolescence, and we were still alive! Our self-esteem increased because we knew we were tough and we didn't give up. Images of a high school graduation procession with me in a wheelchair and on oxygen no longer haunted my thoughts as they had in junior high school. Like any adolescents, both of us had an awakened sense of invulnerability. We believed that if we worked hard at taking care of our health, we could beat the odds and manage to stay well until a new medical breakthrough came along. We became experts in controlling our disease.

Chapter 11

No Escape

Ana

I am happy Isa and me are still alive.

—Ana, age fourteen

Our family was about to go on vacation, but the mood felt strained. Mama and Dad had had a big fight the night before, and Mama had stormed out of the house. She hadn't returned until that morning. Things were calmer, but there was harsh silence in the car as we drove to Lake Arrowhead, where we planned to stay for a few days.

Mama had gone to the mall during her escape and bought new wool pants, which she was wearing, and she was happily telling us about the sale at May Company.

Dad tried to get us excited about the upcoming adventure.

"Ryuta, there should be good fishing in the lake, if we get up early," Dad strained to make conversation over the blaring radio.

"Cool," Ryuta replied.

"Did you pack some bait?"

Ryuta hesitated. His head was turned away from Dad as he peered out the window. ZZ Top's "Legs" was playing on the radio, and Ryuta was strumming his fingers. The delay made it seem like they were ignoring each other.

Finally, he replied. "Yeah, I got some roe and flies I used on the last scout trip."

"Nice."

The strained conversation continued through the remainder of the drive until we arrived at Lake Arrowhead.

We had rented a small, one-room cabin near the lake. The next morning, we went fishing. Ryuta loved to fish, though anyone overhearing the stilted conversation in the car would never have guessed it. Isa and I caught a few trout ourselves, and when we had enough, we returned to our cabin.

"I'm tired," I said.

"What you need is a good long walk," Dad said. Dad always felt that exercise and fresh air were the cure for any malaise. I wanted to prove to him that I was strong enough to hike. So, the family bundled up and went out.

"It's freezing!" Ryuta complained, huddling in his puffy down coat.

"Just walk faster," Dad said.

My heart was racing, and my breath quickened from the high elevation. When I walked, my head pounded, and, as Dad raced ahead, I fell farther and farther behind. The fall scenery was soothing, and we could see the glimmer of the lake as we ascended a hilly trail. Wispy cirrus clouds dotted the sky. They looked to me just like the cloudy patches in the X-ray of my lungs. Perspiration collected beneath the wool sweater and jacket I had piled on to protect me from the chilly air. I complained to Mama, who was also affected by the altitude and walked as slowly as I did.

"Reiner, slow down, Ana-chan is having trouble," she cried out.

"The harder it is, the stronger she will become," he called back. But eventually, Dad did slow down, and when I caught up with him, he pulled off his belt, clipped it around his belt loop, and said, "Here, Ana-chan, hold onto this end, and I'll pull you up."

There was no stopping Dad. He was on a mission to hike with his family, and, by golly, he was going to hike. To him, this was a slow-going trail; he was accustomed to twice the elevation and three times the grade. But it helped me to hold on to him, and I leaned back as he pulled me up the mountain.

Later in the afternoon, my lungs started to bleed. The altitude was too much. All we had wanted was a nice family getaway from illness and reality, but there was no escape. Being in nature was healing; the yellow aspen trees swayed in the breeze while the wind made the leaves dance about. But once I bled, I couldn't focus on the beauty.

The bleeding subsided, and we stayed the night.

The cabin was dark when I heard the clatter of cups from the kitchenette and smelled the aroma of coffee. Mama and Dad always rose before us, and when the coffee was ready they sat in the dim light that came from behind the curtains. Ryuta snored and Isa lay motionless in her cot. I pretended to sleep, enjoying the sounds of my parents.

"It is nice to get away with the children, Reiner," Mama whispered.

"Yah, this is a nice place," Dad said, in a scratchy morning voice.

"It is getting harder for the girls."

"Mmm."

"We must enjoy every moment we have with them. You know, they have lived so long, but things have been so difficult since they entered junior high. Perhaps the end is coming soon."

I cringed.

"We have given them a good life," Dad said.

There was a pause.

"Reiner, we must be strong. We must both help each other out because it will be very difficult as they get sicker."

"Yah."

I wanted to get up and tell them I was okay, and they shouldn't talk like this. I was so sorry to put them through the pain of having to know that Isa and I could die soon. Yet it was comforting that they were actually having a conversation. This was the first time I had heard them talk this way.

Perhaps, when all was said and done, our cystic fibrosis had brought my parents closer. Mama used to say she stayed married to Dad only because of us, that if we hadn't had CF she would have left him long ago. While those comments were burdensome, at this quiet moment as I overheard what they presumed was a secret chat, I was glad they were together. They needed each other.

Later that morning, I started bleeding again, and it became clear that I was going to ruin our vacation, and we would have to return to sea level. Isa and Ryuta protested, and I wanted to stay. There was an Oktoberfest celebration at the lake that I knew would please Dad, and the plan was to hike around Big Bear, but I whined about my headache, and we packed the car and left.

Sitting in the front seat, Dad commented to me, "It is too much for you to be in nature, yah? Hmm. You are really becoming a city girl." I knew he was disappointed in me; for a German and a Stenzel, not being a nature enthusiast and heavy-duty hiker was indeed a failure.

"No, *Vater*" (pronounced "fa-taed"), "I really want to hike," I protested, "I love the outdoors." By addressing Dad in German, I hoped to gain his favor.

When we got home, I went right to the hospital. Dr. Robbie told me my days at high elevation were over. I could no longer hike in the Sierras, ski at Mammoth, or enjoy the snow in the local mountains. It was a devastating sentence for me, and I know for Dad, too. Our family culture of outdoor living had become painfully limited.

Throughout our childhood, Uncle Juichi was our closest relative. Since immigrating to the United States in 1964, he had worked hard to achieve his American Dream, having founded a successful boat company, Arima Marine International, in Seattle, Washington. Muscular and tan from boating and golfing, his thin lips hidden by a narrow moustache, he looked just like General Tojo. Juichi also had Mama's round face, high cheekbones, and short stature. A stoic bachelor, Juichi had no children of his own, but he had a special fondness for his twin nieces. Although reserved and serious in nature, he had a wry sense of humor, which occasionally showed itself and made us giggle. He had suffered from tuberculosis as a teenager and spent an entire year in a sanatorium. Doctors had removed a major part of one of his lungs, and he had a large scar (like my belly scar) to show for it. His illness had forced him to change his educational plans and drop out of a prominent men's college. He understood what Isa and I were going through.

When Isa and I were thirteen, Uncle Juichi invited us to Japan for the New Year holiday. We had just been discharged from the hospital on Christmas day, 1985. Isa's lungs were still bleeding; nonetheless, Dr. Robbie gave permission for our early discharge.

At the airport, Ryuta and my parents stood with us at the gate. Mama's voice quivered with nervousness. "Isa-chan, I hope you are well enough for this trip. Don't you overdo it." She turned to Juichi and told him in Japanese, "You call us right away if Isa-chan gets worse."

"*Hai, hai,*" Juichi agreed, hoisting our heavy bags packed with medical supplies.

Isa told Mama not to worry; she was sure it would stop.

It was time to depart. Ryuta waved at me while I picked up my bags. "Have fun. Bring me back some *kabutomushi* beetles."

He then put his arm around Isa's shoulders. "Bye, Isa. Have a nice trip. I hope you stay well. I love you." It was the first time we had ever heard those words from him.

When we arrived in Tokyo, we were greeted by Uncle Yuzo, our mother's younger brother, outside the airport. Our breath could be seen in the crisp late December air in Tokyo.

Yuzo's home was made comfortable by space heaters and the traditional *kotatsu*, a low table with a heater beneath it that was draped with a thick blanket. As we sat on the floor, tucking our legs beneath the table, the warmth of the *kotatsu* soothed our chilled legs. Our cousins Yuki and Yuji stared at us with fascination, giggling and squirming while Aunt Kiyoko smiled politely and commented on how much we had grown. Obachan, who lived with Yuzo's family, was most familiar and welcoming. She invited us to her small bedroom, where she showed us photographs from her youth.

Our attempts to communicate were a mishmash of our broken Japanese and their broken English accompanied by a lot of smiling and nodding. We cordially shared gifts that we had brought from America and photographs of life back home.

It was time for therapy, and after we used our nebulizers, we laid on the living room floor while Obachan and Uncle Juichi gave us *pan-paka-pan*, their best attempts at chest percussion. I hid my red, puffy face as I coughed. Yuko and my cousins remembered our therapies from 1980, but now our coughs were louder and more productive. I was on display. Yuzo asked questions, and we answered them casually, hiding our feeling of awkwardness. We knew we seemed peculiar to them, not only because we were American relatives, but also because we had this strange disease. Though we were related by blood, they were, in essence, strangers.

The next morning, Yuki, Yuji, Isa, and I roamed the neighborhood, with its long concrete alleyways, narrow streets, and nostalgic scents of Japan— the faint smell of the bakery down the street and the burning foliage. The cold air whipped color into our cheeks and turned our breath to puffs of steam. We found a playground, and Yuki and Yuji jumped on a bouncing bar. Isa started to climb it.

"You better not jump on that, or you'll bleed," I warned.

"No, I won't." She hopped on the bar and nothing happened. On the way back home we broke into a jog. We were soon coughing and breathless, but we felt good.

When we got to Yuzo's home, Isa said, "See, I told you I could stop my bleeds. We're in Japan! I have to be well. When there's a will, there's a way." She was right. For years, in the weeks after CF camp, our white blood cell counts were always lower than usual, proving to us that happiness creates health.

A few days later, we learned the real reason for Juichi's invitation. Our relatives had made arrangements for us to meet a healer, who could reportedly sense the ailments of sick people and heal them through the power of touch.

The healer, a man in his mid-fifties dressed in a black minister's suit, met us in a downtown Tokyo hotel room. A cross hung from his neck. My uncles spoke formal Japanese with him, as Isa and I sat on the bed, trying to grasp the foreign conversation.

"This man may be able to heal your disease," Juichi said. "He has cured people of cancer and has become famous throughout Japan."

I looked with skepticism at the ordinary man, searching for some special aura or air of mysticism about him. He smelled of cigarette smoke, and his black hair was smooth and glossy against his forehead like a crow's feathers.

The healer placed his large, soft hand firmly on Isa's chest, just above her sternum. His eyes looked off into the distance as if he noticed a speck on the wall, and he froze in thought.

"She breathes hard, and her heart works hard. It may be enlarged. Her lungs are filled with sputum."

Not too impressive to me, as I always knew our hearts raced faster than most, to compensate for our damaged lungs.

After a short examination of us both, the healer conferred with my uncles again in formal Japanese. Then, the session came to an end with traditional bowing, gracious words of gratitude, and farewells. The healer left the hotel room. Much to my disappointment, I was not cured.

The next day, Juichi explained that the healer was willing to try his curative magic on us for ten thousand dollars each. Juichi was considering hiring him. He could have the money wired that evening. Even as a naive thirteen-year-old, I was full of skepticism.

"Why would he charge so much money?" I asked Juichi. "Jesus could cure people, and he didn't charge any fees. If this guy says he's a Christian, and he could really cure people, he shouldn't charge for it."

It was a huge disappointment. But I was touched that Juichi was so concerned about our health that he would even consider this costly endeavor. Maybe a better cure awaited us someday.

Chapter 12

Noticing Ryuta

Ana

Dear God, Bless Ryuta and let his troubles be solved. Let him stop doing bad deeds. I know that deep down he's got a lot of painful feelings.

—Ana, age fourteen

Our worsening health forced Isa, me, and our parents, to focus inward.
In survival mode, friends, pop culture, and leisure became low priorities.
At the same time, Ryuta compensated for our isolation and thrived socially. He fell right into the Pacific Palisades culture of surfing, skiing, and wild
high school parties. Isa and I envied Ryuta's popularity. As Ryuta became
more conscious of our parents' foreignness, he decided to abandon our
family ways and affiliate with his friends' families.

Mama and Dad had bought their home in 1972, and since then, Pacific
Palisades had evolved from a middle-class bedroom community into an affluent suburb. Ryuta's peers were the sons and daughters of successful
Hollywood producers, wealthy judges, executives, and corporate lawyers.
He envied his friends, who received fancy cars for their sixteenth birthdays.
Ryuta was at first drawn to their power and prestige and later to their easy
access to money and fame. He believed that these families defined success
in America. To him, Dad's career in academia could not compare to the
high-profile jobs of his friends' parents. Dad had no Mercedes, no trust
fund, and no endless supply of cash.

As Mama and Dad spent the evenings doing our therapy in the living room, Ryuta hid behind closed doors in his bedroom. He spent as little time with the family as possible. He rarely spoke beyond the occasional grunt or derogatory remark. There were signs that Ryuta was slipping away from our family.

One day, while Mama was practicing her favorite piano piece, Beethoven's *Pathetique,* downstairs, I had just finished doing laundry. I carried a pile of his clean clothes upstairs, planning to leave the clothes at his door because the room was usually off-limits to visitors. But that day, the door was slightly ajar, and the temptation was too much. I entered and observed the surroundings. Piles of clothes, books, and papers were scattered all over like a bomb had gone off. The walls were decorated with posters of Jim Morrison, Janis Joplin, and surfing icons. His waxed surfboard rested against the wall. Incense and candles littered his bedside table. A can of spray paint lay in the corner on a box.

I dropped the pile of folded laundry on the bed and peered out the window. A flash of blue on the roof outside caught my eye. I leaned over his bed and pulled the curtain aside. The screen had been torn off and was laying on the roof. I realized this must be the way Ryuta snuck out at night. Spray-painted on the roof in large bold blue letters was the sentence *Jenny Is A Bitch.* It was written so that it could be read from our neighbor's home. Jenny was our childhood friend next door. She had become a popular, rebellious teenager, and Ryuta had been spending more time with her over the last few years. I was pissed that he dared vandalize our home. Mama and Dad, of course, had no idea.

I glanced at his wallet on the table. Just for fun, my curious fingers opened it. To my surprise, my fifteen-year-old brother had a California driver's license. I looked at the photo and thought it must have been a stretch for any officer to believe that the bearer of this juvenile face was old enough to drive. Then I looked more closely at the information on the license: Josh E. Cohen, born 1965. *My lucky brother can pass as a white Jewish guy.* He must have been up to no good, but it wasn't my place to tell on him. I remembered Christmas shopping with him the year before, when I had watched him proudly obtain a nice keychain for Mama with a "five-finger discount." I hadn't told then, and I wouldn't tell now.

When Ryuta's friends came over, Ana and I were inevitably doing house chores or therapy, looking as unattractive as ever. I don't think Ryuta ever explained our CF to his friends, and he must have been embarrassed by how we looked. His cool friends made me nervous with their cuteness, their spiked, bleached hair, and their suntanned skin. To me, they represented the Southern California culture in the movies: they were into good-looking girls, surfing, volleyball, fast cars, and wild parties.

While Ana and I prided ourselves on academic achievement, Ryuta began to focus less and less on his schoolwork. Although he was intelligent, he chose not to take honors classes. I seldom saw him studying. He took classes in drama and chose work-study for which he worked at the local supermarket bagging groceries for rich people and celebrities. He and his buddies regularly wrote themselves permission slips excusing them from morning classes, and then they all went surfing in the morning when the waves were good.

At one point, Ryuta came up with enough cash to buy a used motorcycle. He roared around the neighborhood when Mama and Dad were at work. I worried about him since he didn't even wear a helmet. For several weeks he parked the motorcycle on the side of the house and covered it, and my clueless parents had no idea. As expected, once they discovered it, Ryuta was forced to sell it immediately.

During his tenth-grade year, my mother started to suspect that something wasn't right. Ryuta was failing his classes. She received phone calls from school stating that Ryuta had been truant on several occasions. One day, the principal asked our parents and those of Ryuta's buddies to come to his office around the time when the boys would check into school after surfing. Sure enough, the boys were caught.

That evening, there was a tense discussion in the dining room. Isa and I were excluded, but we hid at the top of the stairs, our ears straining to catch every word.

"Ryuta! How could you?" Mama's shrill voice was at its highest pitch.

"You guys don't get it. School isn't everything. It's not that big of a deal." Ryuta's voice was low.

"You are the son of a world-renowned physicist. You were such a good child. We have given you so much. You must take school more seriously. It is your future." There was silence.

Dad cleared his throat. He finally spoke: "You are grounded. No more surfing."

"It's not just school, Ryu-chan. It is the motorcycle, the sneaking out at night, your time away from our family, your friends' negative influence. Even Akie told me that she saw you smoking on the street with your friends."

I was shocked. After all he saw us going through, he was smoking? Having outgrown his mild childhood asthma, he was the healthy one, and yet, he was purposely destroying his health. I couldn't understand that. I would have done anything to have healthy lungs, to be able to do the things he could do like go out with friends, surf, hike, run . . . how pathetic.

The discussion got more heated as Mama and Dad made accusations about drinking and drugs, about how one of his buddies had been arrested for drug possession, how things were spiraling out of control. I was annoyed. Ryuta's friend was a total loser; like all drug users, he took his health for granted. As the interrogation went on, Ryuta's voice finally broke, and he began to sob. He choked out an explanation, saying how backward Mama and Dad were, how he was ignored, how he hated our family, and how Dad mistreated him and his friends. I suddenly felt sorry for him.

Mama blamed Dad for not being a good father. She blamed us for taking her attention away from Ryuta. She blamed herself for being so caught up in her own depression, her job, and her classes. My brother's rebellion forced us to realize that our family's problems were not just about CF or an unstable interracial marriage. There was another person on the sidelines who had been ignored for years.

Ryuta finally got the attention he wanted when my parents forced him to attend family therapy. After these sessions, Ryuta would march to his room, slamming the door. Dad would stomp out alone for a brisk night-time walk. Mama would go straight to bed. The lines of communication were still closed, despite outside intervention.

In the ensuing months, arguments continued at home after the meetings. Accusations would echo around the dining room, followed by tantrums and harsh words, "I wish I was never born!" and "Reiner, you are in de-nial!" Dad would scoff at Mama's prying, "You are not my shrink!" He would stiffen up, his eyes revealing his discomfort, at any request to share his feelings.

It was a blessing that Ryuta's problems were addressed in time. He nev-er became the academic nerds his sisters were, but his grades stabilized, and he was accepted into a reputable college by his senior year of high school. As he showed his acceptance letter to me, he said, "I can't wait to leave home and never come back." Yet, to our parents, his acceptance to college made up for the problems he had caused them. He had turned him-self around.

Chapter 13

Therapy or Die

Ana

We are caught in an eternal Greek tragedy, a drama that you had no choice whether you wanted to be in or not. It's like fighting an impossible battle, against an enemy that is overwhelming, relentless and unmerciful. In ancient Greece, the only honorable way that warriors could leave the field was to be carried off on their shields. So it is, with our little CF drama, the only way that you, me and others can leave the field is on our shields. Whether we want this struggle or not, this is our fate. It matters not if we get tired, suffer uncountable wounds, desire to be with our loved ones, long to direct our energies into other avenues of life, CF always, always, always pulls us back to the battle field.

—Terry Phelan, CF adult, age forty-seven

Katie, a pale girl with a square face and flared nostrils, was the sickest of the Flamingos at camp. Perfectly feathered canary yellow hair surrounded a face made puffy, especially around the eyes, by retained fluid. The puffiness was a clear signal that her heart was failing. Other prominent characteristics—scrawny legs with practically no calf muscles, knee bones that jutted out like large hinges, and bulbous, lavender-tinged fingertips—were classic signs of CF. Her enlarged chest moved rapidly with each breath. When she spoke, congestion rattled in her deep voice, and her back and neck arched as she gasped contantly for air, leaving anyone watching in no doubt that she was struggling against an advanced case of lung disease. Despite her physical chaos, Katie exuded a sense of order. Her clothes were meticulously ironed, the seams perfectly flat and stiff like those of a school-girl's uniform. In her suitcase, each day's clothing was neatly folded and organized in large ziplock bags. Smaller bags held the earrings and under-pants that were to match each day's outfit.

As the only child of a single mom who worked as an airline stewardess, Katie was precocious and independent, preferring neatness and isolation to spontaneity and gregariousness. At times, the energy of a cabin full of rowdy and rambunctious teens was too much for her to bear. She was the level-headed, sophisticated Flamingo who called the group to order. Katie was so proper; she never shared our reputation for having mouths like truck drivers.

At night, after the counselors left for their evening meetings, heavy con-sumption of Red Vines and Sunkist Fruit Gems turned our sedate card games into wild parties. Accusations of cheating flew and food fights erupted while Madonna's *Like a Virgin* blasted from our cassette player. When the rowdiness got out of hand, Katie would shout, "Girls! Behave! Calm down! You guys are crazy." She peered through the cabin windows, alert for the flashlight beams of approaching counselors. She didn't want to get into trouble for being up past lights-out. "The counselors are com-ing!" she'd cry, and instantly we'd all jump onto our bunks and feign sleep.

During the day Katie struggled to keep up with the rest of us. As we marched along on the camp's dusty roads she dragged behind, slowly putting one foot forward with each breath. She reminded me of Opa. At the top of a hill, she'd stop, her chest heaving and her face turning purple.

"You . . . [*breath, breath, breath*] . . . girls go . . . [*breath, breath*] . . . ahead," she'd force out. "I need . . . to rest."

Karen would answer, "It's okay, Katie. Take your time." We were usual-ly late to the next event, and I would wriggle impatiently. But we didn't want her to feel left out. As Katie's labored breathing moved the secretions in her lungs, she coughed convulsively, her lungs rumbling and shaking like a revving motor. After she had expelled all her air, her purple face would turn upward and she would manage one big gasp only to begin coughing again, expelling more air and spewing out mouthfuls of mucus. She was like an aging salmon swimming upstream, spawning her mucus before dying.

One afternoon, we marched back to the cabin after lunch. The sweat poured from Katie's brow as she stepped onto the cool concrete floor of the cabin. She sat on her bunk, sighing with relief at having survived the uphill climb to her safe refuge. In a second, she exploded into a coughing fit, only this time it was too much for her body to bear. She retched as her lungs shook, and in an instant the smell of vomit permeated the room.

"Oh, my God," she cried. "I'm so sorry . . . I'm so sorry," she said over and over again as she looked down at her clothes and bed covered with vomit. "I'm so embarrassed."

"It's okay, Katie," Karen consoled. "It happens. Don't worry about it." She stepped over to the supplies cabinet and pulled out paper towels, handing them to Katie to clean herself off. "I've done that before."

"Me, too," I said, although I couldn't remember exactly when.

"Yeah, just blame it on the camp food," Isa said. We all started laughing.

Katie didn't seem to notice her differences or even how sick she was. She even boasted about not having to spend time in the hospital. "I've been do-ing really well," she gasped. "My doctors haven't put me in the hospital for the past five years." I couldn't understand that. She seemed so sick to me. *Wouldn't a hospitalization do her good?* I wondered. Although Isa and I were the skinniest and spent more time in the hospital than any of the other Flamingos, we were also the most energetic and athletic. We blasted through the swimming pool during the group races, trained from our swim-team days. Maybe "doing time" at Kaiser had paid off after all.

Over the years we learned to love Katie. She came to our home for sleep-overs a few times, and all of us attended Karen's sweet sixteen party. But we could not always see past Katie's disease. She embodied everything about CF that we didn't want: her horrifying cough, her gasping voice, her slowness. As teenage girls, we spent so much time in front of the mirror, trying to look beautiful . . . and normal. If we looked healthy, people would treat us like we were normal. The thought of our disease changing how we looked terrified us. I wanted to hide it. Though Katie was beautiful, CF was ugly. It *made* Katie ugly.

In 1989, when we were seventeen, our social worker, Alice, referred us to the Make-A-Wish Foundation. The cancer kids in the hospital had told us that the Make-A-Wish Foundation granted wishes to sick and dying kids as a sort of compensation for their suffering. Some of the kids wished for trips to Disney World or for shopping sprees. For months, we debated what we would wish for. Finally, we decided that our wish was to travel to Eu-rope with Karen as a joint-wish to see Oma again. Karen said she wanted to visit Germany to see "Hitler's castle." We were taken aback by her ig-norance about Germany. Ultimately, we opted to have our own wishes, and she chose a shopping spree at Target.

We were humbled by the foundation's gift, which deemed our life of recurrent hospitalizations from CF worthy of a pampered European adventure. A week before the trip, we went to the local Make-A-Wish office to pick up our tickets and saw Katie's name on the board under "Wish Requested." I wondered what she wished for. She was the one truly worthy of a wish. Our privileged life had already granted us extensive travel, and we weren't as sick as Katie. And we definitely didn't feel like we were dying.

Despite our doubts, we headed off on a three-week vacation to London, Paris, and finally Germany. We had been pumped full of antibiotics the week before, and we were in the best health possible. Mom and Dad joined us on the trip, but Ryuta, uninterested in family vacations, stayed home. In London we visited Buckingham Palace, the Tower of London, and Westminster Abbey, all the while receiving royal treatment: we were given private tours, put up in a luxury hotel, and provided with spending money. In Paris, we stood on top of the Eiffel Tower, climbed to the top of Notre Dame Cathedral, and admired the *Mona Lisa* in the Louvre. Our enthusiasm gave us energy, and our health dared not fail us. It was the adventure of a lifetime. We returned from Europe with immense respect and gratitude for the Make-A-Wish Foundation's generosity.

Immediately after arriving home we left for CF camp, our suitcases full of German chocolates and *Haribo* gummy bears to share with the Flamingos. Excited about spending a week with our beloved friends, we were surprised to find Katie's name absent from the cabin roster. "Where's Katie?" we asked our counselor, Denise.

"I'm not sure," she replied. "She didn't sign up this year."

I couldn't believe it. The last time I had talked to her, she had said she was coming. We had to call her.

That evening we marched to the camp pay phone and called Katie's home. We got the answering machine and heard the recording of Katie's rough, congested voice saying "We can't come to the phone right now, so please leave a message." Beep.

"Hi, Katie, it's Ana," I replied. "We're at camp. Just wondering where you are. Hope you're not in the hospital. Give us a call here. . . . We miss you!"

That evening, the camp musicians entered our cabin without the energy and laughter that usually characterized the first night of camp. Even in the dull cabin light, we could see the sadness in Doc Harwood's eyes. He leaned his large bass cello against a wall.

"Girls," he said, "I'm afraid we have some bad news." Katie's mom had gotten our message and called the camp that evening. Katie had died three weeks earlier, on July 12. She was only seventeen. Karen bowed her head, and few moments later I saw her tears start to fall. Tears welled up in my eyes, too, and my body began to quiver uncontrollably. In an instant a roomful of teenage girls was crying silently.

The strum of acoustic guitars began and merged into soothing chords. I felt Denise's arms embrace me. She hugged my bony shoulders as she softly hummed the melody. Bob Flanagan's strong voice cried out the poetic lyrics of Bob Dylan's "I Shall Be Released": words about a man who cannot be blamed, who cries loud, who anticipates his fall and expects any day his release from oppression.

The words hung in the air like the mist from our nebulizers. Katie had finally been released, freed from the cruel illness that brought labored breathing, convulsive coughing fits, blue lips, and vomiting after meals. The mood was somber after the musicians left the cabin. Silence and grief married as we sat, now dry-eyed. Then, moving mechanically, we started our treatments.

Finally, Karen took her nebulizer out of her mouth and said, "Which one of us is next?"

"I don't know," Isa whispered. The hum of the machines drowned out her voice.

Karen spoke up. "Well, Katie didn't even make it to the life expectancy. It's nineteen now." The life expectancy of people with CF had been increasing significantly over the last decade, thanks to advances in medical care. "Guess I've got two more years to go."

"Don't say that, Karen!" Isa cried. "You've gotta have hope! Those numbers mean nothing for you! They're just statistics. *Median* life expectancy means half of us will live to be over nineteen, just as half of us will die before we're nineteen. You've gotta beat the odds." Isa was repeating Dr. Robbie's lecture, trying to persuade Karen that she shouldn't give up.

"Yeah," I put my nebulizer down and went to sit on Karen's bunk. We were both wearing the flamingo T-shirts I had painted for everyone in the cabin. I reached for her hand. Karen's eyes, red and swollen, looked deep into mine.

"We're going to beat this disease . . . as long as we have each other," I said. I wanted her to have hope. I needed her.

The previous year, we had witnessed the extinction of the oldest girls' cabin. It had belonged to a group called the Pink Ladies. With their deaths, the Flamingo cabin had risen to the rank of the oldest girls' cabin, and we had assumed the esteemed position of role models to the younger girls. Like flamingos, we lived beautiful yet fragile lives. Now, so suddenly, the first of our flock had fallen, and the reality of what it meant to be in the oldest girls' cabin stared at us in the face.

Over the years, we had lost many camp friends. We had attended more funerals than our parents had, all for people under the age of forty-five. We had mourned each death with copious tears, disbelief and fear shattering the protective glass walls we had constructed in our minds. We had learned about all the ways that people with CF died. Most suffered slow, prolonged deaths as their lungs withered away from chronic damage. Some died suddenly from particularly virulent infections. One young woman died of rejection after an experimental lung transplant. A few died of massive lung bleeds. One died of heatstroke.

Over the years I had become numb. Tears no longer fell. Instead, I had reached a state of exasperation. But the sorrow of these losses did not outweigh the joy of knowing each individual. Our friends had made us who we were: they taught us how to laugh, how to cry, how to play pranks on the guys, how to assert ourselves, and how to live and grow in this world with CF. Each friend possessed unique qualities and had lessons to share. That was their legacy. When our futures seemed bleak and unknown, they gave us faith that there was a higher reason for all of this, that we were all in this together.

As my friends died one by one, I put on my mental armor by telling myself, *That's their story, not mine.* Maybe something went wrong to cause them to succumb to CF; *I* was doing the right thing to help me thrive with CF. My time would come, someday, but I was determined to get to the back of the line we were all standing in. I was certain that many of my CF comrades would go to their graves long before it was my turn.

"Reiner, it is your turn to do Ana's treatment," Mama said. Dad went on with his writing at the dinner table. Mama was already halfway finished with Isa's pounding, and the pat-pat of her hands sounded weak.

I looked at Dad, but he didn't budge.

"*Vater,* can I please have therapy?" I asked as I approached him.

Dad cleared his throat, the way he did when he was annoyed. I looked down at his writing, a series of complex equations in Greek letters that looked like chicken scratches to me. "Yah, one moment!" he exclaimed, burrowing his head deeper into his research paper.

The pressure in my chest was expanding with each minute. *He always does this,* I thought. *He waits and waits to do therapy until Isa is finished so Mama can start me.* I knew his procrastination tactics well. *God, I hope he doesn't go into the garage,* I thought. He often avoided helping with therapy by suddenly having the urge to wax his skis or fix something with his soldering iron just as I asked as politely as I could for therapy. My anxiety grew; each minute that passed meant my night got later and later, and that meant less sleep. I had a test in first period, and should have been studying, rather than waiting.

I entered the living room where Isa lay across Mama's lap on one half of the sofa. Ryuta was sprawled across the other half, the TV remote in his hand.

I asked Ryuta to move so that I could start therapy.

Slowly, he lifted himself up to a sitting position. I settled myself over a pile of pillows. I pulled my feet up so I wouldn't accidentally kick Ryuta. The waiting continued.

Awkwardly, I began to pound my chest, trying to gather the strength to percuss hard and concentrate on coughing.

I thought about Katie, who had had to do her own pounding so often when her mom was out of town. No wonder she had died.

Finally, Mama said, "Ryu-chan, can't you start Ana-chan?"

Ryuta rarely helped with therapy. But he turned his body to me while his eyes remained fixed on the TV. Without a word, he reached over and started to percuss my back. I stared at the rip in the knee of his Levi's. His pats were deliberate and slow. His touch felt strange.

After a while, Dad finally came to the living room.

Ryuta immediately got up. "G'night," he said.

I thanked him for his help.

"Sure," he said, already heading upstairs.

I got up as Dad sat down and tucked my flannel top into my pajama pants. I lay my ninety-pound body over his lap. Since Ryuta had worked on my back, I changed positions and lay on my back so Dad could percuss the front of my chest. He took the remote, flicked the channels, and turned up the volume. We watched the Los Angeles news, filled with crime stories. Dad pounded me with his padlike hands.

Suddenly, he paused and said, "You have something in your pocket." I was mortified. I was seventeen, and my Hershey Kiss-breast buds jutted out of my emaciated chest, begging for some body fat to prove to the world that they existed. I was too embarrassed to tell him, *Vater, those are my tits!* I turned onto my side.

Just then a story came on the news about the Hubble telescope. He stopped pounding. "Shh!" he muttered over my coughing and cupped his hands behind his ears. I wanted to disappear. *I'm just in the way. He cares more about hearing the TV than clearing the poison killing me.* I held my body in position, too scared to confront him.

By now, Mama had gone to bed, and Isa was resting on the couch, recovering from a rigorous half hour of coughing.

"*Vater,* I can do Ana's therapy," she said.

Thanks for saving me, I thought.

He ignored her, still concentrating intensely on the news. I coughed, hoping to spur him. Moments passed, and I shot Isa a pleading look.

Isa repeated, "*Vater,* if you want to watch TV, I can help."

God, I loved her. Only she knew exactly how I felt at times like these. She had been there.

"Nein! I can do it!" Dad said, snapping out of his TV-induced trance. He started to vigorously pound, as if he were compensating for his lapse. He pounded harder and harder, and the skin on my chest sizzled. My head jarred. I could feel my brain shake in its juices. I started coughing; his pounding worked, but I could feel his anger, his frustration, his hatred of this menial task he had to perform every day on one of us. As I poured out the mucus from my lungs, I was wounded. *Does my Dad hate me?*

Dr. Robbie insisted that we do chest percussion four times a day and that we take our treatments extremely seriously. During chest percussion, Mama hated when we lay motionless. "Mama is making such an effort!" she would say. "Don't you just lie there! Cough! Cough harder!"

We were adamantly disciplined to comply with our aerosols as directed. To distract ourselves while we were tied down for half an hour several times a day, we did homework, painted T-shirts, wrote, folded laundry, anything. Chest percussion morning and night was nonnegotiable. I remembered Dad's warning to us as kids: "Every treatment you miss is one day less of your life." Besides, we couldn't breathe during the day or sleep through the night if we skipped these treatments. We rarely skipped an evening chest percussion—except when we came back late from an event, like our prom. When we were sick, we tried to do two chest percussion treatments in the middle of the day, but this usually was too tedious; we relied instead on exercise or forced expiratory breathing during the day. During our years in junior high school, Dad drove the Volkswagen van to work and came back to school for our lunch break so that we each could do a breathing treatment in the van using his homemade generator. When we were in high school, Ryuta drove us to school and left the keys with us so that we could do our lunchtime treatments. The treatments helped open up our airways and get us oxygenated for the rest of the day at school. Ryuta even got special permission to park the van in the nearby teachers' parking lot.

One of the best inventions ever made was a nebulizer that could run off a battery. The portable machines freed us to do aerosol therapy anywhere. We did it on roadtrips. We did it in an airplane. On a boat. In public bathrooms. In the bushes at day camp. In a tent on a camping trip. On hiking trails. While walking the dog. At Disneyland's infirmary. On the bullet train in Japan. Behind the temples in Kyoto.

In public, the only challenges were the embarrassment of the noisy coughing fits that accompanied therapy and the unfeminine tendency to expectorate and produce large amounts of dirty tissues. Isa and I learned to cough silently or to muffle our coughs using tissues or towels to cover our mouths. If I used a public bathroom stall to do aerosol therapy, it was not unusual to hear someone ask, "Are you alright in there? Do you need help?" The ghastly hissing of rumbling lungs and pouring mucus—worse than a smoker's cough—was a sound that could frighten anyone and send curious observers running the opposite direction. Bob Flanagan told us once that people with CF were "like a Foster's Freeze machine spewing out sundaes of sickness." He was right. Pour, pour, pour. Our cups overflowed, and we were drowning.

As we grew older, Isa and I came to depend on each other for chest percussion, sparing Mama and Dad the awkward imposition. Our therapies became longer and more intense as our disease progressed, and we became more self-conscious about letting in someone new to this grotesque scene.

"You look gross," I would tell Isa during therapy.

"You look the same!" she'd say.

We could demand from each other what we could not ask of anyone else: "Do it harder! Do it faster! Do it on that spot longer! Just do anything to make the tightness go away."

I'd stand up and, while placing my hands down on her chest, lean toward her, and with all my physical might I would shake and hit her as much as my physical and emotional strength could handle.

"That's good!" she'd exclaim while coughing up blobs.

We grew to know each others' bodies intimately and even joked about the perverted nature of chest therapy. We knew our bad spots, areas of the chest where we could feel particular plugs and congestion. We could read each other's coughs—whether one was tight, bleeding, getting out a mucus plug or moving deeper junk from the lower airways. We knew to avoid hitting the stomach, spine, liver, and breasts without having to be told. By the end of one person's therapy, we'd both be sweating and exhausted, but we'd wash up and start right over by changing places. We fought often about who was doing her treatments longer, who pounded harder, or whose turn it was to start therapy. We developed the stamina to endure forty-five minutes of pounding and forty-five minutes of getting pounded, and our therapies became arduous one-and-a-half-hour ordeals. Therapy could have continued for hours, since we just kept coughing up more and more junk; however, we needed to limit ourselves for the sake of sleep and sanity. But through our dependence on each other we became independent from our parents.

Chapter 14

Stanford Twins

Ana

Things to do when CF is cured:
Be a real Stanford student
Hike the Appalachian Trail with Dad
Go jogging
Make a difference

—Ana, age nineteen

"Ana!!!" Isa shrieked. I was bundled up in my favorite Japanese gauze blanket, lost in a dreamworld while my body ached from a fever that had kept me home from school. With the senior prom coming up, I had to make myself well.

Isa's scream sent a shiver up my spine. *Oh God,* I thought, *Moui's dead.* Our dog, Moui, had been suffering from bronchitis in her old age, and we had resorted to giving her regular nebulizer treatments with our machines. My thoughts raced; I knew the dreaded moment of her passing had finally come.

"Ana!" Isa called again, her voice quivered. "Come down, quick!" I raced down the stairs, light-headed from standing up so quickly, rubbing the fuzzy clouds out of my eyes. Isa stood at the bottom of the stairs holding two large white envelopes.

"We got in!" she yelled. I grabbed an envelope. Across the front, large red letters exclaimed, "Welcome to Stanford." In a state of disbelief, I swore I was still dreaming. By now Isa was tearing into her envelope. "Oh my God! Oh my God! We did it!" She was ecstatic, jumping up and down. It was a miracle. Only one in ten applicants were accepted for admission to Stanford, and we had both made it!

In the ensuing weeks, Mama and Dad huddled around the dining table, poring over financial and mortgage papers and student loan applications. They were already paying for Ryuta's college tuition in Colorado, and Mama's income as a newly hired social worker was paying back her own graduate student loans. Mama spent long hours on the telephone with Uncle Juichi, who offered to help us financially. Our uncle, like our parents, believed a good education was very important, and they were all determined to make our rare opportunity a reality.

Eventually, we took out a series of student loans, not knowing if we would make enough money or even live long enough to pay them back. *What a great country America is!* I thought. *Even students with terminal diseases could qualify for large chunks of money from the government!*

Dr. Robbie grinned when we told him the news at our next clinic visit. "You can join the rest of the spoiled rich kids at Stanford." His son had attended Stanford's rival, the University of California at Berkeley.

"What do you really think, Dr. Robbie?" Mama asked, raising her eyebrows with concern. "Do you think they are healthy enough to go away for college?" Dr. Robbie stood up from his stool and approached us. He looked seriously into our eager faces. "You have to go where your dreams are. You haven't let CF stop you so far, so I don't think you guys are going to let CF stop you from going to Stanford."

I couldn't wait to share the news with Karen. She was a year older and had already started her freshman year at the University of Nevada, Las Vegas. "College life is great. I love my nursing program," she had written in a recent letter. "I can't wait till you can experience it yourselves."

I picked up the phone one evening and called her.

"Guess what?" I said, excited. "Isa and I got into Stanford!"

"You did?!" There was silence followed by a quick laugh. "You got into Stanford?! Stanford?! I'm so proud of you!"

"I can't believe it. I mean, the admissions people actually chose us . . . both of us. I mean, do you know what kind of kids go to Stanford? " I paused. "Overachievers, child prodigies, kids of our nation's leaders even." It struck me. I wasn't one of them.

"Karen, do you think we got in just because we have CF and the admissions people felt sorry for us? Or because of affirmative action?"

"Of course not!" she replied. "Don't you dare think that! Think about all you've done—keeping up with your classes in the hospital, your T-shirt business, your "Life at Kaiser" book . . . duh. They'd be stupid not to admit you guys."

I smiled. She had a way of stroking my ego. I was grateful that the admissions department saw us as individuals with unique stories, plus I felt really lucky.

"Karen, this is one step towards becoming adults. When we're done with college, let's live together, okay?"

"I'd love to. I promise."

For one moment, I ignored the "what-ifs" that whispered deep in my heart: the "what-ifs" about CF, about my future, about death. For a moment, we were two best friends with high hopes and dreams of a real future.

Karen continued, "Wow. My two best friends are going to Stanford. My Stanford twins. I'm so proud."

Stanford twins. It sounded cute, but it made me want to puke. Everyone expected us to go to college together. What had begun as a convenience for therapy became a deep conviction that if we didn't give each other chest percussion, we would die. Since we didn't want to die, being stuck together was the price of survival.

Over the course of the summer, we received information about Stanford's areas of study. I became fascinated by the program on human biology, a major that combined biology with social sciences like anthropology, psychology, and sociology. Later, Isa flipped through her orientation booklet and, sure enough, she stated, "Wow. This looks really cool. Oh, my God, this is totally up my alley. Human Biology." Ugh. There was no escape. Could we ever be different? When Isa went to the prom with her friend Josh, I didn't have a date. I went with them; we shared a date! How pathetic.

Although our love for each other was deep, Isa also had an itch to be separate. A few weeks before we left for Stanford, our family sat around the dinner table discussing the move. Steam rose from bowls of fried noodles; the smell of soy sauce and ginger filled the air.

"Make sure you pack warm clothes," Mama said. "It is much colder in Northern California. You must take all precautions to avoid the cold." Our health was always the first thing on Mama's mind. "Bring what you can fit into the car. In the fall your father and I will visit your dorm to bring winter clothes."

"What will your dormitory be like?" Dad asked.

Isa lifted noodles on chopsticks from her bowl and made slurping noises as she ate. We were going to miss home cooking. "We're being placed in the guest room of a freshman dorm called Larkin. It's the only room with a private bathroom, to avoid germs."

"Good," Dad said. "Health comes first. Do your best in your classes but take good care of yourselves."

I hid my deep-seated uncertainty about whether we were healthy enough to survive college, let alone graduate. Class of '94. A lot could happen in four years.

Isa turned to me. "We may be living together, but we have to make an effort to have separate lives."

"I know," I said, leaning on my elbows. "It's bad enough having to go to the same college. I wish we didn't have to share a dorm room, too."

Isa said, "That's harsh, Ana. We have no choice."

Mama's eyes squinted. "Don't be so insensitive to your sister, Ana-chan. You always see the negative side. Be positive, like your sister. It is because you have each other that you can leave home for college. You should be grateful."

I frowned and wove my fingers through hair I'd recently had permed in an attempt to look different from Isa. "But I just want to be my own person. I don't want to be tied to you always."

"Me, too," Isa snarled.

We arrived on the Stanford campus in a used jeep that Uncle Juichi had bought for us, which rumbled and shook as its feeble engine gasped its last breaths after the four hundred-mile drive north from Los Angeles. It was a warm September afternoon, and the campus bustled with sixteen hundred beaming freshmen eager to embark on a new chapter of their lives, ready to leave their parents behind in the final transition from adolescence.

During the first night in the dorm, all of the residents gathered in the lounge for a meeting to introduce themselves. There was energy buzzing beneath the high ceilings of Larkin Hall. I looked around. Everyone was attractive, healthy, and outgoing. I hid in the corner, feeling small and insignificant as students recounted their impressive backgrounds. It seemed as if everyone was a former valedictorian, community leader, or high school sports star.

"Hi, my name's Chris. I'm from Boulder, Colorado. I just came back from spending the summer in Bolivia, working with a humanitarian group to build shelters for the native people."

"Hi, I'm Notah. I'm from Albuquerque. I play golf. I plan to be on the Stanford Golf team and hopefully go pro. It's really cool to be here."

Suddenly, the "T-shirt Twins" and "Life at Kaiser" seemed like preschool artwork and childish diaries compared to the achievements of our dorm-mates. I shrank further down in my seat. *What am I doing here?*

"Isa," I pleaded just before the meeting. "We have to try to be indepen-dent. You stay on that side of the room and I'll stay over here. We have to make an effort for people to know us as individuals." We made rules: "When I wear my hair up, you wear your hair down. You wear contacts and I wear glasses. Don't wear that outfit because I'm wearing this and the colors are too similar. When we introduce ourselves, I'll talk about T-shirt Twins and you talk about something else."

After a few hours, the number of students left to introduce themselves diminished. After much procrastination, I finally stood up from the couch at the other end of the lounge and introduced myself. I held up a sweatshirt adorned with roses that I had painted and invited the students to place their orders. Then I sat down. I glanced at Isa. She gave me a look of ap-proval. I hadn't even mentioned her or the fact that our business was called "T-shirt Twins."

The meeting was followed by a mix-and-mingle social.

"Hi, I'm Ana. Nice to meet you," I said to Virginia, a short, Hispanic woman.

"Didn't I just meet you?" she asked.

"Oh, no, you probably met my twin sister," I explained. "She's stand-ing over there." I pointed to Isa, banished to the other side of the room by our rules.

"Wow! Twins . . . that's so cool. And you both got in? And you're in the same dorm?"

"Yeah, we have a health problem so we have to stick together." I wanted to make it very clear that Isa and I were in the same dorm room for special circumstances. I joked casually about the benefits of having a twin at Stan-ford: a two-for-the-price-of-one scholarship, saving money by sharing text-books, taking turns going to class.

Each person I met inevitably discovered that I was a twin, and, by the end of the evening, I had met several people with whom I connected . . . but so had Isa. Ultimately, we migrated toward each other and began the familiar process of sharing friends. We were still the Stenzel twins and al-ways would be.

The following week was a blur of attending orientation meetings, finding our way around campus, and meeting new people. The campus crawled with the hustle and bustle of students on bikes or Rollerblades or walking with determination to their destinations. Ours was the one hun-dredth freshman class to enter Stanford, and commemorative celebrations occurred throughout orientation week. The entire freshman class sat in Frost Amphitheater one afternoon desperately fanning themselves with their orientation programs in the triple-digit temperature. In the distance we could see the rolling foothills covered with oak trees and the Hoover Tower surrounded by the Spanish-style red rooftops of the campus buildings. Both the attractive scenery and the university president's speech seemed to welcome us to campus.

"You are the future leaders of the world," President Donald Kennedy proclaimed. "Look around you. You are among the finest of your peers. You have made it into the Stanford community because of your academic excellence and achievements of your past. We welcome you to continue to strive for excellence at this great institution." President Kennedy was making every effort to convince us young and excited freshmen that we belonged here, massaging our self-esteem so that we (or in our case, our parents, who had just refinanced our home) would feel justified in paying the costly tuition for membership into this elite academic country club.

I listened to President Kennedy's message with skepticism. It seemed to me little more than propaganda. The echo of his voice was drowned out by my apprehension and self-doubt. *Can I live up to this reputation? What have I gotten myself into?* My father's mantra rang in my ears: "Always, remember, first comes health. Then comes school. Just do your best and make the most of your college experience." That's what I intended to do.

Shortly after arriving at Stanford, we made a doctor's appointment at Kaiser Hospital in Santa Clara, about fifteen miles south of Stanford. It belonged to the Kaiser conglomerate of managed-care hospitals located throughout California, and we were destined to go there for our medical care because of Dad's insurance policy. Unlike the Kaiser Hospital we were familiar with in Los Angeles, the Kaiser in Northern California was an actual Cystic Fibrosis Care Center, accredited by the national Cystic Fibrosis Foundation. Per the CF Foundation protocol, an entourage of specialists waited to see us: two pulmonologists (including Stanford's renowned Dr. Norman Lewiston), a dietician, a social worker, a respiratory therapist, and a genetic counselor. This was a far cry from our hospital in Los Angeles, where only Dr. Robbie seemed to know what CF was. For the first time in years, I took a pulmonary function test (or PFT), in which I blew into a machine that measured my lung capacity. Apparently, using white blood cell counts to measure the degree of lung infection was obsolete, and pulmonary function tests more accurately assessed lung damage. My lung capacity was 53 percent of normal. I was devastated. Isa's lungs were at 65 percent.

"I thought that if your mother let you leave home for college, that you'd be much healthier than this! And you do four treatments every day?" our new pulmonologist, Dr. Jodi Lulla, asked matter-of-factly. Dr. Lulla was a petite, eagle-eyed East Indian woman. She seemed gentle and frail, yet her words were tactless.

"Why are you on Cotazym?" she asked, disturbed that we were taking the sort of powdered enzymes that had been prescribed in the seventies. "These are not effective. You should be taking enteric-coated enzymes instead. They dissolve in the small intestines and help you absorb your nutrients. The powder is destroyed by the stomach acid; it's no good. And you need to take a multivitamin, and calcium for your bones."

Dr. Lulla prescribed a new brand of pancreatic enzymes, the kind other kids at CF camp had used and that we had asked for years ago, which promised us the hope of better nutrition and weight gain.

"You are eighteen and have not had a period yet? Have you ever seen an endocrinologist?"

"No. My doctor in Los Angeles said I don't get periods because I'm too skinny and my body's preoccupied fighting CF," I said.

"That's not always true. We have plenty of women with CF having periods." Her bony fingers turned the pages of the medical records I had brought from Los Angeles. Looking up at me, she glared, "Your history shows that you have been in the hospital multiple times a year. Haven't you ever wanted to do home IV therapy?"

"What's that?" I asked, perplexed.

She explained that many patients at the center were able to infuse intravenous antibiotics for several weeks at home, avoiding hospitalization. This outpatient service had begun when the AIDS epidemic revolutionized patient care, and it allowed people the freedom to carry on with their normal activities. This had never been offered to us as an option in Los Angeles.

From the respiratory therapist, we learned about new methods to clear the lungs. These methods entailed breathing through a kazoolike device called a positive expiratory pressure (PEP) mask, which would dislodge the mucus in the lungs by providing high pressure within the airways. Another therapy device was the "chest vest," an inflatable vinyl vest that resembled a life jacket, that, when connected to an air compressor, would inflate and shake vigorously. It was the first of its kind, invented to provide independence to people with CF.

We learned about the CF Foundation standards of care, including the requirements that all CF patients visit the clinic and provide a sputum culture every three months and that they have a PFT every six months or at each visit. These standards were set to monitor symptoms and treat them before they became serious. This close monitoring offered promises of improved health for all CF patients.

While the clinic visit gave me confidence in our new CF care, I left in tears at the dismal reality of my lung capacity. What kind of care had I gotten in Southern California? Would I have been healthier if I had taken the right kind of pancreatic enzymes like the kids at CF camp had? Could some of my past hospitalizations have been avoided? I felt betrayed by health insurance that had locked us into one hospital. I was angry with my parents for accepting the care without questioning. Most of all, I resented Dr. Robbie, a man whose wisdom I had trusted all my life. I voiced my resentment, but Isa said, "At least we're still alive. We left L. A. just in time." She was right; Katie had gone to a CF Center and died anyway.

Stanford University was an epicenter for CF research and care. The Children's Hospital at Stanford had over three hundred CF patients and one of the best CF centers in the nation. A local group of parents and grandparents of children with CF had formed an independent nonprofit called Cystic Fibrosis Research, Inc. (CFRI). They held monthly meetings at Stanford, where speakers provided updates on CF research—even research that was happening right on campus. The executive director of CFRI, Ann Robinson, welcomed us to the community as though we were long-lost friends. She was Mama's age, and her wispy white hair and robust size were the signs of a dedicated CF mother who struggled to provide the best care for her teenaged son with CF. She had a photographic memory of the CF world's who's who and an encyclopedic knowledge of CF. For hours, she spoke passionately about her son's digestive problems and the discoveries she had made to improve his nutritional status by following a nonconventional diet.

"You have to question everything your doctor says," Ann chided us. "They aren't gods. They don't know everything. You have to be persistent." She chuckled. "Some of the doctors don't like me. They think I'm a difficult CF mother."

"Aren't you afraid of them getting mad at you? I mean, we depend on them for good care, and they kind of *have* to like us," I commented.

"I don't care. I'm doing it all for my son."

Ann coached us on asserting ourselves with our doctors. Her wisdom fueled my resentment. I would no longer passively accept the care given to me, assuming that it was the best. Past assumptions had been proven false. After that moment, I promised myself I would do everything in my power to obtain the most advanced CF care and that I would question and collaborate in my health care. This was clearly the only way to survive.

Within a few weeks, Kaiser approved us to try the "chest vest" and one was delivered to our dorm room.

"I hope this works," I said to Isa, as I snapped the vest closed. "Maybe this is our ticket to independence."

I turned on the big machine, a metallic box that resembled a small refrigerator. It sounded like a vacuum cleaner. In an instant, the vest swelled up, and it shook vigorously in pulsating motions.

"Thhiissss feeeeeelllsss fuunnnyy . . . " I stammered to Isa, my head bouncing with the vibrations. I could feel my skin heating up from the vinyl and my chest quickly felt compressed. There was no sensation to cough, no dislodging of mucus.

As I attempted to cough as Mama had taught me—squeezing my lungs like a sponge—I felt nothing but a sense of suffocation and heat. I tried to distract myself by reading, but the words on the page danced wildly with every pulsation of the vest.

Half an hour into the treatment, there was a loud knock on the door.

"What's going on in there?" A voice called. I stopped the machine, quickly unhooked the vest, and walked toward the door. I felt sweat on my forehead, and my wrinkled clothes stuck to my chest.

A sporty Asian guy stood at the door. He was wearing a T-shirt that read *Stanford Fencing.* "I heard a strange noise. Are you guys okay?"

"Yeah, we're okay. My sister and I have health problems. We have a lung disease called cystic fibrosis, and we have to do medical treatments." The lengthy explanation began.

He scoffed. "You guys spend so much time in your room. You're locked up in there all day, why do you even bother coming out?"

"We have our reasons," I replied, nonchalantly, pretending that his comment didn't bother me.

"Okay, whatever . . . hey, there's a keg party tonight on the north wing. You guys should check it out. See ya later." He stepped away and left. I closed the door.

"How stupid," Isa said, her nebulizer hanging out of her mouth. "Taking their health for granted." She shook her head.

"We're such goody-two-shoes. I know plenty of people with CF who'd go to that keg party over doing therapy."

I hated being different. Yet partying was not attractive to me, as my lungs closed up with some asthmatic reaction after only one beer. I knew I had to do something to share with the other students why Isa and I were so different. Within weeks, I had joined a disabled students' speaker's bureau, which educated students about living with disabilities and chronic illnesses. I finally acknowledged publicly that I was, in fact, very different from most Stanford students.

Chapter 15

A Lost Leader

Ana

Some people who die are more present than those who are living.

—Ana, age nineteen

Having just finished our first quarter at college, Isa and I arrived in Pacific Palisades for winter break. We were planning to visit Karen. I was exhausted from final exams, but the thought of seeing Karen energized me. But on the morning of December 17, 1990, we received a phone call from Kathy, Karen's younger sister. Her voice quivered on the other line. "You have to come now. Karen's in a coma, and they don't think she has much time left. She wanted to see you."

"No!" I cried. "What happened!?" The rest of the conversation passed in a blur. I called Mama and Dad, and they came home from work immediately. We quickly threw our belongings into bags and began a mad dash on Interstate 15 from Los Angeles to Las Vegas. Maybe this was just a false alarm, an overreaction to another CF scare, and we held out hope of seeing Karen's smiling face. We arrived at the hospital just as the desert moon was rising, and I could see the first star. It was 5:30 P.M., and my world crumbled.

Kathy appeared in the hallway as we raced toward Karen's room. There were people standing, their heads bowed, outside the door; they were talking quietly, and some were hugging. Kathy's face was red and streaked with tears. She rushed to embrace me.

"I'm sorry, I'm so sorry," she sobbed, "it's too late. She passed away at 5:17 . . ."

Isa and I approached the darkened hospital room. We could see Karen lying dead on the bed. She lay almost flat, her face pushed up and her mouth open, frozen as she'd taken her last gasp of air. I shivered as I entered the room. It was still. There was no noise of the oxygen cannula. She looked like she was in a deep sleep. I never expected that the first dead body I'd ever see would be that of my best friend.

Dad froze at the door of the room, his face expressionless. Mama began to cry as she hugged Karen's sobbing mother. I had never seen her cry before. I imagined the grief she would someday feel upon my death. *We cause our parents so much pain,* I thought.

Isa and I stood over Karen. Isa stroked Karen's cold foot. I reluctantly reached out to touch Karen. Her soft auburn hair was pulled back, its long, ribbonlike strands flowing across the pillow. Her thin face was pale and translucent. The black circles of fatigue under her eyes were beginning to fade as death had stopped her blood flow. Her soft, white hands were folded across her belly, showing the characteristic clubbed fingers that we always complained about. A single rose lay atop her crossed arms. Her white legs lay on top of her bed, uncovered and lifeless. I could see the thinness of her bones, evidence of the weight loss that had ravaged her body since the last time I saw her. I bent down to kiss her cheek, to feel her soft skin on my lips for the last time.

I turned back to Kathy. "What happened? I had no idea she was so sick. We would've come earlier. I'm so sorry," I choked out through my tears. Isa held my hand as we embraced her.

"It was a bad infection," she said. "She couldn't hold on any longer. She was so tired. She wanted you to know that she did the best she could."

The next day, our parents headed back to Los Angeles, leaving Isa and me in Las Vegas with Karen's family to attend her funeral. Her home felt empty without her presence. We shared memories of Karen, alternating between laughter and tears. We looked at pictures and looked around her bedroom, where a trashcan filled with her dirty tissues sat next to an unmade rented hospital bed. At first, it felt like Karen was just away. Everything seemed surreal to me, as if I were floating in a nightmare from which I would soon awaken.

The end-stage CF I had known from camp meant a gradual decline. Karen, Isa, and I would often predict which kids would not return to camp the following year because we could see them dying already—their emaciated bodies, ghostlike faces, their breathlessness, and their thunderous coughs.

But Karen had been a joyful, energetic wild woman just a few months earlier. She had attended our high school graduation in June, when we pranced around our graduation party in matching baby-doll dresses. We had spent the following week going to Disneyland, the beach, the mall. Then we had all gone to CF camp. Now, six months later, she was dead. My hopes of living with Karen after college dissolved. Our belief that CF was controllable—with therapy, hospitalizations, and exercise—shattered.

We had always spoken of the will to live and the power of the mind over the body. In the fall, I had known she was ill and hospitalized. She had talked about getting a feeding tube for nutrition because she had lost so much weight.

"Karen," I begged during our last phone conversation, "you've got to take better care of yourself. Please try to think positively. You know how powerful our minds can be."

"I know," she agreed. "I'm trying to be positive and fight. I really am." She had sounded tired. I could hear breathlessness in her voice.

"I want to come see you . . . during winter break," I stated. "If you're up to it, maybe we can go skiing at Mt. Charleston."

"I'm not doing so well right now. We'll have to see." The conversation changed as her tone became depressed and distant. "You have a whole new life up there at Stanford. Don't you think you're going to forget about me?" A deep, congested cough followed, ending with a gag and gasp.

"Of course, not!" I defended. "You're my best friend. You mean everything to me! We can still see each other during breaks. I would love for you to visit the campus; it's beautiful up here."

"Yeah, maybe," she sighed. "But life is different now. You guys have moved on."

In the days following her death, I played our last conversation over and over in my mind. Had she felt abandoned? Had that played a role in her rapid decline? What could I have said differently, had I known the end was near? My new life at Stanford had been a great distraction from knowing how sick Karen had become in just a few months and how she was slowly slipping away. Kathy told me that Karen had felt Isa and I hadn't understood, that we had pushed her too much to take control of her disease at a point when she felt so helpless. I had even sent her a book on biofeedback and the role of positive thinking on health. *Damn me!*

At the wake, Karen's body lay dressed in a pink, frilly dress, the one she had worn so proudly at her high school graduation the previous year. Her red hair was sculpted into a perfect mold of feathered curls. Her face was powdered and painted artificially with bright pink lipstick and rouge. I stared at her stiff, lifeless body, sickened by the potent smells of formaldehyde and carnations that adorned her coffin.

I leaned over her and whispered, "This is not how I want to remember you. They've made you up into some sort of mannequin. You were so much more beautiful in real life."

Dad picked Isa and me up from the airport when we returned from Las Vegas. The ride home was awkward. Dad's questions focused on the facts of her funeral: How many people attended? Where was she buried? Who spoke at the service?

When we arrived home, Dad opened the door just as Mama came rushing from the kitchen to stop us. The aroma of *sukiyaki* filled my nostrils.

"Wait!" she said, wiping her hands on her apron. "Don't you come in, yet!"

We paused at the doorway. She shuffled back into the kitchen in her slippers and returned with a carton of Morton's salt. She poured a handful of salt into the palm of her hand and threw it at me. She poured another handful and threw it at Isa. We blinked our eyes as the salt sprinkled our clothes and fell softly to the ground.

"Mama, what in the world are you doing?" I asked.

"Mama is cleaning you. This is a Japanese custom. You must not enter the house after a funeral with the spirit of the dead. It is bad luck. This salt will cleanse you."

"Mama, this is foolish," I replied. We all chuckled, but Mama was serious. And besides, salt or no salt, Karen's spirit would always be with us.

The day after we returned home from the funeral, on December 21, I was admitted to the hospital with a raging lung infection. The pressure of final exams and the trauma of Karen's death had brought my health to an all-time low.

It was the early morning of my third day at Kaiser. The sunrise slowly turned the dark night sky to a glowing orange. Outside I could hear a bus rumbling on Sunset Boulevard as the city awakened. I squirmed in bed, struggling to find a comfortable position on the plastic mattress. Suddenly, a nurse entered and turned on the light. *Damn,* I thought, *another roommate.*

Within minutes, two paramedics were pushing a gurney into the room.

"Ana-chan, you won't believe who is here," a familiar voice said.

I looked up, shocked to see my parents standing beside the paramedics. On the stretcher lay Isa, her face ghostly pale behind an oxygen mask. Her eyes were closed, her breathing audible.

I sat up. "What happened?"

Isa was the strong one. Her health hadn't seemed to suffer from the events of the past week. What was she doing here?

Dad sat down on my bed. "Your sister bled very badly last night. We have been in the emergency room in Santa Monica all night long." For the first time, I saw wrinkles on his bronzed skin. There was dried blood on his sleeve.

Mama continued, "We almost lost her. Mama was so scared." She looked to the floor.

Isa awoke as the paramedics lifted her onto the bed next to mine.

"Hi, Ana," she said. "Surprise."

"You look awful. What happened?" I got out of bed, and pushed my IV pole toward her. Dried blood on her neck streaked behind her hairline.

"I don't know. All I remember was coughing up so much blood, so much blood . . . " Her voice trailed off. "It just wouldn't stop."

"Don't you talk too much, Isa. You must rest." Mama pulled the covers over Isa's shoulders.

Just then, Dr. Robbie entered the room. He glistened from a fresh shave and smelled of mild cologne. "Good morning, Mr. and Mrs. Stenzel."

Mama and Dad stood up and shook hands with him.

"I'm glad you made it here," he said, as he rubbed Isa's back. "This was a close call." He turned back to my parents. Sternly he said, "With Isa's history, it was just a matter of time before she experienced a life-threatening lung bleed like this."

Dad looked at Dr. Robbie with concern in his eyes. "She bled so much. And she was unconscious for some time." He paused. "How will her brain be affected?"

Dr. Robbie reassured Dad that Isa's mental status was unaffected by the hemorrhagic shock. He explained that the chronic lung infection had eaten away at her larger pulmonary blood vessels, causing the massive bleed.

"We'll just keep you here for a few weeks and pump you full of antibiotics to kill those bugs," he told Isa.

"I'm so glad we had oxygen at home," Mama stated. "We forgot to return one tank when the girls left for college. We never thought we would actually use it for such an emergency."

Later, when Dr. Robbie and my parents left, Isa told me her story.

"I remember going to bed last night, watching the eucalyptus tree swaying in the wind from our window. The stars were so clear. I was thinking about Karen, that maybe she was up there in Heaven . . . how much I missed her, why she died. . . . Then, in the middle of the night, something forceful woke me and I sat up suddenly. I exploded with a totally powerful cough, stronger than I've ever had, with, like, you know, that watery salty taste. I couldn't breathe, and the blood just kept pouring . . . I gasped for air but couldn't get any. The last thing I remember was a pool of darkness on my bed."

Dad had been asleep downstairs but awoke when he heard Isa moaning.

He'd gone up to her bedroom to check on her and been horrified to see her lying in a pool of blood. It had soaked her face, her pillow, her hair. Her eyes were closed and her chest was gurgling. He screamed for Mama and ran back downstairs, his feet pounding hard against the oak floor. Isa recalled watching him run, seeing the terror in his face, and hearing him on the phone, giving our address. "She has cystic fibrosis. And there has been a lot of bleeding." Mama was scurrying about downstairs, "Oh my goodness, oh my goodness."

Isa said she heard everything and that she could see my parents panic and flutter about, yet she couldn't move. A light above her was brilliant but foggy, and she felt strangely at peace.

"It was kind of cool. It felt pretty neat," she said.

"Wow . . . sounds like you had a real near-death experience?" I asked.

"Yeah," she replied. "I saw everything . . . from above . . . Mama and Dad at my bedside, tinkering with the oxygen tank, them slipping the O^2 over my face. That felt so good. I think I woke up then. I heard the voices of the paramedics, of Dad telling me I'll be fine . . . to hang on. But I couldn't respond. It was as if I was paralyzed. It was so weird." She shook her head and repeated, "So weird."

Then she turned to me and held out her hand. I grabbed it. "I think I saw Karen," she said.

I smiled.

"She was calling me, but she said I wasn't ready to be with her." Her eyes welled up. "It was her, really her."

My mouth widened. "You're so lucky you saw her . . . I still can't believe she's gone." I looked outside at the Los Angeles skyline. "Maybe it was grief that made you bleed."

It had to be. Isa often held her feelings in. Maybe all those feelings about Karen's death had built up inside of her and then come crashing down in the form of an acute physical reaction.

That night, Isa and I watched the Christmas specials on TV in the pediatric ward. Life really sucked. Karen was dead, and it had happened so fast that we still couldn't quite believe it. I could barely breathe, having been diagnosed with an *Aspergillus* fungal infection in my lungs, and Isa had almost bled to death. We were so blessed to have a chance to go to Stanford, but was that all it would be—a chance? Dr. Robbie believed in us, so did our parents and Uncle Juichi, who had invested in our education. We had let them down. *What were we thinking?* We could pretend to be like everyone else for just a short time, and then our bodies crashed. *Was it all a waste?*

Chapter 16

A Day in the Life

Ana

If I could just have Karen back, healthy and alive again so that we may experience once again the love, fun, and security of childhood. I guess Karen's death was a symbolic abrupt end to my youth—a test of the beginning of adulthood.

—Ana, age nineteen

My next quarter at Stanford began with another session of bustling from class to class and trying to keep up with the pace of student life. A typical day started with a ritual of procrastination that involved hitting the snooze button repeatedly until I had exactly one hour and fifteen minutes before my nine o'clock class. I awoke first, feeling tired and not the least bit refreshed. I shuddered, faintly recalling hearing Karen's voice in a dream. "Keep living," she had said. "Don't be sad because of me." *Was that really her,* I wondered, *or am I just grieving?*

I pulled off my nasal oxygen cannula as I staggered to the bathroom before starting my treatment. After I had taken a few breaths without the pure oxygen, my morning coughing fit began: a jolt to my cardiovascular system akin to doing fifty jumping jacks immediately after getting out of bed.

I stood before the bathroom mirror and looked at my reflection in the dim morning light. My face was red from coughing, and it had puffed up like a balloon. I had not fully recovered during the last hospitalization over Christmas. I had been treated with high doses of prednisone, a steroid, to decrease the inflammation in my lungs. Prednisone had caused my face to swell and my mood to slide into a deep depression.

In the semidarkness, I assembled my nebulizer pieces, which I'd sterilized the night before and left on the shelf, under a paper towel, to dry. After I filled the medicine cup with Albuterol, a stimulant that opens the airways, I turned on my nebulizer and shouted, "Isa, time to get up. I have a nine o'clock class."

She stirred in bed and mumbled, "Five more minutes." *Always the slow one,* I thought. The nebulizer mist moistened the secretions in my lungs, and I stopped to cough, turning off the machine in between violent fits of coughing. The taste of mucus filled my mouth, salty and fermented. I spat into a tissue. Putting my nebulizer back in my mouth, I drew up a syringe of tobramycin from a small glass vial.

I grabbed another plastic vial filled with clear liquid and squeezed its contents into another nebulizer cup. This magic potion was from the clinical trials for DNAse, the newest and most promising drug for CF. DNAse was an enzyme made through recombinant DNA technology by Genentech, Inc., that helped liquefy the thick mucus in CF lungs. We had learned about a clinical trial for DNAse from an article in the *National Enquirer* and had enrolled in the blind trials in February. Although we both participated in the trial, qualifying for it was a major feat for me. A minimum lung capacity of 40 percent was needed to qualify; mine was 42 percent. The clinical trials were my only hope to survive Stanford. I silently prayed that this was the real drug, not the placebo.

Systematically, I filled a small paper cup with my morning pills—enzymes, bronchodilators, vitamins, antibiotics. I grabbed my T-shirt, jeans, and a pair of earrings, dressing myself in less than two minutes and brushing my hair while I inhaled the Albuterol.

"Isa, get up!" I yelled. "I'm starting DNAse now." That was her cue.

Her morning coughing fit was drowned out by the buzz of the nebulizer machine coming from her side of the room. She flicked her light on and opened up a textbook. I squinted: Ecology.

"How can you start studying already?" I asked. "That light's giving me a sinus headache."

"I have a midterm tomorrow. I have to study as much as possible. Just deal, okay?" Isa was majoring in human biology with a focus in wildlife conservation, determined to pursue a career as a conservation biologist, an environmentalist, or something that would allow her to work in nature. *Fat chance,* I thought. *She can't even start her day without electricity.*

After about ten minutes, my nebulizer sputtered, signaling that the DNAse had run out. I turned off the machine and dashed to the bathroom to wash my face and brush my teeth. I grabbed my glasses and keys and rushed out the door, heading toward the cafeteria. The halls were empty; few students were awake at this hour.

In the cafeteria, two sorority girls stood in line, talking about Rush.

"Oh, my God, Heather," one said, as she flicked her blond hair over her forehead. "I'm totally gonna rush with the Tri-Delts in the spring. I swear I hit it off with one of the girls at the party last night. If I don't get in, I'll just, like, totally die."

"Don't worry about it," the other one said. "You can also try to get into Theta. I'll talk to my sorority sisters and they'll make it happen for you. I promise."

I couldn't believe that Rush was such a priority. I looked at the girls. They epitomized health: smooth, tanned skin; blonde, flowing hair; muscular arms and legs. They seemed to coast through college life without struggles, seemingly happy-go-lucky and so carefree. They didn't have to worry about their friends dying or about dying themselves.

Ignoring their stares, I grabbed two bowls of cereal, two quesadillas, and two glasses of juice and put them on my tray. I was not bulimic, like some of the girls; I was just hoarding for two. With a tray full of food, I marched back to our dorm room, arriving just as Isa was finishing her nebulizer.

"Quick," I demanded as I put the tray on my desk, "I only have about fifteen minutes for therapy."

"You should've gotten up earlier," she nagged. She closed her textbook.

"I wouldn't talk," I replied. I leaned toward her. "Isa, do I smell? I don't have time to shower."

She put her head toward my neck and sniffed. "No, but your hair is pretty greasy. You better put it in a ponytail."

I kicked off my Birkenstocks and dove onto the pile of pillows assembled on her bed. I set the timer for fifteen minutes and turned on the radio. Celine Dion's voice drowned out our percussion noise. Isa began pounding my back, her hands encased in mittens. We wore mittens to muffle the loud clapping noise.

"You're doing me too softly. I need it harder. I need it in the upper right lobe; I'm junky there." I demanded. Since I'd begun the clinical trials, mucus seemed to flow out of my lungs with less effort. The goo that clogged my lungs appeared thinner, like mustard rather than mud.

"My mucus is so disgusting, like it's festering from the depths of my lungs. I think I have the real drug." I said. My breath reeked of *Pseudomonas*.

"You're so lucky. I don't feel a thing. I probably have the placebo." She stopped pounding and scratched her forehead. "But that's okay. You needed it more."

Isa's lung capacity was over 60 percent; she had qualified for the DNAse clinical trials without even trying.

"Well, I'll let you have a whiff of it later," I replied. It wasn't fair that she had the placebo. I could let her have a hit of my nebulizer pipe if it helped her feel better, too.

When my time was up, we switched positions, and she lay on the pillows. I grabbed my other nebulizer and started my tobramycin inhalation as I donned the mittens. I pounded Isa's back. No time for a back rub or back scratch this morning; we plunged straight into the misery. As I pounded her chest, I felt the skin on my hands split from the impact.

"This isn't going to be enough therapy." Isa said. "You better come home after class so we can finish. I need more." I hated her nagging. In my resentment, I hit harder. She liked that.

"I can't. I have a HAPA meeting at noon." In my attempt to jump on the bandwagon of extracurricular activities, I had joined a student group called HAPA, an appropriate acronym for the Half Asian People's Association. It was a social network of fellow racial mutts who couldn't quite fit in and lived culturally dual lives. "I'll do you more this evening."

Then Isa said, "We'll have to meet at 7:30 sharp for therapy because I have *taiko* practice tonight at 9:30." Isa was strong enough to play Japanese drums.

"Fine, but you better not be late. I hate waiting for you." I envied Isa the energy to go to her Japanese drumming practice till midnight.

The timer finally rang. I had twelve minutes to get to class. My head pounded from hyperventilating as I vigorously inhaled the antibiotic, trying not to waste a drop. I turned off the nebulizer.

In five minutes, I gulped down a cold quesadilla and a soggy bowlful of cereal and guzzled the juice with the dozen pills from my paper cup. I grabbed my keys and my backpack and shuffled into my Birkenstocks. As I walked out of the dorm I gathered my messy hair into a ponytail. I didn't care how I looked, only that I could breathe. Outside, a light rain began to fall, and the oak trees swayed. I hustled onto my bicycle and began panting after only a few spins of the pedals. I huffed and puffed to class, coughing and spitting up mucus as the early morning bike ride moved more secretions. Like a dog leaving its trail, I was leaving my mark on the Stanford campus.

I slid into my seat just as the professor began his monotonous rambling. Within minutes, I was fighting to stay awake in the dark, oxygen-deprived, crowded lecture hall. I avoided the instructor's gaze, hoping not to be a victim of his inquiries. My mind wandered, touching on Karen. I felt drowsy and unfocused. Aristotle's writings were written on the overhead—absurd intellectualism and meaningless bullshit to me. The eloquent, erudite responses of the other students impressed me. I wondered how they could care so much about Aristotle. I thought, *I really don't give a shit. I am not a real Stanford student.*

Behind me, I heard a fraternity brother whisper to his buddy, "Dude, I partied so hard last night, I'm so hung over. I got up fuckin' five minutes ago." He pulled his sweatshirt hood over his tousled hair as he leaned back in his seat, relaxed.

A mother of a woman with CF once said to me, "No one really realizes how much it takes for people with CF just to show up." She was so right.

Chapter 17

Blossoming

Isa

As selfish as it may seem, I became involved with Christianity so that I could someday go to Heaven when I die to be reunited with my best friend.

—Isa, age nineteen

When I returned to Stanford after winter break, I sought spiritual support through Stanford Memorial Church. I was trying to make sense of Karen's death, Ana's precarious health, and my near-death experience. I was bargaining with God. I needed to understand what Karen had done to deserve to die and what I could do for God to help Ana and me stay healthy in college.

The words of the pastor at Karen's funeral resonated in my mind: "As believers in Christ, we will see our beloved Karen again in Heaven. But those who do not live in Jesus will never see their loved ones again, for they will not enter the Kingdom of Heaven." Karen had talked to me about her faith. Growing up, I had prayed regularly but still felt skeptical of organized religion. I wanted to be a good Christian, but I had too many questions. But if I wanted to see Karen again, I had to believe.

I remembered the nice chaplain who had visited us when we were hospitalized as young teens. He gave us a book, "Getting to Know God," but

I looked at him with loathing. Chaplains, and religion for that matter, were for people who were dying. I wasn't dying and didn't need to talk to him. Now, death was staring me in the face, and I was ready to explore faith.

I also thought of Rick, a CF camp counselor with long scraggly brown hair and a beard who resembled Jesus. Rick had been coming to CF camp since its inception in 1965; he had first attended as a camper. He told me that his family prayed a lot, and after years of treatments for CF, he learned that he had been misdiagnosed and just had asthma. Rick became a born-again Christian and insisted that if one had enough faith, the Lord answered prayers. I wished I had that much faith.

I decided to be baptized on Easter Sunday in 1991. Ana was on her own spiritual quest, and she decided to join me. On Easter morning, Ana and I rushed through therapy to make it to church in time. As I coughed and spit during chest percussion, I felt wetness between my legs. I finished therapy early, thinking urinary incontinence had kicked in again, a common problem in women with CF. I rushed to the bathroom, where I was taken aback to see a crimson stain on my underwear. I was stunned. I hadn't felt any warning. *How could this be? This wasn't supposed to happen, not to me!* I thought. I hated that "womanness" had crept over me. I hated my body for putting an end to my childhood and my secret so suddenly. But I should have known. I was growing. Just a few months earlier, Ana and I had giggled as we clumsily bought our first padded bras at Macy's.

I cleaned myself up and then, having had no time to prepare, I placed a bulky pad of rolled toilet paper in my underwear. We rushed to church in time for the baptism. I wore a pink satin dress for the occasion. I prayed that I wouldn't be dipped into a bath for the baptism. I imagined being soaked and leaving disintegrated, messy toilet paper floating in the holy water. Luckily, it wasn't an immersion baptism; the minister simply splashed holy water on my forehead, and I survived the ceremony leak-free. Needless to say, accepting Jesus Christ as my personal savior was not the only thing on my mind that day.

I was finally a real woman. The new enzymes prescribed by Dr. Lulla combined with the high-calorie dorm food were working, and I had gained nearly ten pounds in a few months. So, despite the nuisance of periods, a step toward health was a prayer answered.

God answered our prayers for health again with the DNAse clinical trials. Following a six-month blind study in which I was certain I had the placebo, I received the open-label drug and reaped the benefits that Ana had felt during the study. She had described it as magic, and I agreed. Over the next few years, I continued to gain weight, and my lung function soared to 70 percent of normal. Best of all, Ana's lung capacity had improved to 55 percent of normal. At the age of twenty, she, too, finally started her period. During her last Christmas hospitalization, Dr. Robbie had suggested that Ana look into getting a lung transplant. DNAse, now called Pulmozyme, helped postpone Ana's need for one.

"Damn, pork chop!" Ryuta said to me as he pinched my round cheek during one of his visits to Stanford. "That Pulmozyme's gotten out of control, hasn't it? What are you weighing in at?"

"I'm 135! Can you believe it, Ryuta?" I said, proud to share my weight.

"That's great, Isa. Just great." He patted my back. Ana and I had grown four inches in college; our eyes were nearly level with Ryuta's now.

After starting Pulmozyme, I felt like a different person. I could hang out with friends late into the night. I could pour my energies in extracurricular activities such as teaching environmental education, playing *taiko* drums, or working as a tour guide. As I walked backward through the Spanish arches of the Main Quad, rattling off statistics about student life, I knew that I looked to tourists like any other Stanford student. I was almost normal. Sure, I still spent hours each day taking care of myself, doing treatments, and taking medications. Our dorm room still looked like a hospital room. But my efforts were paying off.

Home IV therapy became a routine part of college life. Small plastic bottles with self-deflating balloons filled with antibiotics could be carried in my pocket while I went to class, gave a tour, or went out with friends. Infusions lasted half an hour to an hour, every six to eight hours, around the clock, and, when they were coupled with therapy, exhaustion was inevitable. My veins, still weakened from years of abuse, tolerated IVs, but each time the IV went bad and I needed a new one, I had to drive half an hour to Kaiser's infusion center to have it restarted by a nurse.

One Saturday morning, I rushed to flush and disconnect the IV line on my forearm before heading off for *taiko* practice. I had been one of the founding members of Stanford's *taiko* club. We built drums out of wine barrels and cowhide and performed for school and community events. That morning, after stretching and warm-up, I grabbed my *bachi* sticks and stood behind a drum. The song began as players raised their *bachi,* mine stretching past those of the other, more petite Japanese-American women, and, in unison, slammed them down on the drums. The floor and windows vibrated. My muscular legs squatted and flexed as I jumped around the drums, synchronized to the music. My arms, strengthened by years of performing chest percussion, pounded rhythmically against the tight skins.

Don! A dull drone echoed when I pounded the center of the cowhide head. *Ka!* A high-pitched snap sounded when I hit the edge of the barrel.

"Hit harder!" yelled Hiroshi, one of the leaders. I hesitated, knowing my IV was being jarred with each strike. But I couldn't let up; the rhythm exhilarated me, and I hit harder. The song flowed through crescendos, racing and slowing, mimicking the energy of a dancing dragon. Some other players yelled, "*Yoi!*" and I joined in, hollering and laughing. *Can you believe it, Karen? This is for you,* I thought.

As the song reached a powerful climax, I slammed my *bachi* down for its final *Don.* I was panting heavily and in an instant exploded into a coughing fit. I walked to the corner of the room, my red face toward the wall. The intense workout was truly cathartic.

"You okay?" Hiroshi yelled across the room. He already knew my story.

I nodded as I caught my breath. I rubbed the gauze that covered my IV site. I had to make sure the needle was still in.

"What's wrong with your arm?" asked Susan, another player, as she approached me. Susan was a freshman, and this was just our second practice together.

"Oh, I'm just taking IV medication," I said, casually.

"Oh." She looked blankly at me. "Well, you don't look sick . . ."

I was still adjusting to reactions like hers. Before Pulmozyme, I had looked scrawny and malnourished; now it was becoming more difficult to convince people that I had a serious health problem.

My friendship with Bob has taught me immensely about individual coping mechanisms towards illness and death. Too often, health care professionals are quick to define pathology when someone deals with illness or pain in an unconventional manner.

—Isa, age twenty-two, in a class paper

As we attained physical maturity, Ana and I found the curtain rising to reveal a new stage: sexuality. I remained painfully self-conscious and shy about my newfound sexuality, but Ana reveled in her emerging curiosity. Her interest in genetic counseling led her to become involved in women's health. She got involved in HIV education, distributing condoms and literature to students. She professed an expertise about sexuality despite her naïveté and inexperience. Like me, she had yet to find a real boyfriend. Part of her fascination with sex grew out of a discovery about our mentor at CF camp, Bob Flanagan. Who Bob Flanagan really was had been revealed to us the previous summer. It was our first year at camp without Karen, and we were depressed and lonely. I mentioned to Bob that I didn't know if we wanted to attend camp anymore. "If you don't come, I won't come," he said. We opened up to Bob as adult peers then, and he confided in us is true identity as an S&M artist.

We had known for years that Bob was an artist but never that he was an "artist of pain": one who made a living through art, poetry, music, and sadomasochism. He was adorned with tongue, nipple, and penis piercings and with tattoos. He had been inspired to turn "sickness into sickness," as he put it, and to sublimate his CF into an art form and a means to sexual pleasure. Bob attributed his longevity with CF to his ability to "fight pain with pain": mastering his suffering through ritualized and professional sadomasochism. He thrived on exercises of suffocation, hanging, and self-piercing, all the while sending the message that the pain he inflicted on himself was nothing compared to the pain of his disease. We learned that since his twenties Bob had been a performance artist in sadomasochistic theater, and was renowned in the black-leather community for his disturbing exhibitions at museums throughout the United States. He had published several collections of his poetry and prose, such as *The Wedding of Everything*, *The Fuck Journal* and *The Kid Is a Man*. He had even appeared in the Nine Inch Nails music video for "Happiness Is Slavery" and in Michael Tolkin's film *The New Age*. Bob had been one of the first artists to bring the suffering caused by cystic fibrosis into the mainstream art and literature communities. During our junior year of college, Bob told us that he was working on a sexually explicit autobiography, which was later published by RE/Search under the title *Bob Flanagan: Supermasochist*. All of us youngsters with CF admired his pain tolerance and internalized his confessions and his message, "Getting older with CF really sucks."

During our senior year, Ana and I took our friend Hayley Wester to a San Francisco erotica club to see Bob Flanagan perform. Hayley, a freshman who also had CF, was a petite Texan whose silky blonde hair hung past her rounded shoulders. She was artistic and creative, and we thought she'd appreciate meeting an entertainer with CF.

Following a provocative reading by lesbian artist Susie Bright, Bob appeared on stage, oxygen tank in tow. At forty-one, he was gaunt, and his voice was roughened by congestion. Ana, Hayley, and I sat on the edge of our seats. *My very own superstar,* I thought. Around us sat people with all types of piercings, leather, spiked collars, and dyed hair. Gay couples clung to each other. *God bless America,* I thought. *This is true freedom.* The room was hazy with smoke, and the three of us sputtered through the readings.

Bob proceeded to read his eloquent self-analysis, "Why?" in which he spoke of his path toward S&M: ". . . because it feels good; because it gives me an erection; because it makes me come; because I'm sick; because there was so much sickness; because I say FUCK THE SICKNESS; . . . because they tied me to the crib so I wouldn't hurt myself . . ." He cursed as much as we did in our young CF-camp days. Ana sat with a huge grin. Hayley and I watched Bob, mouths agape.

After the show, the three of us walked back to the car, and on cue, we all exploded into coughing fits. When we had collected ourselves, we started to drive back to Stanford.

"Wow," said Hayley, "that was . . . uh . . . very interesting." I smiled, and wondered how her parents would feel if they knew their proper Texas-bred daughter had just been to an erotica show. And that her sweet Japanese CF friends were contributing to her delinquency.

Ana said, "I think I can understand how life with CF could lead to S&M. After all, CF is all about pain . . . stomach aches, IVs, coughing, and getting pounded. It's totally about being poked and prodded. We have to put up with it for survival." Ana's excitement peaked with this new realization. She continued, "CF is totally a lifestyle of bondage and of physical and emotional masochism. It all makes sense to me."

Hayley agreed. "I think Bob is telling us that life is going to be painful, but we can accept the pain by surprising ourselves with strength."

"I think it's just awesome that Bob found a passion to keep his spirit alive," I said. "I mean, S&M gives him strength, purpose, and a mental release." I turned toward Hayley. In the backseat of the car, she was embraced by colorful reflections from the passing streetlights.

I asked Hayley what her passion was, but she said she still hadn't figured it out. "Same here," I replied. "I need to find the fuel for the fire that will keep me going . . . but I don't think it'll be S&M." I grinned. I felt no repulsion, no disgust, and no need to judge the S&M lifestyle. I had a profound new respect for Bob.

Ana was intrigued by the prospect of testing her own pain threshold. At camp that year, she took out her syringe needles. With the help of Kathy, Karen's sister, she wiped her earlobes with alcohol and stabbed them each three times with the needles. Blood dripped down her earlobes as she announced, "No pain, no gain." I thought it was lame; she was a wannabe Bob Flanagan. But, a few months later Ana and I got flamingos tattooed on our shoulders. As the tattoo needle etched into her shoulder blade, Ana laughed, "This is nothing compared to all those damn IVs."

A few months ago, I didn't even know what CF was. I had only heard the name mentioned in the context of genetic diseases that you knew you didn't want your children to have. For me, CF was a faceless and distant problem. That all has changed dramatically with the entrance into my life of Isa and Ana Stenzel. They have not only taught me about CF, but also a great deal about love, life and understanding. I will never forget them and the special place they now occupy in my heart.

—Andrew, in a letter to Cystic Fibrosis
Research Inc., age twenty-one

With the help of Pulmozyme, my hormones and confidence skyrocketed. I began to experiment with flirting, and, of course, I enjoyed it. But I still had much to learn about what it meant to be a woman and how I could become more comfortable with my changed body.

I met Andrew in the dorm; he worked in the cafeteria. When I appeared for meals, he would often quip, "Ah, back for more?" Or he would grab my meal card, swipe it, and hold up the pocketknife key chain attached to it. "You'll need this for the meatloaf tonight." I look into his stunning blue eyes and smiled. I was hardly bold enough to get to know him more. But then one day, in late January of my senior year, I was doing therapy when someone knocked on the door.

I opened the door. It was Andrew. "Hi," he said. We were the same height, and he had a slight build and receding blond hair. To me, he looked like an all-American white guy.

"Oh, yeah, hi." I smiled. I had pulled the shades during my therapy and worried that he would wonder what I was doing in my room in total darkness. "I know you from food service. What's up?"

"Oh . . . well, I was just walking through the hall and, uh, thought I'd stop by to say hi."

"Oh, well, come on . . . in." I darted over to the windows to open the shades and grabbed a tissue to cover my mucus-filled Dixie cup. After he settled casually on my bed and made a few wisecracks about the posters in my room, he said, "So, uh, what do you do that makes you different from everyone else?"

His question took me by surprise. *Therapy,* I thought, *but I can't tell him about that already.* "Well, I work as a tour guide. Just ten hours a week. I play *taiko,* which is Japanese drumming." I put on a facade of normalcy. We talked and flirted for a while. I admired his warmth and humor. Andrew shared that he was passionate about Democratic Party politics. He loved Broadway musicals and '80s rock 'n' roll.

Andrew turned out to be Prince Charming, who literally came knocking at my door. Over the next few weeks, he invited me to the St. Olaf Choir concert held at Stanford Memorial Church, but he also invited a friend from the dorm to show that this wasn't a real "date." He visited me on the top of Hoover Tower, where I was working as a tour guide. Through the bars hundreds of feet above the ground, I pointed out the Silicon Valley landmarks in the distance.

"Beautiful, beautiful," he exclaimed. Then he looked at me, "And the view isn't bad either."

I grinned and looked away. His compliments embarrassed me. I said, "Oh, Andrew, you're so bold." I had never known anyone who thought I was beautiful.

On March 10, 1994, just three months before graduation, Andrew became the first guy to ask me if he and I could "go together." Startled, I agreed to, but then I sat awkwardly with no idea what to do next. Andrew tried to kiss me that night, but I pulled away.

"Um, I think we should wait before we kiss."

"Oh-kay . . ." he paused to assess the moment. "Did I do something wrong?"

"Oh, no. I just wonder why we have to kiss on the first date."

"Well, I wouldn't want to make you uncomfortable. Uh, have you ever kissed anyone before?"

"Of course." I was sort of telling the truth. I had played spin the bottle at camp many times, but I had never really kissed anyone . . . with feeling. I continued, "I mean, why is it that we have to define the start of a romantic relationship by the moment when we kiss? Is that what dating is all about, getting physical?"

Andrew laughed. "Okay, we don't have to kiss, but we can discuss the philosophy of a kiss for tonight."

Although it seemed like I was playing hard to get, actually I was still painfully self-conscious about my looks and my naïveté.

The next night, Andrew introduced me to his favorite thing to do on a date: slow-dancing to his favorite '80s romantic ballads. I put my arms around his solid shoulders and swayed. He turned me on, and we managed to kiss. I gave Andrew four quick pecks, inhaling his sweet scent, and then moved away to catch my breath. There weren't fireworks, just butterflies. I wasn't short of breath because of my lungs; I was just so worked up and nervous about this newfound intimacy.

In the past, "rice chasers" had approached Ana and me: they were white men with Asian fetishes, who had studied Asian language or culture, had traveled or wanted to travel to Asia, and were otherwise fascinated with all things Asian. They tended to be attracted to Asian women for their exotic ties to a fascinating culture, and when we sensed their fixation, it raised red flags and we ran the other way. I wanted to be liked for who I was, not for the group I belonged to or the way I looked. Andrew showed no outward signs of an Asian fetish; he didn't even like Japanese food.

Andrew said I reminded him of Winnie Cooper on *The Wonder Years*. He liked brunettes who were thin but not too thin. He was genuine and open about his feelings: an absolute must for me. "My criteria for a guy are that he has to be able to cry and play the guitar," I once said. He didn't play the guitar yet, but he had taken voice lessons, and when he serenaded me, I just melted. We talked openly about academics, family, and career goals. He got to know me for who I was instead of knowing me for my disease. I admired his sincerity, his emotional intensity, his social uprightness. We both took our relationship seriously and with a sense of urgency because of our impending graduation.

That same night, after a few more kissing experiments, I sat Andrew down on his bed and got down to business.

"Andrew, I have something to tell you," I confessed.

"What is it?"

I took a deep breath and recited the speech I had rehearsed ever since I first imagined dating.

"I have to tell you that I have a lung problem called cystic fibrosis. It's pretty serious so I have to do respiratory treatments with my sister, and that's why we live together. So I cough a lot and take medicines and do my treatments to stay well." I paused, then hurried on, "So now that we're together I know this is a lot to take in, so if you ever get overwhelmed or can't deal with it, I want you to let me know immediately, rather than letting me get too attached just to get hurt later on. Really, be honest with me if you can't deal."

Andrew's concerned gaze relaxed, and he smiled. "Isa, you can do so much here and you're no different to me than any another student. If you need to take care of yourself, that's one thing. I can deal with that and it seems like you're pretty healthy anyway." He chuckled. "Besides, we're just dating. What's the big deal, anyway? It's not like we're getting married or anything!" He was right, and we both laughed. I needed to stay in the moment and enjoy having a boyfriend who cared about me rather than fear what might come next.

The next day, I had a project on animal tracking in the Stanford foothills. The rest of my conservation biology class had gone on a camping trip to the Sierras to scout marmots. But the lack of electricity and high elevation at the campsite plus the early signs of a lung infection that I'd been feeling kept me from going. Instead, my instructor gave me an independent project. Andrew had already finished his coursework and was almost done with his honors thesis about presidential politics. So he came along.

We walked through tall grass that was waist-high on us both as I scoped out faint trails left by deer. I scribbled on my notepad tracing out the paths. It was a typical Stanford spring day: the blue sky was cloudless and the sun's reflection on the brilliant yellow mustard flowers blinded me. In the distance I could hear the chirping of the red-winged blackbirds.

"So, what do you wanna be when you grow up?" Andrew asked.

"I have no idea," I said.

It was true; I was clueless. I wished I were like Ryuta, who had a clear interest in international relations and economics and had studied Japanese and German; or Ana, who had known since her freshman year that she wanted to be a genetic counselor.

I continued, as we climbed through the shrubs: "I mean, here I am studying environmental stuff, but I don't think I can pursue that. I'm such an environmental poseur. With my CF, I contribute to massive amounts of plastic medical waste; my life depends on animal research; and my day-to-day life requires electricity from the burning of fossil fuels and the development of land for businesses like hospitals and drug companies." I stopped my rant to catch my breath. I couldn't even walk up the hill. I was trying to opt out of environmental work for socially conscious reasons. This was the real reason.

I turned away from Andrew and started coughing. I needed to spit, but that was way too unfeminine.

"Are you okay?" Andrew asked.

"Yeah," I said as I gulped a blob of mucus. What I did for love. "But I've been interested in the psychosocial aspects of illness and disease, so, medical social work appeals to me . . . but part of me wants a job that has nothing to do with health . . . I also took a great class on humans and viruses last fall, which made me think of public health as an option for graduate school . . . so, we'll see."

Enough talk about me. I hated being on the spot, like this was an interview. "What about you? What made you interested in law?"

"I'm not good at anything else. I mean, I have no other options." He smiled humbly.

"Oh, please, c'mon."

Andrew said, "Well, I care about politics, justice. The law impacts every part of our lives. To do what is right in the world, I need to know the law."

Wow. Here was another Stanford student who really seemed to have it all together with his vision for the future. Just like what Donald Kennedy had said way back during freshman year.

A few days later, Andrew's leg started itching, and he broke out with a rash from poison oak. Another reason to give up my environmental career.

A week later, I had another lung bleed and wound up in the hospital. I was forced to let Andrew into my real world. He sent me flowers and asked all about what had happened. After I returned to the dorm, I showed him home IV therapy and let him flush my line. Andrew insisted on learning about my therapy and how to do chest percussion. During our senior trip to Lake Tahoe, he had no problem when I slept next to him with oxygen. He was willing to give Ana percussion as well and accepted our symbiotic unit openly. Dating a twin could be confusing, but he recognized my uniqueness and my personality differences from Ana immediately. To my surprise, he was not scared away. Andrew was becoming a part of my life.

A few weeks before graduation, I entered my dorm room after an evening with Andrew to find Ana crying, alone, on her bed.

"What's wrong? Oh, God, who died?" Tears meant another CF friend had bitten the dust. A wave of panic poured over me.

"No, no, one died," Ana moaned. She grabbed a tissue and blew her nose. "I'm . . . I'm just overwhelmed. I don't know. I'm just so damn emotional. Damn hormones. We weren't missing anything in junior high."

I drew the shades and started to change my clothes. Ana had been emotional even before hormones were in the picture. She took life so seriously, and I could never understand that part of her.

Ana continued, "You're so lucky. You're healthier, stronger, guys are always falling for you first. It's just not fair."

"*Gomen*," I apologized. "I know. Somehow, I've been luckier. I wish it wasn't this way." I didn't have the nerve to tell her my good news, which would crush her even more—I had just heard that I had gotten the job for which we both had applied. It was for a one-year English-teaching position in Japan sponsored by Stanford's Volunteers in Asia Program. I knew that Ana would come to Japan with me anyway—that was a prerequisite to my accepting the job abroad.

She wiped her eyes, which were still pouring buckets. "I . . . I . . . just wish I had what you have." She looked up at me, her eyes intent. "I'm just tired of being the lesser twin."

I tried to rationalize. "Sorry. You aren't lesser . . . you're just different. Besides, having a boyfriend isn't everything . . . okay, well, maybe just the icing on the cake. Remember, that's what Karen used to say. Think of Joi, Rosa, they're like our best friends here. You have them."

"No one will ever be my best friend. That was Karen. I . . . I just wish she was here to see us graduate."

"So do I." I sat down in my bed across from hers.

"I'm totally having a midlife crisis," Ana said. Some students were laughing hysterically in the courtyard. I got up and pulled aside the shade to close the window.

"I know." Growing up was so complicated.

She continued to pour out her thoughts. "Don't *you* get overwhelmed? I mean, we're *graduating*. We've got to find jobs, get health insurance, pay back student loans. And, yeah, I'm healthier than I've ever been, but there's no guarantee it'll last. Doesn't any of that worry you?"

Her panic was contagious.

I flustered for a response. "Of course . . . but I try to stay in the moment. I believe God has a plan for us. Take it one day at a time. For now, we have Mama and Dad's health insurance. We'll defer the loans for a year while we go to Japan. It'll work out."

"God, you sound like Pollyanna."

"I'm just trying to help."

Yes, the future was unknown, but for the first time in our lives, it was not completely dismal. If Pulmozyme had made such a difference in our health, what was next? Tantalized by opportunities after Stanford, we were still sailing in rough waters and needed a lifeboat. Might there be other promising treatments on the horizon from which it wasn't too late for us to reap the benefits?

Andrew and I were caught in the confusion of our newfound relationship. After three short months, we were in love. Finals were over, and graduation was in a few days. We had spent the day touring wineries in Napa Valley. We were tired and sunburned, but the romantic outing had energized our love. We sat on the bed in my dorm room, alone, having "the talk." Laughter could be heard from the other freewheeling seniors out in the hall. Andrew reached over and held my hand.

"Isa, what we have is so incredibly special. You mean so much to me, and I've fallen hard in love. We've got to keep a good thing going."

I leaned on him. "I know. I love you so much, too." Did I know what love was? It had only been three months. Three intense months. "You've changed me, Andrew. I've grown more as a person since I've known you than you can imagine. But I don't know . . . I just don't know what to do." I looked away.

"Let's give it a shot. Lots of couples survive long distance relationships. We can't know for sure, but I think what we have is strong enough to try."

It was so hard to say what I really wanted to say. How did he know all of this? He spoke so honestly, and I owed him the same.

"As much as I love you, Andrew, it just, it feels unrealistic to continue dating when we have no idea where our futures are heading." I spoke slowly and deliberately. "I mean, I'm going to Japan for a year, and you're off to Harvard Law School for three. Who knows who we'll meet, what will happen . . ."

I looked into Andrew's eyes; they were awash with tears. He began to cry, and his face turned redder with each heavy sob. This level of emotional intensity from him was new to me. I had always wanted a boyfriend who could cry, and I had gotten one full force.

"I'm sorry to hurt you, Andrew. I really do love you. I'm just confused. Just scared, really."

The doorknob jiggled, and Ana's voice came through the door, "Yeah, was awesome. See you guys in the morning."

Andrew jolted up, wiping his tears. He sprang for the bathroom that was connected to our room. As Ana opened the door, I quickly followed Andrew into the bathroom and closed the door. This was between Andrew and me.

"*Pleeaase,* I want to be with you. There's nothing I want more. This is so different than anything I've felt before. I feel like you're the one for me . . . the one . . ." he managed to say between sobs.

My God, I was so intimidated by his certainty, and my instinct compelled me to run. I never knew anyone could fall so earnestly in love with me. What had I done to make him feel this way, to deserve this love? I was so confused about my obligations to Ana, my fear of intimacy and letting him further into my unknown future. But I couldn't tell him everything. It was all too complicated. And I felt horrible that it was all up to me to crush him. Two days after graduation, I left my sobbing boyfriend at the edge of Lake Lagunita and said good-bye forever.

A few days after arriving in Los Angeles, I came to my senses. Given my dating history, why had I been so stupid as to turn down this amazingly devoted guy because of my fear of the unknown? He *was* indeed one of a kind. I called him, apologized, and resumed a serious, loyal relationship. Relieved, he welcomed me back with open arms. Over the summer, I visited him at his parents' home, and he visited me at mine. We spent a few romantic weeks together, and it felt right.

When we were together, our love was intense. He yearned for ours to be the perfect relationship of his life, emulating the true romance that his parents had manifested for three decades. We spoke for hours about our insecurities about dating, about our dreams and wishes for the perfect mate, and about a future together. Early in our relationship, I told him that I never wanted to get married, rationalizing that it was just a social convention and institution that limited individual freedom. In the back of my mind, though, I was scared to death of marriage.

Although I tried to ignore it during my Stanford years, I winced at every reminder of my parents' tense marriage. Mama and Dad had become alienated and started sleeping in separate bedrooms. Mama had even changed her name back to her maiden name, Arima. Dad was climbing more mountains, and Mama had bought herself a sports car. They were both having midlife crises. They talked about divorce so often it seemed imminent.

"I finally made my mind up to divorce your father," Mama announced over the phone one day. I was taken aback by her decisiveness. "And so when I bumped into Dr. Robbie at Kaiser, I told him I would get a divorce. You know what he told me? He said, 'If you lose your daughters, are you prepared to handle everything all by yourself?' And I thought long and hard that I could not do it alone. He changed my mind."

Marriage meant feeling stuck. I never wanted that. Besides, all my life I had doubted I would live long enough to marry, and now I had found this perfect someone who could possibly be the one. How could he choose to be part of the insanity of CF culture? He was a smart man, but I wondered if he knew what the future held for us. I was almost relieved that we dated long-distance for the next three years: he didn't have to be exposed to my daily CF routine; constant exposure might have brought him to his senses. Besides, Ana and I needed the time to adjust to having him in the picture on a permanent basis.

Ana and I finished Stanford with no aspirations to be the "future leaders of the world." Leaving behind a vial of Pulmozyme in the Class of '94 time capsule, we graduated with gratitude that we had lived to see all the moments of hard physical and academic work come to fruition in two diplomas, two caps and gowns, one day of celebration and good-byes, and a core of vibrant memories.

Chapter 18

The Next Generation

Isa

"The tragedy of life in modern civilization is going for the 'slam dunk' but seldom being able to do so. Ordinary life seems to get in the way, while our dreams and fantasies remain mostly unfulfilled. While most people live their lives in modern civilization's confusing and often absurd existence, we are fortunate to live out a fantasy—at camp. For one magical week we live the literary romantic's life that the 18th and 19th century poets imagined. Modern civilization is a fraud—the real life lies waiting—at camp. You represent that real life to me—that emotional, from the heart attachment with no strings attached that very few people experience, and the summer camp is where this type of life is cultivated—people relating to people for no reason except to enjoy each other. I think Jesus said all this a couple of thousands of years ago. Few people listened, except us."

—Bob Crabb, in a letter to Ana

A bus pulled up to the Northern California CF camp. Laughter and chatter spilled out from its windows. The bus scattered dust, which was swallowed by the shadows of the redwood trees of the Santa Cruz Mountains. At this camp, each camper was paired with a counselor who would provide one-on-one supervision throughout the week. My camper, Ashley, was nine years old. Like me, she was at this CF camp for the first time. As the campers stepped off the bus, many received hugs from former counselors, known affectionately as *thumpers* because of their roles as chest percussion therapists.

I stared at the children, trying to find Ashley. I peered at each child, looking for the stigma of CF that would tell me I was among my own. It was difficult. The campers appeared healthy—there were few emaciated children, no kids with oxygen tanks or IV poles, no kids with pale faces and blue lips or the clubbed fingers so characteristic of the kids we saw at Southern California CF camp. The San Francisco Bay Area was home to some of the best CF Care Centers in the nation, and it showed.

A plump girl standing by the registration table poked me. "Why do your fingers look like that?" she asked, pointing to my Q-tip fingers.

"Do you have CF?" I asked her.

"Yeah," she replied. Her nail beds were flat.

"Haven't you ever heard of clubbing? It's part of CF."

"You have CF?"

I nodded.

"You're so old!"

I beamed with pride. Now it was my turn to be a CF adult; I had reached a milestone reserved only for the lucky few. Ana and I had made it.

A tiny blonde girl stepped off the bus wearing Tevas and a bright tie-dyed shirt. One of the camp leaders stood by her and yelled out, "Isa Stenzel? Here's Ashley!"

Ashley had a high-pitched voice, bright blue eyes, and flawless, tanned skin. She came from rural Northern California and was the only child in her family with CF. "I have goats and chickens!" she exclaimed as I carried her belongings to her cabin. "We live by the Redwood Park. We live next to a field where my horse lives. Oh, and I don't get poison oak!" Her calloused hands pushed aside the fair hair that fell across her face. This girl was beyond adorable. After we dropped her things off in the cabin, we toured the camp. Barely fifty pounds, she had strong, sinewy legs, and she ran fiercely along the trails alongside the creek.

Over that first week of camp, I began to see that my relationship with Ashley was like the eating of a Twinkie: the first bites were sweet, but each progressive bite was increasingly unappetizing. She was a brat who protested and screamed when it was treatment time. Sometimes, I had to hold her down to make her inhale her tobramycin. She was part of the new CF generation, who didn't do chest percussion but instead blew into a PEP valve, a device that moved secretions by breathing against pressure.

She didn't take her treatments seriously at all. Sometimes she had the

PEP pipe in her mouth but just breathed through her nose. I'd tell her, "Breathe deeply! Ashley, if you want to grow up to be strong and healthy, you have to do it right!" I sounded like my mother. I was a true nag. I brought my portable nebulizer to her cabin so we could do our treatments together. Sometimes, I found her PEP pipe on the cabin floor or under her pillow. And the more I nagged, the more she revolted.

Ashley also resisted the camp activities. At one of the camp's educational workshops on nutrition, there was a contest among the campers to make the highest-calorie milk shake. Ashley poured milk, vegetable oil, chocolate syrup, peanut butter, bananas, and protein powder into the blender and watched as the concoction blended into a brown soup with an astounding eight hundred calories.

"Ewww," she exclaimed. "That's disgusting! I'm not tasting *that*!"

"Oh, come on, Ashley," I replied. "Let's have a contest . . . who can drink this the fastest." I swallowed my cup quickly, feeling the slime of peanut butter and oil slide down my throat.

"Ah, ha . . . you won!" Ashley beamed as she poured her cup into the trash.

For the next five summers, Ashley and I were paired as camper and thumper, and she continued to drive me crazy. Once it took four of us thumpers to carry Ashley by her arms and legs to the talent show. When I tried to walk with her to activities, she kicked me or pulled my hair, laughing. She loved to tease, and once threw herself into a patch of poison oak and then chased me across the camp trying to hug me. One year, I told Ashley's mom at the end of the week, "Her energy, if she directs it into her health care and fulfilling hobbies, will do her well in the long run and keep her alive."

But her spirited zest grew on me, and I fell in love with her. I admired her competitiveness during team games, her witty jokes about doctors. We had a lot in common: she thrived in school, was a tomboy, a nature-lover, and slightly socially awkward. During one educational workshop, Ana and I made a "Transplant Teddy Bear," sewing "old" and "new" lungs that could be switched inside the bear's chest by undoing a zipper. We gave the bear a transplant in front of the kids. Ashley, with precocious insight, was the only one to ask, "Won't the body reject the lungs?"

At one meal, when Ashley protested taking her pills or eating high-calorie foods (all she wanted to eat was watermelon), I told her, "I know pills are annoying, but you just have to deal with this for now. Listen, you'll only have to do this for several more years. By the time you're my age, I am *totally* sure, in fact, I *promise* you, there will be a cure by then." That was 1991, and I was nineteen.

Two years earlier, in 1989, the gene for cystic fibrosis had been discovered by Drs. Francis Collins and Lap-Chee Tsui. Finding the gene was a major breakthrough, and scientists said a cure could be expected within the next ten years.

Over the years, though, there were complex articles in CF newsletters about the gene and protein and sophisticated yet unsuccessful techniques for gene therapy. Most basic science research remained obscure and largely clinically irrelevant. A decade after the gene discovery, the impatient parents who attended CF education events would cast bitter accusations at the researchers who always ended their presentations with "and further research needs to be done."

One year at camp, I remember campers and thumpers hanging out beneath the redwoods while doing arts and crafts, musing about the so-called cure. With a striking maturity forced upon them by circumstance, the kids and adults offered a well-balanced assessment of candid realism and hopefulness.

"I know I need to keep myself healthy until the cure comes."

"That's a crock. The science is so much more complicated than they thought; it'll be years before they find any cure."

"There's not going to be any real cure. There'll be a control for CF, like with diabetes, but I doubt there'll be a magic pill that will totally cure it."

"You see, I'm confident. I think the cure is right around the corner."

"I'm way too sick for a cure. I just don't think I'll be around then."

"What the hell is taking so long? I mean, there is so much fundraising and still no cure."

"Yeah, the idea of a cure is just to give parents of little kids hope. We're too old to benefit from it, because we adults have way too much lung damage to fix our lungs."

"My version of a cure is to get a lung transplant. Maybe those will be more successful some day."

But in the 1990s new drugs were in fact developed: first Pulmozyme; then TOBI, a concentrated form of inhaled tobramycin, and other third- and fourth-generation antibiotics that helped to treat *Pseudomonas*. Better treatments, but still no cure. And with each new breakthrough came more nebulizer treatments, more pills to swallow, more IVs to infuse, and more time and energy to treat the disease that was shortening our lives. More treatments for kids like Ashley to hate.

Support groups were held each afternoon at this camp. We sat in a circle under the towering beams of the camp's central lodge. The late afternoon sun brought a ray of light into the room.

"What's the best part of having CF?" asked the psychologist who led the groups.

A teenage boy raised his hand. "'Cause I'm shooting blanks, I can have sex with as many girls as I want without getting 'em pregnant." The group chuckled.

A discussion ensued. I looked down at Ashley, embarrassed for her. I wondered if she knew most men with CF were sterile. She looked up at me and whispered, "Can girls with CF have babies?"

"Yeah," I said. Good, she got it.

A young thumper spoke up. "Camp is the best part of CF. The love and friends here . . . we connect on so many deeper levels than what exists in the outside world. We are all in this together."

The facilitator paused and glanced around the room.

"I'm just curious. For those of you with CF, if you could take a pill that would cure you of CF, and all the experiences—the memories, relationships, everything—associated with having CF, how many of you would take that pill?"

I looked around. Among the forty or so people in the room, only one skinny arm rose, illuminated by the sunlight entering the room. I heard a cough. I had to think hard about that question. CF had given me so many unique life experiences, and for that I was grateful. I did not raise my hand.

After the group, Ashley opened up. "CF, CF, CF . . . that's all everybody talks about. I mean, don't these people have a life?"

I laughed. She had a point. CF camp had transformed us, restricting our identities, defining us as people with a disease. There was something liberating about not exploring that part of our lives so deeply.

Even though Ashley didn't care for support groups, they were among my favorite times at camp. The messages from these discussions helped us through the journey with CF: *Communicate openly. Embrace life. Recognize its fragility. It is better to love and lose than to never have loved at all. Laugh often and at yourself. Forgive yourself. Cultivate the spirit. Dare to share your story with others. Love others generously. Don't take life too seriously. Tell people you love them. It's quality-of-life that matters more than quantity.* My CF community gave me a passion to keep fighting and ignited my will to live. We all were balancing on a tightrope between sickness and death, hope and fear, truth and denial.

As Ashley matured, our friendship deepened, but her rebellion continued. We talked over the phone about being in the hospital, getting Make-A-Wish Foundation wishes, about school, our families, and her horse, which kept her focused and motivated through her teen years. She rode and trained it regularly, and she taught me a great deal about horsemanship. She still didn't want to do her treatments, but she used horseback riding to clear her lungs. Her turbulent adolescence was marked by more hospitalizations. Her access to healthcare was also limited; there were no CF Care Centers in the rural area where she lived. When she needed to be hospitalized, her mother had to make the five-hour drive to the San Francisco hospital where they stayed together for several weeks.

In her teens, her voice took on a desperate edge as her health deteriorated. It still squeaked, but now it was shaky with frustration rather than strong with confidence.

"I just don't want to have to deal with any of this anymore," she said. "You can do anything because of your sister. You went to college, you've traveled, and you're tall! I wish I had your life!"

Guilt consumed me. She was right; I had been tremendously privileged. I wanted to tell her to take better care of her health, and she could do the same, but I knew those words would fall on deaf ears and could be a lie. It was about so much more than that—about economic privilege, social support, opportunity and geographic proximity to excellent medical care. It was about my own drive to work as hard as possible to stay healthy and functional. And she was right: I did have my sister. Ashley's strong desire to live a normal life, which meant denying CF, was her main drive.

When Ashley was seventeen, I visited her in the hospital. Instead of the tan, energetic girl I remembered, she was pale and blue-tinged; her once defiant voice was breathy and congested. I wanted to cry. She was supposed to be healthier than me. I had broken the promise I had made almost a decade earlier that a cure would be found.

"I fucked up," she confessed, "didn't take care of myself and now look at me."

"Oh, Ashley, I'm so sorry. I wish it wasn't so unfair." I didn't know what else to say.

Then she told me, "I just want to get this stupid disease over with, so I'm getting a lung transplant."

My God, I thought. *What a brave yet impulsive choice. What about the risks?*

She continued, "I don't even want to go through the slow process of waiting on the list," she explained. "That takes too long and I just want to take a year off after high school, get my lungs and then go on to college. I don't want to deal with treatments and hospital stays when I'm in college. I'm going to be healthy with new lungs." She decided to receive a living-related lobar lung transplant; her father and a family friend were willing to donate their largest lung lobes. She received her transplant when she was eighteen.

Through Ashley's struggle, I realize that there are so many ways a young person can deal with an illness as imposing as CF. Was there is a right or wrong way to cope with CF? As a college student, Ashley lived a normal life free of CF. She realized her goals.

And I envied her.

As people with CF were living longer and being treated more aggressively with antibiotics, newer and more virulent strains of bacteria were emerging in their lungs. Some bacteria were resistant to antibiotics; others were more benign. The same bugs might sit dormant in the lungs of one person with CF but cause rapid decline and death in another. A new concept called "cross infection" emerged. New evidence showed that CF patients with virulent strains of bacteria, particularly a rare strain called *burkholderia cepacia,* could transmit these strains to another person with CF through close contact, such as by coughing on each other or holding hands. Experts in CF care and infectious disease recommended screening and isolation of people with CF who harbored dangerous bacteria. It was difficult to quantify the risk of transmission of *burkholderia cepacia,* as well as the common, more benign bacteria that most people with CF had in their lungs, *pseudomonas aeruginosa.* Sputum culture tests had no standardized method of detecting the more dangerous bacteria, and the methods that were used yielded results that could not always be trusted.

The uncertainty created a new generation of hysterical parents afraid of allowing their children to socialize with others with CF and caused ostracism and isolation of those patients with particular infections. Fewer children were sent to camps. For safety, many camps started a screening process to identify any prospective attendees whose recent sputum culture reports showed dangerous bacterial strains; those children were not allowed to attend. People with CF were no longer permitted to be roommates in the hospital and were encouraged to wear masks when close proximity was unavoidable. CF had evolved into an infectious disease. Just as at-risk populations had been taught to consider the concept of safe sex and universal precautions after the emergence of HIV, people with CF have been molded into asking one another, "Is your culture safe?" before any social gathering. Kids received a crash course on microbiology at a young age, and we heard them ask one another questions like, "Do you have methicillin-resistant *staphylococcus aureus* (MRSA), *burkholderia cepacia,* or *pseudomonas aeruginosa* resistant to all antibiotics?" Antibacterial hand gels, disinfectant sprays, masks, and gloves became common sights at CF social functions, just in case. Gone were the days of hugging each other, of sharing a cabin together, all doing therapy in unison, of holding each other as we cried at camp. By the late 1990s most of the CF summer camps in the country were gone. Many CF medical experts discouraged camps due to the risk of cross infection and the fear of litigation. There is now a generation of people with CF who are afraid of being together, who will believe that they are alone in their struggles and won't have the personal connections with CF adults that we cherished so much growing up. Alternatives such as phone mentors and internet chat rooms are the new version of CF support, though, in my opinion, these are never as meaningful as in-person interactions. Ana and I mourn for those who will miss out on the gift of CF camp that our generation received. The friends I met along this common road enriched my life immeasurably.

(Back row, l to r) Grandfather (Sukehisa Arima) and Great-uncle Tsukada; (front row, l to r) Obachan (Tazuko Arima), Mama, Uncle Juichi, Uncle Yuzo, Great-grandmother Honda, and Great-aunt Tsukada, Manchuria, China, 1943

Oma (Ada Stenzel) with Dad (left) and Uncle Jurgen, Breslau, 1943

Isa (left) and Ana, 1972

(l to r) Mama, Ana, Isa, Ryuta, and Obachan, at home in Pacific Palisades, 1973

(l to r) Dad, Ryuta, Mama, Isa, and Ana, 1974

Opa (Georg Stenzel) and Oma (Ada Stenzel) in back
with (l to r) Isa, Ryuta, and Ana, Los Angeles, 1975

Isa (left) and Ana blowing out their
candles at birthday party, 1978

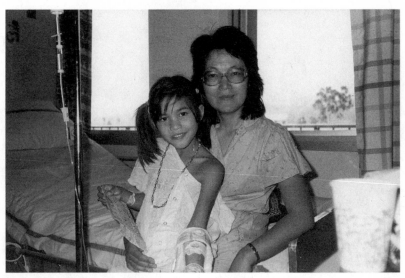

Ana and Mama, Kaiser Hospital, 1979

(l to r) Ryuta, Ana, Dad, and Isa, Japan, 1980

(Back row, l to r) Uncle Yuzo, Mama, Dad, Uncle Juichi, and Aunt Yoko; (front row, l to r) Obachan, Ana, Cousin Yuki, Isa, and Ryuta visiting Grandfather's grave near Mount Fuji, Japan, 1980

CF Camp (top, l to r) Isa, Karen, Michelle, and Renee;
(bottom, l to r) Bob Crabb, Joe, Rocky, Bob Flanagan, 1989

Christmas in the hospital: Mama, Ana, with Ryuta standing behind her, and Isa, 1985

(l to r) Ana, Uncle Juichi, Mama, Obachan, Ryuta, and Isa, Ryuta's birthday party, 1990

(l to r) Isa, Ryuta, and Ana at Stanford graduation, June 12, 1994

Ryuta, Isa, and Ana, at Kyoto's famous golden temple, April 1995. Isa's lungs were bleeding badly, so Ryuta carried her backpack, but we went sightseeing anyway.

Isa and Andrew on their wedding day, June 27, 1998
Photo courtesy of Howard Auzenne

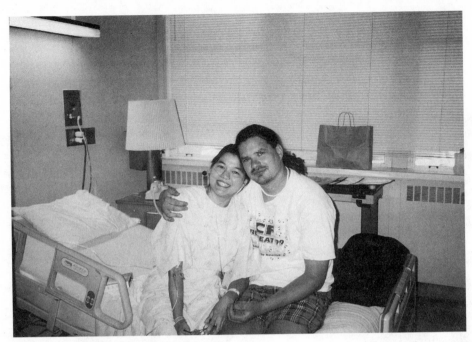

Ana and Rob at Stanford Hospital two hours
before Ana's transplant, June 14, 2000

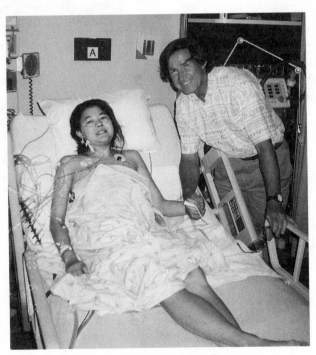

Ana with Dad after her double lung transplant,
June 16, 2000, in Stanford ICU

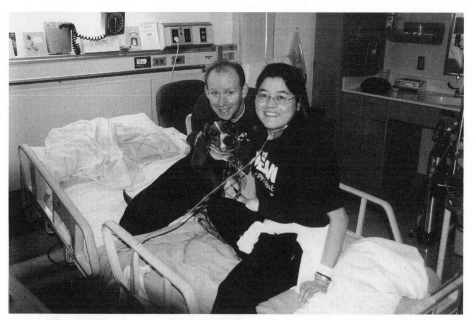

Andrew, Rupie (bassett mix), and Isa at the hospital
three weeks before her transplant, January 2004

Isa and Ana in ICU three days after Isa's transplant, February 9, 2004

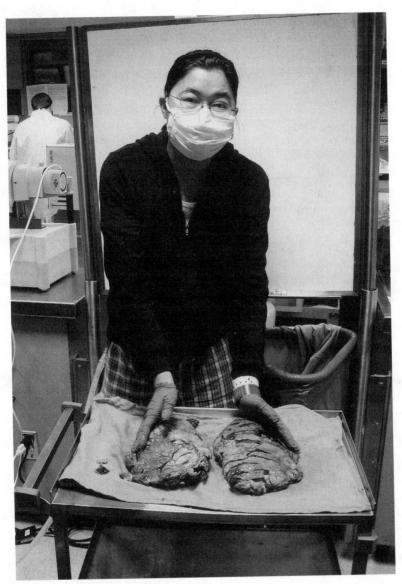

Isa, two weeks after her transplant, saying
goodbye to her old lungs, February 2004

Rupie, Isa, Ryuta, and Ana skiing at Tahoe one year after Isa's transplant, February 2005

(l to r) Isa and Ana at the top of Half Dome,
Yosemite National Park, September 10, 2006

(l to r) Isa kissing Ana, U.S. Transplant Games, Kentucky, June 2006

James Dorn, Ana's donor,
June 28, 1970–June 14, 2000

Xavier Cervantes, Isa's donor,
September 10, 1985–February 4, 2004
Photo courtesy of Lifetouch

Part 2

The Adult Years

Chapter 19

An Adventure in Japan

Isa

Japan is a great place to visit but a miserable place to live.

—Isa, age twenty-two

As the plane descended over southern Japan, I looked through the window at the foreign landscape. In the distance, the blue Seto Inland Sea was littered with fishing boats and hundreds of small, rocky islands covered with thick greenery. Closer by, I saw the concrete sprawl of Takamatsu, a small city in Kagawa prefecture on the northern tip of the island of Shikoku. It was late afternoon, and already I could see the flashing neon lights of downtown in the distance, their bright arrogance advertising Coca-Cola and Sony.

"Can you believe it, Ana?" I asked, pulling down the sleeves of my Stanford sweatshirt. "We're finally here." I grasped her hand and held it tight. Her fingertips were cold. Oxygen deprivation during the ten-hour flight had left its mark. I couldn't wait to breathe fresh air at sea level.

"Yeah," she replied, "are you ready for this?"

"I hope so. Let's just remember . . . whatever happens, health comes first."

Ana tightened her hand around mine. "This is going to be an adventure for both of us. I'm glad at least one of us got the job."

Ana had spent the summer bitter about my getting the English-teaching job that we had both applied for through Stanford's Volunteers in Asia program. We wanted to live life to the fullest, to see the Japan we remembered from 1980 and relive the moments we had loved then: catching praying mantises in a field of tall grass, feeling the pink petals of springtime cherry blossoms falling on our cheeks in the breeze, or tasting the sweetness of a fresh red bean rice cake. Now, we were still alive and healthy enough to travel.

Ana had hoped to find her own freelance English-teaching job. *We* had agreed to come to Japan together, even though deep down inside I knew she had no choice. We were symbiotic again, joined by the needs of our lungs, even more dependent on each other in a foreign country than back home.

While I spent time with Andrew during the summer, Ana prepared for our trip. She ordered massive quantities of medication, hoarding 50 bottles of pancreatic enzymes, 2,000 vials of Tobramycin, 10 bottles of Ciprofloxacin, 20 bottles of Albuterol, 6 boxes of Pulmozyme . . . the list went on and on. Our luggage was packed like that of drug dealers. Fortunately, with a letter from our doctor and our proficient Japanese, we made our way through customs without a hitch.

Once in Takamatsu, Ana and I found our way to our studio apartment in a building named Kubo Mansion, which was provided by my job. It was no mansion. Hidden at the end of a dark hallway on the third floor was an iron door, which opened into a small sunken entranceway. Within the apartment, a tiny range top with two electric burners sat adjacent to a sink that had only cold water; next to the sink sat a mini refrigerator. On the other side of the kitchenette, a sliding rice-paper screen opened up into a small sleeping area composed of six *tatami* mats, the traditional rice mats used as flooring. The room measured eight by twelve feet and reeked of moldy straw. A thick mattress, or *futon,* and an array of blankets were folded neatly in the closet. They were to be spread out each night on the floor as tradition dictated.

That evening Ana and I ventured out to explore our neighborhood. It was the beginning of September, the tail end of the hot and humid Japanese summer. My clothes stuck to my skin like Saran Wrap, and mosquitoes buzzed in my ears. Idle taxis and buses spewed exhaust in our faces. Young children in school uniforms, on their way home from evening tutoring classes, gathered at crosswalks. Old ladies with curved spines hunched over walkers as they struggled through the streets. It seemed like everyone's eyes were upon us. Was it our height? Our twinness? Our mixed race? Could they tell by the way we dressed that we were *gaijin* (foreigners)?

We headed downtown toward bustling streets filled with quaint shops and restaurants. Across from the train station, I saw massive billboards adorned with *kanji* characters that I recognized from childhood Japanese school but had never bothered to memorize. The blaring siren of the crossguard rang in my ears as the ground vibrated with passing commuter trains.

Ana and I settled on a restaurant that served *udon*, a noodle dish that was the delicacy of the region. We stood staring at the plastic food displays in the restaurant's window. Perfect for illiterate foreigners. We chose tempura *udon*, with a side of pickled cabbage, for fifteen hundred yen, about twelve dollars. I wondered how I would maintain my weight paying so much to eat so little.

Stepping inside the restaurant we were overcome by the stench of cigarettes. *Damn smokers*, I thought. *Welcome to the land where over 60 percent of men take their healthy lungs for granted.* I tried not to breathe deeply. My lungs had a tendency to bleed from secondhand smoke. I ordered without looking at the menu, wiping my sweaty forehead with an *oshibori*.

My eyes scanned the claustrophobic restaurant. In the corner was a group of business men wearing navy suits, huddled in lively conversation amid bottles of Sapporo beer and cartons of Mild Sevens. More stares.

We got our food and found a table. I savored my tempura *udon*. This was what being here was all about. With this food, I belonged here.

In the middle of our meal, one of the businessmen approached our table. He reeked of beer and cigarettes; his face was oily and reddened. In Japanese, he mumbled, around the cigarette still between his lips, "Beautiful girls. Come to my hotel with me."

Suddenly his arm came forward, his hand reaching for Ana's bare shoulder. In the sweltering heat, she was wearing a loose silk tank top. Was her comfortable attire unacceptable here? Maybe our American choice of clothing was an inadvertent invitation to strange men.

"Excuse me!" She snapped in Japanese. She pulled away, swatting away his hand. She announced that she was American, was not interested, and demanded that he leave us alone.

His face froze, his eyes widened, "You're American?!" He took a step back and promptly left the restaurant.

I admired Ana's comeback. I would've been speechless with awkwardness. We bore the curse of looking Japanese on the outside, thus attracting this kind of chauvinistic treatment that was probably the norm for Japanese women, but we were fully American on the inside, and Ana, for sure, was not going to tolerate that treatment. It was only our first night in Japan, and the high prices, smoking, and sexism so far were disturbing. Being here as an adult would definitely test my cultural tolerance.

The next day, I started my job teaching English to local medical students while Ana began to search for a freelance English-teaching job. I felt relief, when, after a few weeks, Ana found a handful of part-time teaching opportunities with the help of the Takamatsu International Center. Each day I boarded the train for the thirty-minute ride to the countryside. From the window, I could see vast golden wheat fields, blended with a blue haze from burning foliage. Old hunchbacked farmer's wives gathered fresh cabbage and radishes from their gardens. Once I arrived at my stop, I rushed up a long hill to reach the Kagawa Medical School. In the half-hour walk I soaked up the Japan I loved. I passed by sprawling rice paddies where tiny beads of rice danced in the morning breeze. I passed traditional homes with their authentic blue-gray roof tiles and their old wooden sliding doors under the arching rooftops that created the perfect shady space to hang persimmons out to dry. On the second-floor balconies, plush futon mattresses lay airing, as the sun dried up the moisture that had collected in them the night before.

Most of my students were physicians who wanted help with English conversation or with editing research articles they had written for publication in English medical journals. To help them with their broken English, I often brought newspaper clippings or articles about politics and social issues to stimulate an hour-long dialogue. Since they were doctors, I was open to them about my CF, which offered us discussion material about differences in the doctor-patient relationship, medical systems, and research.

One of my morning conversation classes was made up of several doctors' wives. We sat around sipping tea and nibbling delicate desserts served on elegant dishes as the women giggled and talked about their husbands' schedules, the meats currently on sale, or their kids' accomplishments in school. My mind wandered during the conversations. I thought about how far my mother had come. Since we had started college, she had been working as a pediatric social worker at Kaiser Hospital in Los Angeles with the same nurses who had taken care of Ana and me as children. She had blossomed into an assertive, ambitious, spirited professional. She had joined a gym and a community choir. I looked at these housewives and imagined how stifled and miserable Mama would have been in Japan.

After my morning classes, I whisked myself away to the most private bathroom I could find. I removed my portable nebulizer from my backpack in the bathroom stall. I puffed away while I coughed my brains out. Occasionally, medical students entered the bathroom, and I held in my cough so as to not gross them out. Sometimes, a faceless student would notice me in the next stall, and she would flush the toilet over and over, because allowing the sound of urination to be heard was taboo in Japan. This infuriated me, because there was a drought in Takamatsu, and also with each flush I imagined droplets of bacteria flying into the air as I inhaled from my nebulizer. How foolish, I thought, each of us trying to hide our bodily functions, and this was a medical school!

My English lessons were an opportunity for me to learn about Japanese culture. I heard from one of my students named Saito-san that many physicians did not tell patients the prognosis in cases of terminal cancer to spare them the depression that might come from learning their fate. Even family members said nothing. I could not imagine the truth being concealed from me; much of my appreciation of life came from knowing my time on earth was limited.

Saito-san and I also talked about the stigma of physical difference in Japan. "Are there any disabled people here?" I asked. It had been months, and I had not seen a single person in a wheelchair. Train stations, shopping centers, and temples had no ramps, no handrails, few elevators, and no disabled parking places.

"Most disabled people live in institutions," Saito-san explained. "They do not live in the community, because it is too difficult. It is too much of a burden and shame for the family."

"But what if a disabled person wanted to live at home with their family?"

"Most people accept being in an institution. It's just the way it is."

I thought about Obachan's familiar response to our childhood complaints that something was difficult: "*Shoganai*." It meant "it can't be helped," that one accepted things as they are rather than acting to change them. I wondered, if we had been born in Japan, would we be locked away in an institution, too? I left the discussion grateful that we live in a country where everyone deserves a chance to live a normal life.

I also thought about those two painful words that Saito-san had used— burden and shame—the Japanese values that Mama had ingrained in me. No wonder Mama had placed double-paned windows in our bedrooms and told us to muffle our coughing with folded towels. She wanted to hide the shame of our being different and spare others the disruption of our noisy coughing. Was this why I was always so self-conscious?

At the end of the day, I made the long walk back to the train station. The red ball of fire in the distant sky was like no other sunset I'd seen. Though exhausted, I was pleased that I had the energy to work full time. As a real working adult, I could earn money and support myself, living independently without my parents' assistance. For once, I was contributing to society instead of sucking up its resources, as I had done all my life as a sick person.

We liberally took time off work to explore Japan. Josh, who had been my high school prom date, happened to be studying in northern Japan on a Fulbright scholarship, and we spent a few intermittent weeks touring the country together. We explored the Roppongi nightlife in Tokyo's red-light district; we dipped in a scalding co-ed tub at a hot spring in Atami; we toured the outdoor markets of Kobe; we sat under blooming cherry trees and wandered the Hiroshima Peace Park and Atom Bomb Museum. He happened to be staying over with us when the 6.9 Kobe earthquake struck nearby in the early hours of January 17, 1995. The three of us screamed and hugged one another as our flimsy apartment shook violently. We had known each other nearly half of our lives, and we shared each other's innermost secrets. Ana and I openly coughed, even spit, and did therapy in his presence. Besides, with his lactose intolerance, we competed with embarrassing gastrointestinal-distress stories. Our travels were carefree, with few organized plans. We simply hopped onto the Shinkansen Bullet Train and got off where we wanted to go, hoping to find an affordable hotel near the train station for the night.

On one occasion we wandered around a small town for what seemed like hours looking for a hotel. The sun was setting, and we were getting nervous about finding accommodations. The heavy nebulizer machine in my backpack added to my breathlessness, and I needed a treatment. One hotel after another quoted a price of close to two hundred dollars for the night. Finally we found a clean-looking building with the English word *Motel* written next to various kanji characters in the entry. Inside, it was apparent that this place charged only seven thousand yen, or around seventy dollars, for one night. There was also a list of prices by the hour, presumably for exhausted businessmen who wanted to crash for a few hours in between appointments. We entered and approached the counter. Offering Josh a chance to practice his Japanese, we let him ask for a room. The middle-aged man looked us over, first Ana, then me, and then said to Josh, "No, only one girl allowed." Ana explained that we had a health problem and we had to stay together, but the man insisted. Finally the three of us realized that this was one of Japan's notorious "love motels," offered for one-night stands and extramarital affairs in this supposedly sexually repressed culture.

During my adventure in Japan, Andrew was never far from my thoughts despite his being seven thousand miles away in Boston. We both carried on with our personal lives: my ambition to travel and his academic plans in law school. But we remained deeply committed. We kept in touch daily by email. We also wrote each other love letters and scented them with perfume or cologne. We sent each other audiotapes with reports on our lives; sometimes he sang love songs on his tapes. We wore handkerchiefs for a few days and mailed them to each other for the pheromones.

Our love nauseated Ana. She became an expert at eye-rolling.

"Gawd," she'd say, "that's *so* cheesy."

Andrew visited me in Japan during his winter break. He brought another three month's supply of Pulmozyme, which we needed to get through
the year, impressing my parents with his willingness to help. We visited
Kotohira Castle, situated on a mountaintop in central Shikoku. Getting to
the castle entailed climbing 750 steps. On either side of the stairway were
souvenir shops and snack stands selling barbequed squid or red bean
cakes. We walked arm in arm through dense fog and bitter cold. I could
climb only a few steps at a time before I had to stop to catch my breath and
cough. Andrew was patient. We also toured Shodoshima Island, known for
its large population of free-roaming monkeys, and hiked to its mountain
peak while enduring the stares of hundreds of the curious beasts.

It had been five months since we had seen each other, and we were horny.
I had to schedule private time with Andrew while Ana was out teaching.
It wasn't an easy feat. She came home unexpectedly one time and caught
us in the middle of action. I then asked her to go shopping, go for a walk,
do something, *anything,* so I could be alone with Andrew.

"You are so selfish," Ana complained. "I live here, too. What am I supposed to do, wait outside the door while you make out with Andrew?"

One night, Andrew finished up my therapy after Ana had already fallen
asleep. After we were done, the three of us lay like sardines across the entire floor space. Andrew and I cuddled under the heavy pile of blankets.
We listened for Ana's rapid, deep breathing to make sure she was sound
asleep. Then, we tore each other's pajamas off and wriggled under the covers, me trying not to jar Ana, who was lying just inches away. Suddenly,
Ana shot up. "*Heki?* You okay, Isa? Your breathing alright?"

Andrew and I froze. "Yeah, I'm fine," I said. She lay down and went back
to sleep.

Finally, Andrew and I got ourselves a hotel room, but only after I
promised Ana that we would time our absence to fall before and after giving her therapy. I was keeping something from Ana for the first time, and
I tiptoed around the subject of my intimacy with Andrew for fear of her
judgment.

Sexual intimacy excited me, but I hesitated each step of the way. All my
life I had struggled against my body: it was my enemy; it caused only pain
and discomfort and needed to be constantly monitored for problems. It was
ugly, a source of mucus, gas, diarrhea—only unpleasant bodily functions.
Now, Andrew saw everything about my body as beautiful, as *sexual.* He
showed me that my body could be a source of pleasure I never had imagined. *You mean, I'm supposed to have fun with this body?* Sexuality had been
my lowest priority, and I had a lot to learn. I was open and eager but just
didn't know how. Things were moving very fast. I had gone from being a

little girl with no interest in men just three years earlier to having a mature physical relationship. My confusion slowed our physical exploration and tested Andrew's patience.

With CF came another level of intimacy. "I'm not very comfortable around bodily stuff," Andrew had told me at the beginning of our relationship. "I almost fainted in eighth grade health class during the birth video. Blood and I don't go well together." We joked that now he was dating someone who was all about bodily needs. During our time in Japan, Andrew was becoming an expert at giving me chest percussion. I taught him how to pound my back hard, just the way I liked it, and he thought it was kinky. Occasionally, his hand would slip and he'd pat my butt or stroke my breasts. Therapy turned him on. How convenient! But his aversion to bodily fluids made me even more self-conscious than before. I spit into my paper cup as stealthily as possible.

During one of our therapy sessions at a hotel, my hands slipped, and my cup spilled over the bed. It fell over his lap and yellow-green ooze poured down his leg. "Nasty! Don't look! Close your eyes!" I grabbed a pile of tissues.

"Eeeew!" Andrew yelled. But then he started laughing.

I could practically see his skin tingling with cooties. I said, "I'm so sorry! This is so gross! I'm so embarrassed . . . I can't believe you're attracted to me."

He recovered more quickly than I did and said, "Don't worry, dear. This is a part of you. It's okay."

Andrew left Japan two weeks later. Our relationship was on solid ground, and we were convinced that we were meant to be together.

Chapter 20

Homesick in Japan

Ana

By late January, my breathing was heavier. My mind felt foggy as I struggled to teach my classes. Fatigue and breathlessness engulfed my body, and copious amounts of mucus gurgled in my lungs. I had a raging lung infection, and Isa was struggling, too. How would we survive in Japan for another eight months? We were treating ourselves with only a closetful of American oral antibiotics.

The only controls we could exert over our festering lungs were to decide when to increase the dose of antibiotics and when to increase the duration and intensity of our chest percussion, sometimes pounding each other's chest for a full hour and a half each. After our therapies Isa's shirts would often look like they had been sprinkled with paprika; the sprinkles were the marks left by the bleeding cracks in my hands. Our poor neighbor had to listen to hours of clapping and coughing that passed through the thin walls each evening. One therapy session took nearly four hours. We filled one paper cup, then two, then three.

"Ten ounces in an hour and a half. Not bad," I said, cleaning up my cups and tissues. I let out a long sigh, leaning against the wall. "I feel so much clearer. This is what it was like in the dark ages of CF. No meds. Just therapy."

Isa said how fortunate we were to have the kind of disease where there was something that could be done.

Because of Mama's Japanese citizenship, we were able to obtain medical care through the Japanese national health care system. So we visited a pulmonologist at Kagawa Medical School named Dr. Jiro Fujita. Dr. Fujita spoke fluent English but had never treated anyone with CF. He was fascinated by CF, because it resembled a lung disease he had considerable experience treating—diffuse pan bronchiolitis (DPB). DPB was common in Japanese people and was characterized by copious mucus and chronic *Pseudomonas* infections. Dr. Fujita took pictures of our clubbed fingers and asked for sputum specimens from us for research purposes so that he could study our "American" *Pseudomonas*. He ordered a CT scan of our lungs, the first time we had ever had that test. He had us speak to a class of medical students about cystic fibrosis, and we showed a video on CF camp. When Obachan visited from Tokyo, he checked her blood to look for the CF gene. She turned out not to be a carrier. She told us she knew it was from our grandfather's side.

Visiting Dr. Fujita was a mind-boggling experience. In navigating the health-care system, we had to cope with language barriers and unfamiliar treatment styles. The patients were seen in a communal setting, exposed to one another in large exam rooms, with multiple patients sitting on exam tables that were lined up five feet apart. We were terrified of catching tuberculosis or some other lung infection as it seemed uncustomary to cover one's mouth when coughing or sneezing. To our dismay, the hospital waiting room had smoking and nonsmoking sections. Patients could even smoke in their hospital rooms!

During one appointment in February, Dr. Fujita analyzed my arterial blood gas, and my oxygen levels were in the eighties.

"You know," he said in his thick accent, struggling through words, "you are not so well."

"I know," I replied. I explained that I had used supplemental oxygen during sleep since I was seventeen and wondered if I could get it in Japan, too.

"I am surprised you are so strong with such a low oxygen level." He willingly prescribed an oxygen concentrator, a machine that concentrated oxygen from the air into a fine stream for inhalation. He also prescribed clarithromycin, a macrolide antibiotic, which he hoped would treat our *Pseudomonas*. Clarithromycin had been used for years in Japan for patients with diffuse pan bronchiolitis.

Dr. Fujita was ahead of his time; more than half a decade later, macrolides such as Zithromax would become standard antiinflammatory treatment for CF.

"Can I get some IV antibiotics that I can use at home?" I pleaded.

"We don't not have such a system here. American patients are very independent. But it is not allowed to give IV medications at home in Japan.

If you want we can put you in the hospital here so you can get some antibiotics. But our hospital has a problem with M-R-S-A. It may not be safe for you." I knew that methicillin-resistant *staphyloccocus aureus* was one of the virulent bugs that infected CF patients and forced isolation if contracted. I refused to be hospitalized.

The long winter continued to be hard. Heating, like everything else, was expensive, so Isa and I rarely turned it on. The apartment walls were terribly thin, and when the wind howled outside, we felt a draft inside. When we spoke, our breath could be seen. Our wardrobe was a mismatch of old lady clothes in layers, since Obachan had sent us boxes of her sweaters and undergarments from Tokyo in the fall. "You have no idea how cold it gets in Japan!" she warned us.

The oxygen machine produced some much-needed heat, and in the evenings I found myself huddling under layers of blankets, sipping oxygen, just to stay warm. Isa's lungs started to bleed regularly, and we created a "Y" prong tubing so she, too, could suck on some oxygen. We were so weak! I thought of my parents and grandparents and their trials during the war. As spoiled California girls, we could hardly handle Japan's winter.

By early March, the buds on the plum trees had begun to erupt into cascades of pink blossoms, like kernels bursting into popcorn. It was as if God has snapped his fingers, and nature awakened. One Saturday afternoon in Takamatsu's famous Ritsurin Park, we stared at the multiple shades of pink blossoms against a rare sunny blue sky. Isa and I savored these first signs of spring. I was absorbed by each blossom's unique, delicate beauty. We shook the branches, and the soft petals fell gently like snow. "We survived the winter," I told Isa.

People were taking pictures, having picnics, singing, and drinking *sake* beneath these trees. Even stoic businessmen bent over the branches of blossoms to smell their sweet scent and exclaimed "*Subarashii!*" (Amazing!)

I noticed an old man standing in front of a tree near Isa and me. He was peering at the blossoms, also humbled and reflective at the new sign of spring. He bore the look of a sage, and his features seemed worn, as though he had lived through many harsh winters. Beneath his bald, dark-skinned forehead speckled with age spots sat two deeply set eyes. His long, thin beard hung below his chin, shading the wrinkled skin of his neck. He wore a dark blue robe and straw sandals, like the monks we saw at the local Buddhist temple.

As his gaze wandered from the tree to the crowd, our eyes met. We exchanged smiles, silently acknowledging the beauty. Then, leaning on his cane, he wobbled toward us and said in Japanese, "Good luck in the twenty-first century." He turned and shuffled away.

Isa and I stood speechless. It was 1995. The old man seemed to know he would not see the new century but assumed we would. Why did he choose to give us such hope? Did he know that he was speaking to young people who also doubted they would see the next century? Who was this man? As I felt the warmth of the sun on my back for the first time in months, the warmth of his message energized me. God had sent us an angel in the land of the rising sun.

By late May, we had decided to return home early. Isa's contract was for a year, but our health came first, especially as the humid summer would pose further health risks. Our bodies were tired and called for more intravenous antibiotics in the United States.

During our last month, Ryuta joined us in Kubo Mansion. His job was leading nowhere, and he was deep in credit card debt from college. He was inspired to join the other expatriates in Takamatsu to earn enough money teaching English to repay his debts and to improve his Japanese language skills enough to have an advantage in the job market.

Ryuta, Isa, and I had not lived under the same roof since high school. Our relationship in the past six years had been limited to brief phone conversations and occasional holiday visits. Isa and I wondered what awaited us. As we picked up my brother from the Takamatsu train station, it was as if we were being reunited with a long-lost relative from the past.

I carried Ryuta's mountain bike up the stairs to our apartment and arrived breathless. Once inside, I bent over the sink and had a massive coughing attack.

Ryuta approached me and started to pound my back. "You okay? Thanks for carrying my bike. I could've done it. You should've just told me it was too heavy. Sorry to make you *muri* and overdo it. Why do you always have to *muri*?" *Muri* was the Japanese word for pushing oneself.

I explained that life with CF was all about *muri*. If we didn't *muri*, we would have died a long time ago.

That evening, we laid three futons side by side on the *tatami* mat, completely covering the entire floor like cigars in a box. Immediately, the teasing and tickling reminiscent of childhood began. It was as if we were stuck in the backseat of a car again with boyish Ryuta for a very long road trip.

Ryuta watched in horror as Isa and I performed our prolonged nightly therapy ritual. It had been a long time since he had witnessed us doing treatments.

"Look at your puffy face!" he said, grabbing my red cheeks as I coughed violently. "No wonder you fuckers are so damn smart. You lie around for hours each day with all the blood running into your brains." We laughed loudly.

"I think that's the first compliment you've ever given us," Isa said.

"Welcome to our life, Ryuta," I said. "This is CF as an adult. You better get used to it." I lay on my back, my hips propped up on pillows, as Isa pounded me. My shirt slid up, revealing the scar on my belly. Ryuta flinched. "Goddamn! I forgot you had that! That's gnarly!" He poked at my hard stomach.

Every night we laughed and reminisced about childhood and parental annoyances during our long treatments. We also talked about what life was like in Japan. "You should've charged more," Ryuta criticized, referring to our hourly rate for English classes. He always spoke as if he knew better. "I'm gonna charge 10,000 yen an hour and if I can get another fifteen students, I can make shitloads of money."

"You're so materialistic," Isa said.

"You gotta be. It's all about making money in Japan."

"You're gonna wipe yourself out with so many classes. I'm already giving you ten of mine." I was feeling protective not only of my brother, but also of my students, should the quality of Ryuta's teaching suffer.

"And, it's about the experience of being here, too," Isa remarked. "To see the world. That's why we went to China." Just before Ryuta arrived, we had returned from a fantastic tour of the Great Wall and Beijing with Josh.

But Ryuta was convinced of his financial planning. "See, that's the philosophy that made Mom and Dad make stupid mistakes with their money. They never bothered to invest. They'd be totally rich if they made better choices. Now they're screwed when they retire."

"Well, that's why they're lucky to have you," I joked. Mama and Dad's retirement was the last thing on my mind. "That's the one advantage of having CF; we don't have to worry about stuff like that. It's all on you."

"Tshh. Don't talk like that."

"Sorry, but it's true. . . . One day you'll be the only child left. Aren't you amazed it hasn't happened yet?"

He said nothing. He picked up the remote and flicked on the TV.

The days with Ryuta were some of the most memorable times in Japan. Even though our lives had taken different paths in the last six years, we rewove our bond in just a few weeks of traveling around Shikoku, visiting Kyoto, and socializing with our friends. The adolescent Ryuta had been filled with emotional resentments, passivity, and rebellion. The adult was full of wit, humor, and ambitions. I loved him.

Our last few weeks in Japan were hectic. Isa and I finished up our classes, packed, and said our good-byes. We were leaving Asia, knowing that we would probably never return. As the airplane took off, heading east toward the Pacific Ocean, I peered down for a last glimpse of the blue waters of the

Seto Inland Sea. I bid farewell to the land I had called home for the past ten months. I had inhaled all the wonders of Japan—the food, the shopping, the countryside, my students—and had treasured each moment I was there. Despite the struggle of living in Japan, it was another chapter in our splendid life that was coming to an end. But when the plane landed, I felt renewed appreciation for America, my real home.

Chapter 21

Going Downhill

Ana

It's Saturday, 1:30 in the afternoon. My body lies here, broken and aching. Lungs rumbling like a southwest thunderstorm, spewing poison with every cough, heaving, labored at every breath as I lay here alone feeling eighty years old. I ask myself is this the life I want to live? Long hours each day of the week only to collapse like a tired dog on weekends while my friends enjoy the weekend off I lay here regaining the energy I lost and strengthening myself for the burdens to come.

—Ana, age twenty-four

Two months after returning from Japan, following hospital tune-ups and a restful summer, we embarked on another beginning: graduate school at the University of California, Berkeley. After signing for more student loans, I started a master's degree program in genetic counseling. Isa began a dual master's program in social work and public health.

A few days after classes started, I began to huff and puff at the slightest exertion. Wearing my *I climbed the Great Wall* sweatshirt, I would drag myself up the stairs to my new apartment. With each wheezy breath, my lungs demanded to know how I could have neglected them for so long.

Isa and I began attending the Cystic Fibrosis Care Center at Kaiser Hospital in nearby Oakland. Our new doctor was a pediatric pulmonologist named Dr. Gregory Shay, a caring man in his mid-forties with gray hair, blue eyes, and frantic energy.

In early 1996, a visit with Dr. Shay brought the devastating realization that I was losing control over my CF. As always, the clinic visit started with a pulmonary function test; the "Blow Job," as I called it, was a pivotal moment of each clinic visit.

I pulled my hair into a ponytail, rolled up my sleeves, and disconnected my bra strap. Nothing, not even a rubber band around my chest, would get in the way of my effort to blow as hard and as long as I could. I pleaded to the lung gods for big numbers as fervently as someone preparing to spin the Wheel of Fortune.

With my lips engulfing the mouthpiece and a plastic clip pinching my nose, I leaned forward toward the machine. My lungs wheezed and rattled as I forced myself to expel every ounce of air into the hose connected to a computer. The respiratory therapist monitoring the test yelled, "Keep blowing! Keep blowing! More! More!" My face turned red, mauve, then purple, as my jugular bulged like a burrowing banana slug on my neck.

I felt wetness in my underpants as urine leaked from incontinence. I looked up at the monitor. A blinking red light flashed "CAUTION: Severe Obstruction." I cringed with disgust as sweat dripped down my brow and my head pounded.

After I recovered from an explosive coughing fit, I said, "That sucks! Let me try again. I can do better." I tried again. And again. The numbers hardly changed. *Damn.*

The respiratory therapist joked, "My God! Don't die on me!" as she scribbled in the chart, "Patient performed spirometry test with maximum effort." My trials were done. My lung capacity was at 30 percent of normal, my lowest ever.

"Are you doing too much?" Dr. Shay asked. I leaned over his shoulder, glancing at my chart to read what he had scribbled: *Advanced-stage CF.*

"I don't think so," I replied. My classes weren't that hard, but the long hours at my genetic counseling internship were draining me.

"Well, maybe you need to think about cutting back." *Cutting back?!*

"You know, your numbers have been dropping steadily over the last few months," Dr. Shay said. "And you just got off of IVs in August. . . . Have you ever thought about getting a lung transplant?" Dr. Shay asked, rather nonchalantly, while staring at my chart. "It's something you better start thinking about."

I wriggled on the exam table and crossed my arms. "I was told to consider a lung transplant back in 1991 . . . but I didn't think I needed it yet. Look how far I've come since then. Maybe I just need IVs again." I paused. "Maybe I just blew badly today."

The news hit me like lightning. For so many years, I had prided myself on controlling my CF through aggressive care. Now, no matter how much effort I made to take care of myself, there were no positive returns. I was overcome with fear at the thought of giving in to this disease. *What would my professors think?* I cried as I drove toward Berkeley for my evening genetics class. In class, I sat silently while the professor's monotonous lecture slid past my ears: "Let's discuss the selective advantage of X-linked color blindness. Why was this trait beneficial to our species?" I felt completely out of place. I thought, *I'm fucking dying.* Being a graduate student was just a sideshow to the dramatic spectacle of my reality.

"Thirty percent lung function is your new baseline," Dr. Shay said at the next clinic visit.

"I refuse to believe that," I said. "Please don't give up on me. . . . Maybe it's stress. Maybe it's Aspergillosis. Or an allergy. Maybe if I exercised more . . . " I grasped for explanations. "Can't I try Sporanox? What about allergy testing? What else can I do?"

"Your labs show no indication of an allergy or acute reaction. You're already following an aggressive regimen . . . it's just that your numbers show that your lungs are irreversibly damaged," Dr. Shay responded.

Later, my frustration turned to anger. "They just don't care!" I cried to Isa. "They don't suggest anything new unless I ask. They are giving up on me." But I knew that there was only so much Dr. Shay could do.

As the differences in our health became more apparent, I relied on Isa to do more of the physical jobs around the apartment, like vacuuming and taking out the trash. It seemed unfair that I was so much sicker than she. Why did our treatments work for her and not for me? Isa did my therapy with such rigor, trying desperately to clear out my lungs with her thumping. At times, she was so exhausted that she'd say, "Let's take a five-minute break," and we'd fall asleep hunched over each other in the middle of the treatment. On several occasions, we woke up at three o'clock in the morning and found we'd knocked over a cup of mucus onto the carpet. We would get up, exchange places, and I would then do Isa's percussion for another hour.

As the diagnosis of "advanced-stage CF" sank in, I felt even worse. I could not longer remember how it felt to walk without being short of breath. I redefined myself from a person living with CF to a person beginning to die of CF. Using full-time oxygen and home IV antibiotics and sleeping ten hours a day joined doing therapy and having mucus pour out of my lungs as routine.

As my sense of control over my CF diminished, I blamed myself for not doing enough. My thoughts became a continuous stream of "shoulds": *I should exercise. I should do more therapy. I should go in the hospital.* The catch-

22 engulfed me. *If I do exercise, I'll burn calories that I need to preserve. If I do more therapy, I'll lose sleep. If I go into the hospital, I'll get behind in my classes.* My head spun.

Four days before my twenty-fourth birthday, my hero, Bob Flanagan, finally died after years of struggling with end-stage CF. His last words to me were "Getting older with CF really sucks." There was no long lecture, no instruction sheet, only his honest statement that life was going to get harder. And now I was standing in line behind him.

It was six in the morning. I was slumped over the toilet seat, having awoken with the familiar "pop" followed by the gurgling of a lung bleed. My bleeds had become another daily hassle, completely unpredictable, surprising me in class, on the train, in the supermarket. This bleed began when I rolled over in bed. It came in a deluge, yanking me out of sleep and sending me bolting, half-dazed, into the bathroom. I looked into the bowl, the splashes of crimson against the white porcelain looked like a sick form of modern art.

My head pounding, I staggered to Isa's bed, where she lay still sleeping. "Isa, get up. I think I have to go in." *Damn.*

I surrendered to being hospitalized like a wounded soldier being carried from his last battle. My body needed rest.

"I have cystic fibrosis," I confessed with shame to one of my professors from a pay phone in Kaiser's admitting department. "I won't be able to make it to class for the next few weeks."

My professor was surprised. "I heard there was someone in the class with CF. I had no idea it was you."

"I know, I'm the wrong race," I replied. At least I wouldn't have to explain what CF was or why I needed to be hospitalized. Learning about CF was part of the genetics curriculum.

My professor suggested that class be held at the hospital so that I could attend. I hesitated. I tried so hard to separate my two lives, that of a normal graduate student and that of a sick person just trying to breathe. But my two lives had now merged.

Later that week, the class of eight showed up in my hospital room so that I could participate. Although touched by their willingness to accommodate, I was embarrassed to be seen hooked up to IVs and oxygen. I officially became the "token" genetically mutated person in the genetic counseling program. My classmates finally entered *my* world.

Shortly after being admitted, I realized that I had made a mistake, even though I was too sick to be anywhere else. I realized there had been a decline in the quality of patient care since our childhood hospitalizations. There were just too many patients and too few nurses to provide good-quality care. When I had the energy, I tried to assert my needs. I watched the nurses to make sure that I didn't fall victim to some fatal medical mistake.

One night, I awoke to find another patient's medication hanging on my IV pole. Another time, I watched in horror as a nurse dropped an open syringe on the bed, picked it up, and attempted to insert it into my IV site.

"Excuse me," I said, "that's not sterile anymore. Can you please use a new needle?"

The nurse glared. "I don't need patients to tell me how to do my job." She stormed out of the room, slamming the needle into the sharps box by the door.

Bitch.

During therapy, I lay motionless as the weak chest percussion of the unconditioned respiratory therapists failed to loosen the mucus plastered to my lungs. I needed Isa. The respiratory therapy department, like that of nursing, was severely understaffed. One respiratory therapist asked, "Can you just use an inhaler today? I just don't have time to give you a treatment." Another therapist requested that I use a useless mechanical chest vibrator to do my own chest percussion. "You CF patients are so demanding. I just don't have the strength to percuss as hard as you want it."

The ignorance about CF, even among the medical personnel, shocked me:

"So when did you come down with cystic fibrosis?"

"I was born with it. It's a genetic disease."

"My friend's cousin has CF. Did you get it from your mom or dad?"

"It's recessive. They both carried the gene."

One nurse even asked, "So when did you notice problems with your breasts?"

What??!! She thought cystic fibrosis was the same thing as fibrocystic disease of the breast!

"I want to spread the word about CF," I remember saying in a television interview as a child. I was tired of having to explain to curious visitors why I was in the hospital and what CF was. I was reminded why I entered the genetic counseling program: to do my part to remedy society's ignorance about CF.

Every hour in the hospital provoked more stress. Embittered by the poor care and unable to distract myself, I was forced to confront my declining health. I cried at night. *What did I do to deserve this? Is God abandoning me?* A shrink showed up at my bedside at the recommendation of an observant nurse to address my "anxiety and depression." Recurrent thoughts of impending death haunted me. I feared leaving Isa alone so that in time she, too, would die of a lonesome heart and sick lungs. I did not want to die consumed by fear, anger, and frustration.

It was during this misery that I accepted being listed for a lung transplant. There was no alternative. I was being dragged, kicking and screaming, into advanced-stage CF and was ready to look it straight in the eye and holler, "Fuck you!"

Just before my twenty-fifth birthday, Kaiser's transplant program referred me to Stanford Hospital for the official transplant evaluation. Over two days, I would undergo extensive pulmonary and cardiac function tests, a psychological evaluation, and a physical examination by Stanford's transplant team. The team included several pulmonologists, nurses, a social worker, respiratory therapists, surgeons, and the usual entourage of medical residents and fellows. Mama and Dad flew up to join me for this lengthy process.

Dr. James Theodore was the founder and director of Stanford's renowned lung transplant program. A large man with snow-capped hair and a broad grin, he strutted around the clinic wrapped in an aura of power. But beneath his intimidating presence and gruff style was a grandfatherly figure who cared deeply about his patients. He could accept or reject a patient for the transplant waiting list depending on his assessment of their physical and mental strength and their ability to survive the surgery and comply with the rigorous aftercare. He rejoiced in the transplant successes and mourned the losses.

Dr. Theodore was notorious for interrogating patients. When he interviewed me, he sat back in his chair, folded his arms across his robust chest, and fired questions at me:

"Well, how long do you think you're going to live?"

I leaned forward and replied, "About three years, maybe more." My fingers felt cold, and I tucked them under my legs to warm them.

"Have you prepared your will?" he asked.

Mama and Dad glanced at each other. "It's done," I said.

"Tell us why you think we should list you."

"I want a better quality of life. I'm losing my ability to function." My oxygen tank hissed.

"Are you compliant with your treatments? If you're not after transplant, it will kill you and will kill you fast and painfully."

"I'm obsessed with therapy."

"You're going to have to give this transplant everything you've got. Transplant is not for wimps."

"My mentor was a masochist. I think I can handle it." I smiled at him, but he did not smile back.

"Who'll be your caregivers? You know, this whole process takes just as much toll on the caregivers as it will on you."

Mama interjected, "We are prepared to do anything." She tucked her hair behind her ears, revealing gray roots.

"You have to be sick enough to need a transplant but well enough to survive the surgery and recovery. Fifty percent of lung recipients are alive in five years. Right now, those are better odds than what you've got with your present lung function."

Then he rattled off a laundry list of potential complications: high blood pressure, kidney failure, stroke, cancer.

"With lung transplantation, you're trading one disease for another. Lung transplantation is not lifesaving, it is life-prolonging. There are no guarantees. You will be immunosuppressed for the rest of your life." His eyes looked stern, his face solemn. His folded arms rested on his enormous belly.

"Complications like infections or rejection can occur at any time. Chronic rejection of posttransplanted lungs feels similar to end-stage CF. It's a miserable way to die. You have to trust us. You people with CF are so damn stubborn, and think you know it all. But after your transplant, you can't just go and take care of yourself like you do with your CF. One false move without medical guidance and you could die."

My parents sat silently through most of the interview. At the end of the session, the social worker turned to Dad and asked how he felt about the transplant. "It's scary," he said. "But I will do whatever it takes to support this decision. It gives us hope." That was the first time in my life I had heard my father truly express his feelings.

Dr. Theodore's in-your-face approach was designed to weed out those in denial from those who had a realistic understanding of what lay ahead. Due to the shortage of donor organs, organ transplants were reserved for those who fulfilled strict medical and psychological criteria. Candidates had to be compliant, realistic, and aware of the risks and limitations of lung transplantation. They needed a passionate will to live if they were to meet the physical and emotional demands of the surgery, its potential complications, and the recovery.

Several months after the evaluation process, I received a call from Stanford; I had qualified for the transplant list.

"Congratulations!" Mama said over the telephone in a gleeful voice. "This is wonderful news!"

"Yeah, right. How can you congratulate me?" I asked. "I'm officially sick enough to need new lungs."

"Yes, but the process went so smoothly for you, and for that we have to be grateful."

She had a point, but I still didn't feel like celebrating.

I thought about my other friends with CF who had been rejected from the list because they had lung infections that were resistant to all anti-biotics, lacked adequate insurance, or had no support system. Even Bob Flanagan had been rejected because he was deemed too sick to survive the surgery. I thought of the old days at Kaiser and Maricela and the other kids with cancer who had died. At least Isa and I had a disease in which the diseased part could be removed and replaced with a new one. I *was* lucky.

As I tried to sleep that night, fear and uncertainty flooded my mind. I couldn't stop the questions. *Will I survive? Is it worth the risk? What if I have complications and die earlier than if I just hold onto my CF? Am I choosing the easy way out by getting a transplant rather than facing advanced CF?* There were no straight answers. I had to just trust in the journey that was unfolding.

Within a few weeks, I received a pager, which would ring when lungs became available. I anticipated waiting two years. I needed that time to prepare.

A few months after I was placed on the list my friend Hayley was called for her lung transplant. We had kept in touch since our evening at Bob Flanagan's show years ago in college. She was listed for a transplant in 1995 when she was a sophomore at Stanford. Her health had rapidly deteriorated; keeping up with the demands of student life, on top of a not-so-mild case of CF, was just too much for her. Yet, she was still determined to become a physician. Shortly after being listed, she told me, "I'll get a transplant and recover for a year. Then I'll finish Stanford and start medical school by 2000." I admired her composure and courage.

But, in the most divinely unjust way, her lung transplant failed, leaving her on a ventilator for weeks, struggling against a blood infection that made her white blood cell count skyrocket to 70,000 and permanently damaged her new lungs. Isa and I visited her several months into her hospital stay; she was still wearing an oxygen mask, her frail body reduced to an emaciated, immobile, and thoroughly traumatized mess.

"I never thought it would go this way, that I'd come so close to death," she said, breaking down. We watched her, shedding our own tears.

"If I don't make it," she cried, "please know how much I love you both. You are like my sisters." She weakly turned her head and looked at me. "And don't let this scare you. Don't let this be the way you think of transplants."

Hayley survived, and eight months later, she received a second transplant, this time a new heart and lungs. After she woke up in the intensive care unit, she scribbled on paper, "I'm alive! I'm alive!" Over the next two weeks, she regained her strength, and her lungs functioned beautifully. Then, suddenly, she became drowsy and confused. She died later that week as her brain was ravaged by a fungal infection brought on by immuno-suppression.

Hayley's death shocked me as much as Karen's had, though we were hardly as close. The unfairness, her minimizing of the risks, the lost potential of a bright Stanford student, and my own painful survivor's guilt crushed me like a ton of bricks. I dreaded the thought that my transplant might fail like hers. I wanted to scream at God's cruelty, my blood boiling, *Why? Why Hayley? Why did she have to go through such relentless, meaningless suffering, for nothing?* She could've had more of a chance. Why was I the one to get to graduate from Stanford, travel abroad, and go to graduate school? And she had nothing.

I found Hayley's death an especially cruel irony in the modern times of cystic fibrosis. It was so much worse than it had been years before, when we watched the scrawny little six-year-olds at CF camp shrivel up and die. People in our generation had a carrot dangling in their faces: a normal life, a chance to realize ambitions, the potential to excel academically and thrive vocationally, and the opportunity to fall in love, all because we were living longer with CF. *Tease me with a good time,* written in the bathroom stall of life—a cruel universe had tempted Hayley, and then the rug had been pulled out from under her. That was the unintended cruelty of a technology that lets us live with CF into the most promising days of our lives.

A package arrived on my doorstep in the winter of 1997. It was a small box, neatly bound, with a return address from Takamatsu, Japan. The package, reminiscent of our time overseas, was a welcome surprise.

The package was from the doctors' wives who had taken Isa's conversation classes. Isa and I peered into the package, our eyes dazzled by dozens of brilliant colors. Inside, wrapped carefully, were bundles of delicate paper cranes. They were strung up horizontally by thread, packed tightly together in twenty separate bundles of fifty cranes, each crane made from a different color of origami. Together, they lit up the room. It was *senbazuru*—a thousand paper cranes—made by the meticulous and gracious efforts of Isa's students, women across the world whom we barely knew.

I had read the Japanese story of *Sadako and the Thousand Paper Cranes* in elementary school. Japanese folklore says that making a thousand paper cranes grants all wishes for health and peace. Sadako was a young girl who was diagnosed with cancer shortly after the atomic bomb was dropped on Hiroshima. Sadako and her friends desperately folded paper cranes, hoping to save her life, but she died before all one thousand cranes could be completed. A memorial stands for her in Hiroshima, close to the epicenter of the bombing. Now it is a pilgrimage site for those wishing for world peace and cures for disease. Travelers arrive laden with their own *senbazu-ru*, which they leave, covering the memorial with thousands of bundles.

My fingertips caressed the paper cranes. Each one was folded perfectly from a tiny two-by-two-inch piece of colored origami. The accompanying letter read, "We know you have health struggles. Our families made the *senbazuru* for you to wish you good health next year." *How did they know I needed such a message of hope?* Perhaps the power of the cranes would bring me health. I had to believe.

Chapter 22

Three's a Crowd

Ana

I think your sister hates me.

—Letter from Andrew
to Isa, 1997

I often wondered if declining health was related to stress, for it was also in the summer of 1996 that the challenge of living with Andrew began. Andrew moved in with us, having found a summer internship at a Bay Area law firm. Now that the lovebirds were finally together, their affections for each other made up for their two years apart. In our close living quarters, I saw an Andrew who was new to me, different from the harmless undergraduate who had dated my sister. There were things about Andrew's personality that I found difficult to accept. He was a Stanford- and Harvard-educated intellectual who felt that life could be controlled through careful planning and effort. His life had unfolded with little struggle, so he lacked flexibility and perspective.

One Saturday morning, I awoke to the sound of moaning in Isa's bedroom. *Great,* I thought, *they're fucking.* That just grossed me out. I turned my back to the wall and tried to fall back to sleep. A short time later, I was awakened again by faint singing and giggling, as Andrew, in his schmaltzy romanticism, serenaded her in bed. *Forget it. There was no way I'm going back to sleep.* I got up and headed to the kitchen.

In a few minutes, I heard their bedroom door open and then Isa's cough-ing sounds emanating from the bathroom, followed by Andrew's footsteps pounding the floor as he headed to the bathroom in his boxers.

"Turtle dove," he said, "are you okay in there?" He stood with his face pressed to the door.

"I'm fine, babe," Isa's voice replied.

"What should I have for breakfast, my love?" he asked the closed door.

"Whatever you want, dear," she said. I could hear the sound of water running.

"Well, what do you want me to eat?" Andrew asked.

Just then, the door opened, and Isa emerged. "Let's see what we have." The two lovers entered the kitchen, holding hands.

"Morning, Ana," Isa said. She was wearing her boxer shorts printed with *Someone at Harvard Loves Me.*

"Hi," I said, trying to hide my irritation as I buried my face in a genetics article and gobbled my cereal. I ignored Andrew.

Isa walked to the balcony to open the door. A cool breeze entered the liv-ing room, and the hum of traffic filtered into the apartment.

Andrew followed. She then walked to the front door and opened it to grab the morning paper. Andrew followed her again, like a puppy dog. *He's smothering her,* I thought.

"Andrew, can you make juice?" Isa asked when she returned to the kitchen.

"Of course, dear, anything for you. Let me first kiss your cheek, sweet-heart." He bent over and kissed her cheek. I turned my back. Andrew pulled open the freezer door. A can of frozen orange juice concentrate rolled out of the freezer and slammed to the floor, then bounced off his toe.

"Owww!!" he cried, "goddamn it!! Son of a goddamn bitch!" He hol-lered, as he slammed the freezer door shut. "Fuckin' bastard!!" He began to pant and moan. He fell to the floor, grabbed the orange juice canister and pounded it on the floor, like a child trying to break his toy.

"Stop, Andrew, stop!" Isa .said, grabbing it from him. "You're going to break it and spill it." He got up, his face beet red and limped to the couch.

"Goddamn it!" he continued. "It hurts, it hurts . . ." he moaned and lay on the couch, putting his arms above his head as a scarlet hue began to spread beneath his thinning blond hair.

Isa followed him and knelt beside the couch. "It's okay, babe. Let me get some ice for you."

I looked up. I was dying of CF, and he sat immobilized over a bruised foot. *Jesus,* I thought. *Get a grip.* I retreated to my own room.

Isa and I, despite being identical twins, were different in more ways than ever. She loved him; I found him irritating. In the years that we lived to-gether, our personality differences had created a symbiotic dynamic that worked, a dynamic that was based on mutual support, equity, and balance. If I was sick, Isa was well. If Isa was sick, I was well. If I was pissed off, Isa was happy (this was the usual case). If I was happy, Isa was pissed off (rarely). Andrew's presence now drove a wedge into the relationship that had sustained us for so long. Andrew's dominating personality controlled their relationship, and Isa relished in her more passive role. She became someone I didn't understand and wished not to be around. Our arguments escalated. She couldn't understand why I couldn't just accept Andrew. As annoyed as I was at Andrew's quirks, I couldn't confront him. Instead, I simply complained to Isa, so she carried the burden of my grievances, torn between her twin and her boyfriend.

To make matters worse, I was dateless, single, and destined to lifelong virginity. The mere thought of having energy, health, and time for a rela-tionship, let alone of finding someone who would fall in love with an in-valid like me, was unimaginable. Life was not fair.

Chapter 23

A Heavy Burden

Isa

I returned from Japan burdened by the knowledge that the trip had negatively impacted Ana's health. It was my fault she had gone to Japan; she hadn't really had a choice. Now, the shit was hitting the fan; she was sick all the time with a raging lung infection that could not be controlled.

Once at Berkeley, the rat race of "normal" student life began. I took six classes in public health and social work each semester. Three days a week, I had an internship at a social-service agency over an hour away by train. I joined the board of directors at Cystic Fibrosis Research, Inc. (CFRI) as well as committees that planned educational events. Ana and I regularly spoke to hospitals and drug companies about living with CF. Summers brought demanding internships at the VA hospital and Genentech, Inc., the makers of Pulmozyme. The busier I was, the less I focused on our health struggles.

But ten months in Japan without IV antibiotics had taken a toll on my health as well. The strength I had gained from *taiko* drumming at Stanford had been depleted, and my shortness of breath during any exercise made me increasingly anxious. My lungs still bled regularly, and routine home IVs took longer to control my lung infections. Yet, I had no right to complain. Ana's lung function was a good 20 percent lower than mine.

I began to feel that my health-care providers were not taking my complaints seriously. In their eyes, my disease was mild compared to Ana's. When Ana and I went to clinic together, I tried to explain that, while Ana was sicker, I was feeling worse than ever. The CF social worker kept using words like *enmeshed* and *need to differentiate,* which infuriated me. The staff finally placed us in separate exam rooms or made us come to appointments at different times.

Ana's desperate advocacy for new and improved treatments allowed her to start a new inhaled antibiotic called Colistin and use a new nebulizer called an intrapulmonary percussive ventilator, or IPV.

"Can I also try the IPV and Colistin?" I asked Dr. Shay.

"Well, I can try to get you the IPV, but it will be hard to justify with your lung function. And as far as Colistin is concerned, you don't really need it."

"Well, I obviously have *pseudomonas.* Colistin seems to help Ana."

"She has more antibiotic resistance than you do. Colistin is most effective for people whose *pseudomonas* is multi-resistant."

"Dr. Fujita in Japan said I had a mucoid strain, and that's harder to treat with antibiotics. So, am I just supposed to wait until I get sicker to reap the benefits of new drugs?" I exploded, "Shouldn't there be a preventative focus? Maybe it'll help prevent multi-resistance. I want to do everything possible to keep myself from being in Ana's shoes." Poor Dr. Shay. He always had to deal with angry patients. After my incessant pestering, he finally gave in. Like Ana, I was desperate.

For class I had to peruse the DSM-IV, a mental health manual. I was sure I was going crazy and entertained myself with diagnoses: 300.02 Generalized Anxiety Disorder; 300.4 Dysthymic Disorder; V61.8 Sibling Relational Problem; 301.6 Dependent Personality Disorder. Would Dr. Shay think I had a somatization disorder or hypochondriasis? Did I just want the same attention as my sister? Of course not! I was grateful for being healthier. Yet, my therapy routine still took the same amount of time as Ana's. Graduate school and the stress of Ana's decline left me perpetually exhausted. If I was supposed to be the healthy one, why was life so hard?

I began to torment myself, as if I needed to suffer as much as Ana. Nighttime panic attacks disrupted my sleep, and my pillow was often soaked with tears. What would I do if she died? We had come into the world together as a single cell, and I wanted to die with her. I'd rather we both died in a head-on car wreck or in a plane that took a nosedive, huddling together in our last moments. Womb to tomb. That would be fair. Being left behind would be the ultimate punishment for being the healthier twin. For the first time I imagined my life without Ana: could I be strong enough to find a will to live by myself? Andrew was a source of passion for survival, but was he enough?

Andrew became the sounding board for my frustrations. "Andrew, I'm so afraid of the day when I'll be as sick as Ana. It has only been a year since Stanford and I already feel a whole lot weaker."

"You still seem strong," he said. "You're doing everything you can to stay healthy right now." He was right. Besides my therapy regimen, I had joined the YMCA to swim regularly. I had had sinus surgery to prevent drainage into my lungs. I had gotten my IPV machine. I *was* doing everything.

But I felt another weight. It was just a matter of time until he'd feel the helplessness I was feeling watching Ana decline. I worried that he could not handle my decline. Would he run away? I never wanted to cause him hardship or distress. I wanted him to be strong. If we were going to stick together, he needed to be strong.

"Oh, shit."

CF camp had taught me that profanity was a healthy form of emotional expression. It suited the moment. Even with my nightlight, I saw the swollen chubbiness of my arm. The burning sensation that had woken me was a sure sign that my IV was infiltrated.

I looked at the clock: 1:15. I clamped the IV and disconnected myself from my portable pump.

Doing home IV therapy meant I had the freedom to use IV antibiotics while continuing to go to graduate school, exercise, and enjoy home-cooked meals. It also meant I could avoid the germs and stress of being in the hospital. But at these times, home IVs were a nightmare.

Now that my IV had slipped out of the vein, getting a new IV placed would require a dreaded trip to the emergency room and a wait that could last several hours. But I had three classes in the morning, and I refused to imagine that an ER visit would interrupt my precious night. What I really needed was a home-health nurse, but Kaiser was too cheap to send one unless the patient was critically ill and homebound. I had to wake Ana.

I got up and barged into her room, flicking on the light. A slight breeze from an open window chilled the room; Ana's labored breathing always made her feel hot. Hours earlier, the fresh air had been contaminated by cannabis smoke from the hippies in the apartment next door, and the faint scent still hung in the room. I strained to see in the bright light.

"Ana, get up. Sorry to wake you. Can you start my IV? The damn thing is screwed."

Ana groaned and rolled over. "Oh, for God's sake. Get a port." Ana had gotten a port-a-cath, a built-in catheter in the chest that offers permanent venous access for infusions, in her sophomore year of college. It was the first physical reminder of having a more severe stage of CF, one that required routine IV antibiotics. The port was a small lump in her chest that was noticeable even when it was not accessed for infusions. Her keloid scar was a small but obvious bulge. Because I wasn't using as many antibiotic treatments as she was, and overall I had better veins, I dreaded the idea of getting an artificial implant in my otherwise natural body. I worried about whether Andrew would find the scar and lump, usually placed above the breast, unattractive.

I wished my arms could tolerate the newer PICC lines (peripherally inserted central catheters), semipermanent spaghetti-length catheters that were fed into a large vein in the bicep area and could last several weeks. But for some reason, my veins revolted against those lines, and within hours my arm would swell up with severe irritation.

While Ana roused herself, I dug through the disorganized boxes of medical equipment in the hallway closet. Through the years of home IVs, we had collected a stash of tubing, needles, betadine, and other supplies. One of our hospital nurses had given us a small supply of angiocath needles, unintentionally giving us "permission" to start our own IVs. Angiocaths were plastic catheters with steel needles. The needle was removed after it hit a vein, leaving only the catheter, which allowed for a longer-lasting IV with increased flexibility around the site.

I brought the supplies to Ana's bed. She washed her hands as I untaped my defunct IV, wincing as the tape tore out several hairs. In one sweep of my hand, I easily pulled the plastic catheter from the arm, dropped it, and placed a gauze with pressure onto the sore, puffy spot. I sighed with relief.

"Here's a good vein," I instructed Ana, as I held out my left arm. A juicy vein ran from the top side of the forearm to the underside. Ana tightened the tourniquet around my arm and began slapping the vein to make it pop up. She prepped the catheter with a small extension tubing, flushing them both with sterile saline. After years of witnessing nurses go through this routine, she could do it with her eyes closed.

"Ready?" she asked. "Let's get this sucker in and done with. I hope it doesn't roll."

"Sometimes it blows. Go easy when you hit the vein. God, I can't believe we're doing this."

With intense concentration, we held our breath as Ana pierced my skin with the needle. The pinch of pain was nothing; it was more nerve-racking to worry about whether we were competent to do this.

In an instant, a small amount of blood filled the catheter.

"You're in! Now feed it in gently," I instructed. Ana carefully glided the plastic catheter into my arm as she pulled the steel needle out. Then, she slowly injected saline to flush the line. Like an eruption, the insertion site rose steadily with a blue-tinged color.

"Damn! It's blown. God, what did I do wrong?" Ana hissed.

"I was afraid of that. Try not feeding the catheter in right away. Or, maybe you pushed the needle in too far."

We prepared to try again. Our stash of needles was limited; once the catheter was separated from the steel needle it could not be reused. Ana made another attempt on the same vein, but it blew again, causing another large round blue bruise. I was starting to look like a junkie.

Tens of minutes passed. We explored my arms and hands looking for another vein. My veins had been abused for years, and the options were limited. In the silent concentration of our search, I could hear the faint swooshing flow of the oxygen through Ana's nose prongs.

"Sorry, Ana, to keep you awake," I said.

"*Shoganai.* It can't be helped," she replied. "You'd be doing the same for me."

Ana tried again on my left hand. After digging the needle into my flesh fishing for another vein, we gave up and pulled out the needle. Another needle wasted. I refused to let her prick the small veins in my right hand. I needed to take notes the next day in class. We laughed at the insanity of being both masochistic and self-reliant—a perfect combination for the occasion.

I had a small but obvious vein on the area below the inside of my wrist, crossing the base of my inner forearm. It was a tender spot, but the vein was highly visible, and we decided to give it a shot. I wiped the area with alcohol, and Ana prepped the last angiocath needle.

"This better work," she said. "Why the fuck is this so hard? It looks so easy when the nurses do it. I feel like I'm doing everything they are."

"Is it the toughness of my skin?" I asked. "We're just not used to this. But try again. I don't mind the pain."

"Flanagan would be proud," Ana laughed. She pierced the tender spot, and it stung. In an instant, though, bright scarlet expelled into the catheter and she was in.

"Don't thread the needle yet!" I told her. "See if it flushes first. If it doesn't blow, then thread it. If it blows, take it out and we can reuse it."

Ana pressed her thumb again the syringe and injected saline against resistance. The blood washed away from the catheter, but instantly my hand was filled with a hot, stinging feeling that ran up my arm.

"Ooooww!" I squealed. "That hurts like hell!" I could handle plenty of pain, but this was different. After the burning sensation, my hand had gone numb.

"It won't go in," Ana grimaced.

"My God, I think we hit an artery! Holy shit!" I panted. "You went too deep! Take it out! Take it out!"

We learned very quickly not to inject fluid into an artery. She pulled out the catheter immediately, in her haste dropping the needle on the floor. I applied pressure to stop the heavy bleeding from my wrist. "This is ridiculous," we chuckled. Laughter was the only way to cope with this torture.

We were out of angiocaths but had plenty of plain steel needles that were used to draw medication out of glass vials. They were the only option. I offered my antecubital vein, the vein inside the elbow that is most reliable for blood draws, but only reluctantly, because this meant I could not bend my elbow. Ana finally succeeded in starting an IV, and she taped down the steel needle carefully. I then instructed her to tape my arm to a book so I wouldn't bend it while I slept. My infusion was restarted, and it flowed nicely into the large vein. We finally turned the lights off and went back to bed. I had been up for an hour; avoiding a trip to the ER hadn't spared us an eventful night.

I went to class the next morning with that steel needle still in place, trying not to bend my arm or to let my classmates notice that it was rigid. Later that afternoon, the irritation caused by the needle became unbearable, so I removed it. I surrendered to the hospital and the help of the experts.

Nights like these finally persuaded Ana and me to resign ourselves to state assistance. California was one of the few states in the nation that offered public health insurance to all people with cystic fibrosis, regardless of their income. Genetically Handicapped Person's Program (GHPP) had been established to provide medical coverage to adults with astronomical medical costs, namely, those with specified genetic diseases such as CF, hemophilia, and sickle-cell disease. My monthly pharmacy bills often reached four thousand dollars, and without Kaiser or GHPP I simply could not afford to stay healthy. As clients of GHPP, Ana and I received services that Kaiser denied, such as home-health visits. For a short time, a nice respiratory therapist came to my apartment to provide chest percussion to me when Ana or Andrew was not available. In graduate school, Ana and I were fortunate to receive medically dependent coverage under my parents' insurance. I worried constantly about health insurance after graduate school, but luckily, I knew GHPP was always an option. For many of my CF friends who had to work part-time or were denied insurance due to the preexisting condition exclusion, GHPP provided the only safety net for healthcare coverage.

Aging with cystic fibrosis brought a new bodily challenge: DIOS (distal intestinal obstruction syndrome). DIOS means God in Spanish, which is appropriate, because when DIOS happened, it *was* all-powerful and all-knowing.

Warning signs crept up slowly. Totally different from my childhood *pon-*

pon-itai, the familiar pain could be triggered by hot weather, forgetting to drink every hour, stress, greasy American food, or forgetting to take my enzymes. Once, I was too busy to notice that it had been days, and my belly was huge. Earlier that day, a cashier at the supermarket had asked me when I was due. "Oh, I'm not pregnant," I said. "I'm just constipated." I smiled.

My upper intestines talked to me first. They churned and stiffened, hardening in convulsive fits every few minutes as my bowel knotted up like stiff ropes, pulsating and trying to flow but unable to do so. Soon, the pain permeated my abdomen, cramps ebbed and flowed in shooting sensations, forming hard, distended rock formations that protruded, dancing from my belly in rhythmic upheaval.

"You have golf balls in your intestines," Dr. Shay commented, after an abdominal X-ray revealed the culprit causing my pain.

"I knew you're full of shit," Ana joked, as I reported on his diagnosis when I returned home.

"And *you* thought Andrew was a pain in the ass," I teased, sitting hunched over. "*This* is the real thing."

Throughout the day, I had resorted to various remedies in attempts to cure the pain. I had increased my fluid intake, taken over-the-counter laxatives, and consumed more vegetables, but the pulsating pain did not respond. There was no action down below.

I removed my tight jeans, which strangled my midsection, and searched for the right comfortable outfit. I did not own a muumuu, but a cotton nightgown served as maternity wear for the evening, allowing my fullness to protrude to its natural capacity.

By evening, the nausea had started. My mouth filled with salty saliva. This was the real thing and had the potential to become very serious. It was time for the mother of all laxatives, the last resort: GoLytely. "GoLytely" was a misnomer. "Flash Flood" was more appropriate.

GoLytely was a powder consisting of polyethylene glycol, similar to an ingredient in antifreeze. The electrolyte powder came in a gallon jug that I filled with water and mixed vigorously until it dissolved. I had to attempt to drink the entire gallon within an hour. The fluid fizzled and bubbled as the electrolytes dissolved. The potion would absorb fluid into the bowel, serving as a sort of Drano for the clogged plumbing that created the pain. The particulars of this lengthy process had to be just right: on an empty stomach, six hours before or after other medications, and definitely, definitely, definitely within the privacy of one's own home.

The first quart went down easily. The cool, slightly cherry-flavored, clear liquid was comforting. *Surely my pain will soon be over,* I thought. Within half an hour I attempted to guzzle my second quart. With each cup, I became more uncomfortable, as my already distended abdomen began to feel waterlogged. By the third quart I had to lay down, chilled to the bone by the sudden flood of cold water into my system. Goosebumps waxed and waned on my skin. My rock-solid intestines knotted constantly, as if to scream, "What are you doing to me?" while my full stomach pressed up against my chest, joining the internal mayhem, shouting, "No more fluid, please!"

Lying flat, I used a straw to sip my last quart. I closed my eyes, drawing the liquid in methodically, rhythmically, one mouthful at a time while I listened intently to the sound of each gulp between deep, steady breaths. *Keep it down, keep it down.* I held in my cough. Surely I'd hurl if I had a coughing attack. Images of worst-case scenarios raced through my head: Being admitted to the hospital. Losing my privacy and being poked and prodded by nasogastric tubes and enemas. Abdominal surgery. Prolonged recovery and weight loss.

I flashed back to the moment as the slurping sound of the straw against the bottom of the glass told me that I had reached the end. In one last gulp, I was satisfied: one gallon of GoLytely down in one hour without vomiting. Now, I just had to wait. Curled up in a fetal position, wrapped in a blanket for warmth, I lay there, belly distended and rock hard, pain excruciating. I held my cold, sickened belly with warm hands. It was tender to the touch, like a rubber ball. *Is this what it feels like to be pregnant? Except for this, I will never know.* How different my belly was from Ana's! Her railroad-track scar from her last intestinal surgery reminded me of what could happen.

I befriended the pain. It made me stronger. It made me appreciate the pain-free days, reminding me that CF attacked the gastrointestinal system as relentlessly as the lungs. Shitting was as much a part of CF as spitting.

Within an hour my intestines began their loud cries. They fizzled, churned, moaned, and squealed in agony as fluid migrated in, expanding the already full lumen. The magic potion was kicking in. The nostalgic sensation of having to go to the bathroom was finally returning. I held out for as long as possible, allowing the brew to marinate within my bowel for maximum effect.

At last I could wait no longer. For the next two hours, the porcelain bowl became my confidant, the recipient of a deluge of semidigested waste. The smell of toxic shit polluted the bathroom. But I was cleansed.

Just as suddenly as it had come, the pain subsided. I felt whole once more. I could welcome the sight and smell of food again. GoLytely had worked its magic.

There's a popular joke in the CF community:
Question: What's more important, having sex or having a bowel movement?
Answer: Try going a week without each and you'll find out.
You can say that again.

Chapter 24

The Question

Isa

Christmas 1996: The day my life changed forever. I'm happy for Isa and Andrew but not for me. I'm fearful for my survival and well-being. Can she be as true to him as she is to me?

—Ana, age twenty-four

The fire crackled, casting a dim light and warming our bodies. It was Christmas Eve 1996, and I was visiting Andrew at his parents' home in Portales, New Mexico. His parents had gone to bed early, and Andrew and I swayed to a raw version of our song, Guns 'N' Roses' "November Rain." Before me stood a bushy Christmas tree, crowded with colorful ornaments from Andrew's past. The smell of pine mixed with fire comforted me as I held Andrew close.

Andrew fidgeted, and his eyes wandered away from mine, as if he were examining the room. "Are you okay?" I asked him. "I mean, you seem kind of removed."

"Oh, no, I'm fine," he assured me.

The last note of the romantic melody echoed through the still house. When the song came to a close, Andrew pulled me toward the couch. "Let's sit and cuddle."

I sat down, but he turned and knelt in front of me. He reached over to the end table next to the couch and pulled open a drawer.

His voice quivering, he whispered, "I've wanted to ask you this for a while now." The firelight reflected in his watering eyes. He pulled out a small box and clutched it to his chest. My heart pounded, and I thought, *Oh, my God, is this happening?*

He held my hands and peered into my eyes. "I know we don't know what will happen in the future. But, one thing is for sure, I love you with all my heart, and I want to be with you for the rest of your life."

I couldn't keep my mouth from falling open. He lifted the lid of the small box, and I let out a gasp. The ring was brilliant.

"So, here goes: Isa, will you marry me? Will you be my wife?"

I blinked back tears. "Are you sure? Are you sure?"

"Yes, more than anything."

I had no doubts. He was the best thing that had ever happened to me. "Yes, of course. I would be honored to be your wife," I grinned and put my arms around him.

When I was released from his embrace, Andrew slipped the ring on my finger, and we kissed. I held my lips against his, drinking him in, inhaling his sweet fragrance.

After we collected ourselves, we approached his parents' bedroom. When we knocked, they opened the door excitedly, revealing a tray of champagne and flutes on a bedside table. Mrs. Byrnes's round blue eyes sparkled beneath her short curls, and she beamed at us. His dad stood next to her. He was the spitting image of Andrew—or rather the Andrew of thirty years in the future—a shiny forehead, a smooth upper lip, straight, long nose, and tender gaze that bestowed immediate comfort.

"Did you say yes?" Andrew's mother asked me.

"Of course!"

"Yeah!" she cheered. "Congratulations! We're thrilled to have you in the family!" She embraced us both, and Mr. Byrnes joined in the group hug.

I called Mama and Dad right away. "Mama, Andrew asked me to marry him!"

There was silence.

Finally it was broken. "Oh my goodness," Mama said. "What a surprise." There was another pause. I had heard no joy in her voice, just concern, as if she had heard bad news at a doctor's visit. "Does he really know what he's getting into?"

I spoke to Dad next, who was genuinely pleased. "Isa-chan, congratulations to you both. What a fine moment."

The phone was passed to Ana, but all I could hear was sobbing. Finally she said, "I can't talk right now. I just . . . I just can't deal." I hung up the phone and burst into tears in front of Andrew and his parents.

"My parents are the most happily married couple I've ever known." Andrew's words from our first date echoed in my mind. The Byrneses were indeed wonderful. Margaret and Larry both worked in education: Larry had served as a dean of education at various universities throughout the country during his career. Margaret worked as an educational consultant and taught award-winning workshops around the world. Their relationship seemed perfect; they rarely fought, they shared tasks, they communicated well, and they had similar expectations of each other.

Andrew's sister, Mary, was completely normal compared to my brother. She was charming and always interested in establishing a relationship with me. She maintained frequent and honest communication with her parents and brother from her home in Colorado. The Byrneses also kept in touch with a slew of relatives; they were a tight-knit, relationship-focused, loving, humor-filled family.

Margaret and Larry were thrilled at how happy I made their son. They were concerned about my health, and I tried to educate them about cystic fibrosis, but they certainly did not dwell on it. They were bright people, and they knew the ramifications of having a daughter-in-law with CF. But they kept their concerns to themselves.

When I returned home for the rest of the holiday, my parents had gotten over the initial shock. Dad was impressed with the size of my diamond and already starting to talk about the wedding budget. Although it would be years before Ana could find peace with my marriage to Andrew, she had composed herself enough to talk about the wedding. Mama, though, remained distant until dinner the night before Ana and I left for Berkeley.

"It was such a shock, Isa-chan. We never, ever expected you or Ana-chan to get married."

By now, I could confront her. "Your reaction was so awful, Mama. I cried in front of the Byrnes parents."

"I just didn't know what to say. He was just your boyfriend, and it seemed so fast."

"Mama, we've been dating for three years!"

Mama continued to pour out her thoughts, not really hearing me. "He is such a sensitive boy. Does he really know what is ahead of him? He is so in love. I just don't want Andrew to be hurt."

"How could you say that?" I asked. "Andrew knows everything there is to know about CF; he knows the future. But he still made the choice to spend his life with me. . . . He's the only person who sees me for who I am, not just for my disease." I wanted her to know she was in the latter camp.

"Yes, I know. He is a very special boy. But I don't think he really understands how much work it will be to take care of you. Is he really strong enough?"

She just didn't get it. Her belief that we were a burden to her prevented her from understanding that there were people in this world who enjoyed my presence above and beyond "the imposition" of my disease. More Japanese bullshit. My CF was a huge part of my life, but a small part of who I was—my beliefs, values, goals, or personality. I was a person, not just a diagnosis.

"You are the only one who is here voluntarily," the father of a child with CF said to Andrew at a Cystic Fibrosis Research, Inc. educational conference we attended together one summer. Andrew had chosen to have cystic fibrosis in his life. I often asked myself, *What is Andrew getting out of this? Is he some sort of codependent, self-sacrificing martyr?* His love exceeded all reason. My parents' bitter marriage had left me jaded. They each had given things up more out of commitment than out of genuine love. But Andrew's unflinching loyalty defined unconditional marital love.

I came to understand that I was worth it, but I still carried the weight of all that he would give up to be married to me. He needed generous health insurance, and we needed to live near a CF Center. Someday he'd be the sole breadwinner. His hobbies and work would be postponed or given up for visits to the hospital. Most of all, he would have to forgo having children.

We were standing in line at the grocery store one day, and a chubby toddler in front of us started screaming and flailing his arms at his mother. Andrew leaned toward me, rolled his eyes, and whispered the classic Rodney Dangerfield line, "Now I know why tigers eat their young."

I laughed. "Don't you think kids are cute?"

"No, they're annoying."

"You must have some paternal instinct. I mean, it's natural."

"Kids are a pain in the ass. I don't care about having them. I just want you."

"But you have great genes to pass on," I said.

"There're enough bald people in this world," he said.

We had these conversations often; I probed, seeking out Andrew's true feelings about being a father. I knew women with CF who had given birth; biologically it was possible. But pregnancy and parenting, even through adoption, took an enormous toll on the health of the women. I decided never to have children of my own. It was not a devastating loss; I wasn't meant to be a mother. I was just glad to be alive. My engagement to Andrew changed things. I felt sad for his loss. Andrew didn't seem bothered at the prospect of not having children, but maybe he was just protecting me.

Another sacrifice was our physical intimacy. The sicker I became, the harder it was for us to have a normal sex life. Stress and shortness of breath squelched my desire. Sex was like running a mile while breathing through a straw, all for the chance of a few seconds, if that, of pleasure.

Sex was embarrassing. As our sweaty bodies wriggled and danced in bed, my breathing grew louder and heavier. My muscles tightened around him, and I panted like a dying horse. The pressure was building, higher and stronger, until I could stand it no more, and I had to let nature take its course.

"Hold on," I gasped. I rolled quickly over, pulling him out so I wouldn't squeeze him. I exploded in heaving, juicy, violent coughs, releasing my own ejaculate of mucus from my exercised airways. I grabbed tissues and poured out blobs of lung come.

With this climax, I felt release, a great sense of pleasure of renewed breath and air. "I'm so sorry," I muttered.

Andrew rubbed my back. "It's okay, sweetheart, it's okay."

After I recovered, I rolled back on top of Andrew and continued our lovemaking until finally we both came. Other times, just to avoid the discomfort, I lay there like a log while Andrew finished. *I'm a lousy lover.*

It amazed me that Andrew found me sexy after these bittersweet routines. He still wanted to be monogamous, with *me*. After sex, I felt like I had been hit by a truck. I lay in bed, exhausted. Some days, intimacy consisted of holding each other, because sex was simply too strenuous. Weeks went by without any action. I worried about letting him down, not pleasing him, or being a failure as a lover and future wife. But after I confessed all my worries and inadequacies to Andrew, he still understood and loved me.

Tension had been building for days now in our Berkeley apartment. Andrew had graduated several weeks earlier from Harvard and had moved in. He was commuting to Palo Alto for his new job at a law firm. Ana's silences had grown, and I could sense her bad mood.

Ana lay on the bed as I sat facing her. Andrew had gone to work. I pounded Ana's chest as she muffled her cough in a towel and then spit into her cup. My mind escaped the drudgery of therapy with distractions of what to write for my final psychotherapy paper and which statistical program I needed to learn for my epidemiology/biostatistics thesis. I was also thinking about wedding plans for next summer, mentally choosing invitations and considering dresses.

In the distance, a siren blared. Ana's voice broke into my stream of thought. "You're not focused. You're doing therapy like you don't care."

"I do care, I'm just thinking of all the other things I'd rather be doing than therapy."

Ana sucked on her oxygen. "Like escape to be with Andrew."

"You're rude," I accused. "I mean school stuff, wedding stuff." I paused. "It's so obvious you don't like him."

Ana resisted commenting between coughs. "I don't know . . . I don't know," she said, which meant she really wanted to say something hurtful.

"I just . . . I'm just in the way. Maybe you should just go off and marry him and let me die."

Her resignation pissed me off, so I pounded harder. The mattress squeaked with my heavy blows. "How can you even say that? Don't you think I care about you?"

"Well, you don't show it. You're going to abandon me next weekend to go to Napa with him, leaving me to fend for myself for therapy."

It was true. Once in a while, Andrew and I wanted to get away, like when we went to Rome over spring break. Ana could rely on our jackhammer-like mechanical percussor for just one night of therapy. All Andrew and I wanted was a romantic summer getaway. Was that too much to ask?

"It's only for one night."

"You always put yourself first," Ana muttered. "You've always been more selfish."

"You're being just as selfish," I told her. By now my pounding was violent, and rage had curled my hands into fists. "You *bitch.*"

"Ow! Stop it! You're hurting me." Ana scowled as she got up from the bed. Her matted hair covered her contorted face. "What's your goddamn problem, you're a fucking maniac!"

"Well, how am I supposed to respond to your rudeness? Isn't it normal for a couple, an engaged couple, to get away for *one* night? I mean, it's not going to kill you."

"You don't care about my health," Ana cried. "Look at me! I'm listed for a transplant. I can barely breathe. And you are just moving on with your life. I'm just in the way." She started crying, and, immediately, I did, too. We never had such an emotional explosion.

Ana blurted out, "Maybe it's better if I just distance myself. And I don't want to be your maid of honor, either."

Now that was the ultimate insult. I was frozen. "How . . . how could you even say something so cruel! I never knew you had such evil inside of you! . . . It's my wedding. *My* wedding!"

She stood motionless.

"What the hell am I supposed to do, Ana?" I sobbed. "Do you want me to break up with Andrew, so I can take care of you? Would that make you happy? Would that save you from a transplant? I don't think so! I can't believe you would ruin my dreams that way. I'd never forgive you."

I glared at Ana, my soul mate and archnemesis at the moment. We had always relied on each other. The power of two had kept us going. Now it was breaking down.

"No, no," Ana sobbed, "you have to get married. I just don't know what to do."

I blew my nose as tears poured down my face. "You will always be the most important person in my life. But we have to find a way to fit Andrew into our lives. I'm sorry to make your life so hard. But I have mine, too. . . ." I looked away and exhaled. "I just wish you could find someone, too. It would make life so much easier."

"Yeah, right. Rub it in. Look at me." She tugged at the oxygen tube that lay against her face.

"What are we supposed to do?" I cried.

"I don't know. I don't know. . . . We need an instruction book."

Chapter 25

Another Love Triangle

Ana

You were my first new female friend I met after Sonya died. You stayed up and talked to me on the phone and let me listen and grieve. You brought me to the CF community and I fell in love with you and your sister.

—Letter from Rob to Isa, age twenty-six

"I'm moving out," I announced to Isa a month after graduating from Berkeley. She was sitting in front of the computer working on her thesis. She stopped typing and turned to me.

"What?" she exclaimed.

I had been hired for a part-time genetic counseling job about an hour away. "The drive is hell. I don't have energy or time for that commute. I have to move out. It's time."

"Are you sure? That's so risky."

She was right. After so many years of depending on each other for therapy, I wondered if I could actually live alone. But I had to try.

"I just can't live here anymore. Andrew's driving me nuts, and I need my independence. Besides, I'm sure you'll be glad to not have me complain about him anymore."

She didn't disagree. "But how are you going to get therapy?"

"I'll figure it out. Stanford Hospital does outpatient chest percussion for CF adults. Maybe I can get that. And I can use the percussor. It's worth a try."

"Maybe Rob can help you," Isa suggested. Rob was Isa's new friend, and he lived in Redwood City, close to Stanford. She had met him at a CFRI support group, and their friendship had flourished in the last few months.

"Maybe, but I barely know the guy. It would be weird."

"Well, if you get desperate, at least he's someone you can turn to for help."

Rob did not have CF, but he had lost his fiancée, Sonya, to CF a year earlier. He came to the groups to share his experience and offer support to others.

I found a small cottage for rent on a woodsy estate in Atherton, a wealthy community several miles from my job and, coincidentally, only a few miles from Rob's apartment. A few days after my move, I met him at another quarterly CFRI support group.

I saw him sitting across the room when I entered; he smiled and waved at me. *Maybe he thinks I'm Isa,* I thought.

"Welcome to the neighborhood!" he said as we left the group. "We're neighbors! I can throw a rock and hit your house from mine." He patted my back gently.

"Yeah, it's nice to know someone in the area. We'll have to hang out." I was at a loss for words. After spending two years isolated in an all-female graduate program, I felt strange saying anything to a man.

Rob was large, standing six feet, three inches tall and weighing about two hundred pounds. His long, wavy, brown hair was pulled back in a ponytail, and small loops decorated his earlobes. He had the aura of a rock star and the muscles of a mountain biker. He wore flannel shorts and a white T-shirt advertising his latest mountain-bike race. On a chain around his neck, he wore a cross and the engagement ring that had been Sonya's.

In the ensuing weeks, I found contentment in my new independence. Isa and Andrew were happy to have their space and to be liberated from my moodiness at last. Thanks to the Genetically Handicapped Person's Program (GHPP), I enrolled in Stanford's outpatient chest-percussion program and received a treatment from a respiratory therapist each day after work. Rob and I spent increasing amounts of time together.

"I'm free, finally free!" I rejoiced to Rob one evening. "Without Isa, I can do my own thing . . . like hang out with you."

He sat on the carpet of my cottage. I sat across from him on my bed, my tan legs dangling, the carpet tickling my toes. Outside, a breeze rustled through the leaves, sending some falling onto the porch or tapping softly on the roof.

"You have a new life," he said, "to live as your own person."

"Yeah. It feels great to be self-sufficient, finally."

"All the women with CF I've known have been so independent. That's a quality I've always admired."

Rob stood up and approached my stereo. He stepped over my oxygen tubing toward my CD collection.

"Bob Dylan, huh?" he asked. "Isn't that your parents' generation?"

"Yeah . . . I grew up hearing Dylan at CF camp. It was run by hippies who loved the sixties. As for my parents," I scoffed, "they aren't American. They'd have no clue who he is."

Rob sat down next to me on the bed, his eyes dreamy. We talked about sixties music and the songs he used to play in his band. He had spent over ten years as a bass guitarist in a rock band, performing at clubs in San Francisco and Los Angeles. I found myself engrossed in his stories of a life so different from mine.

"Music was cool. It was addictive—the fans, the cheering crowds. I loved it," he continued. "But I left because of the drugs and alcohol. It became self-destructive." He pulled out his wallet and showed me a coin.

"This is my sobriety chip. When I met Sonya, I promised her I'd quit. Now I'm three years clean and sober. I've seen so many friends in the music industry die of overdoses. Such a waste. I didn't want to be one of them. Now, I live my life one day at a time. Just trying to do my best, stay clean, follow the Twelve Steps. Enjoy the finer things in life, family, friends, God."

His face was sincere, almost childlike, as he spoke. I had rarely come across someone outside the CF community who valued life the way we did. Rob's own disease of addiction had made him genuine and introspective. I felt as if I had known him for years. There was no presumption about where our friendship was going and no pressure to impress each other.

It was August 1997, and the annual Northern California CF summer camp was quickly approaching. The "camp" was no longer for children; it was now open only to mature teens and adults with CF and their friends and family members who could follow strict cross infection protocol. Isa and I had convinced Rob to attend because it would be a cathartic, healing experience for his grief. We set out for a week in the mountains to attend the newly named "CF Family Retreat." On a lazy afternoon, sitting on a log under a canopy of redwoods, I confessed, "I don't think I'll ever fall in love."

"Why not?" he asked.

"Why would anyone want to fall in love with someone so sick?"

"You can't help who you fall in love with. I have no regrets about being with Sonya. CF was just a part of her and something I just accepted."

The bushes rustled behind the redwood grove, and a deer appeared. We watched silently for a moment until the deer slipped away.

The sunshine warmed my back as I spoke. "I just can't imagine anyone finding someone with CF attractive—coughing, farting, doing therapy all the time. What a pain in the ass."

"You just learn to look beyond the disease and at the person." He looked at me with his hazel eyes and took a deep breath. "I have a confession to make . . . I have a crush on you."

"Really?" I asked. I felt the need to turn up my oxygen, and I blushed. *No way. This couldn't be true.* I had feelings for him too, but I hesitated. "I wouldn't want to make you go through this again, after losing Sonya. Why would you want to do that again?"

He looked at me. "Either way, we're already friends. If I lose you, it'll be a huge loss anyway. If we get together and it doesn't work out, the worst we could be is friends."

His words were reassuring. The imaginary neon sign on my forehead that read *Not lovable* was dimming.

"Excuse me," I said. I escaped to my car and promptly threw up.

Later that summer, after spending a weekend with Isa in Berkeley, I returned to my Atherton cottage and realized that I had forgotten my key. I had nowhere to go but Rob's apartment.

"I need a place to stay tonight," I told him over the phone. "Can I crash at your place? The only thing is, I need therapy."

"Sure, my home is your home. No problem. Just come over after seven."

That evening, I knocked on his door. He opened it. His hair was loose, and it partially obscured his face, but I could see that his eyes were red and teary. He wore a torn Nirvana T-shirt.

"What's wrong?" I asked.

"Oh, it's been a hard evening. My grief counselor just left. I'm just dealing with a lot right now."

I gave him a hug. I was not used to seeing a man cry.

"I'm here if you need to talk. But if you need your space, I can leave. I don't want to impose."

"No, it's okay. I want you here." He leaned over and hugged me.

I looked around his apartment. It was dark, filthy, and packed with memories of Sonya. Pictures of her hung on the wall; her clothes and makeup still filled the closets, and her expired medication was still in the refrigerator. He shared photos and keepsakes, and I developed a deep understanding of their life together. Pain accompanied this awareness, as there was no doubt that, despite our fledgling relationship, Rob was still attached to Sonya.

Later that night, Rob did my therapy. I had it easy. He needed no training or explanation. I didn't need to hide my massive coughing spells. Rob had seen it all with Sonya: mucus, coughing fits, stomachaches, even vomiting.

"I need it harder, right here," I said, pointing to my right chest, "and faster." It was easy to assert my needs with Rob. "Yeah, that's the spot."

"Sounds like sex," he said. We laughed.

"Sonya's still in your life," I said. "You must have loved her so much." I coughed into a towel.

"Yeah . . . but I know I have to move on. It's just hard. After she died, I just didn't know what to do with myself. All those nights of doing therapy, of helping her, being there for her at the end. Suddenly, she was gone."

"What did you do with yourself?" I asked. I spit into a tissue.

"Oh," he sighed, "there were plenty of nights I sat at that table staring down a bottle of Jack Daniels, about to drink again . . . but then I remembered my promise. I knew if I relapsed, my life would be over." He got up and left the room, only to return a moment later with a long yellow strip of satin.

"I started martial arts . . . kung fu. Spent my nights kicking ass, getting my frustrations out. Here's my yellow belt, my first one. It was great to go somewhere to get my mind off of grieving. It was the best thing I did to survive losing Sonya."

He sat back down again and continued percussing my back.

After therapy, Rob gave me a massage, his large, soft hands caressed my aching back. "Ah, that feels good," I said. He bent down and kissed my neck. Therapy was great foreplay for sex. I turned over and wrapped my arms around his massive shoulders. I wanted him. Intimacy came easily, and our bodies melted together with an unquestionable comfort, free from any of the awkwardness I had anticipated. My conviction that I would die a virgin dissipated. I finally understood Isa's love for Andrew. I now knew what it felt like to be in love.

In the ensuing weeks, each time we made love, Sonya's engagement ring, hung on a chain around Rob's neck, dangled in my face as if her spirit were teasing me. Finally it was too much.

"This is weird," I said on one particular evening. "I don't know how much of this I can take."

"What? Am I squishing you?"

"No, it's not that." I sat up. "It's . . . it's her ring. It's hanging in my face. I'm sure she'd be pissed if she knew you were with me."

Rob looked away. "I'm sorry. Please be patient with me."

At that moment I wanted to tell him how hard it was to be second. How I wanted to be with him and wanted him with me and me alone. But I refrained.

"I know you need time. And I'll give you all the time you need. It's . . . it's just hard for me, too," I said.

"I'm so sorry. I do love you." Rob put his muscular arm around me, and we hugged.

I learned from Rob that love and sorrow come from the same place in the heart.

A month later, I visited Rob's apartment again. Sonya's photos were missing from the bookshelf.

"You took Sonya's pictures down?" I asked.

Rob stood at my side. He rubbed his face with his hands and let out a sigh. "Yeah, it was tough. But . . . it was time." He lifted a photo of him and me—our first photo together—and put it on the shelf. He took my hand in his and led me to the kitchen. "And look at this." He opened the refrigerator. Her medicine was gone.

"Wow," I exclaimed, "that's a huge step. I'm impressed."

"It's time. I've come to accept that life goes on. And my feelings for you are getting stronger. You have my heart and mine alone." His words relieved me. Maybe the love triangle with Sonya was finally dissolving, and Rob would be mine.

On weekends, I left Rob to spend time with Isa in Berkeley. Andrew had moved closer to his office in Palo Alto, and Isa was alone there. One day, Rob confronted me with his resentment about my visiting Isa.

"I don't want a relationship with strings attached," he stated, as I was about to depart for Berkeley.

"What do you mean?" I asked.

"I've already had a relationship like that. Sonya was in the middle of a divorce when she met me. It was so difficult for her to break her ties. I don't want to do that again."

He was the one with strings still attached to Sonya. How could he consider my twin sister a competitor?

"Sorry," I said, heading out the door. "You mean the world to me but I won't abandon my twin for you. You're just going to have to accept that."

On occasion, the two men would join us in the Berkeley apartment for the weekend. Rob and Andrew were striking contrasts. One was tall with too much hair, the other shorter with too little hair. One was profoundly intellectual, the other unacademic. One was averse to sun and sport, the other bronzed from mountain-biking and hiking. One found passion in politics and law, the other rarely voted and had indulged in his share of lawlessness. One was incapacitated by the slightest pain, the other welcomed kicks and punches from martial arts.

Still, they found common ground in their adoration of eighties rock and roll, football, and the Stenzel twins. For the first time, we had help from others—our partners—who willingly gave us therapy as a means of intimacy and for the empowering feeling that they were doing something to help our health.

My family was happy for me that I had found love and someone to help me. But they were cautious.

"Watch out, Ana," Ryuta said when he visited. "Rock star is on the rebound. He just misses CF and wants another sick girlfriend. That's fucked up. I'd be careful if I were you."

His comment pissed me off. "You don't know that. You don't even know him. Gimme a break." But I wondered if my older brother, experienced with a multitude of relationships, knew better.

On one occasion, I called Mama from Rob's apartment. "What are you doing?" she asked. "Your breathing is so heavy."

"Oh, I'm just cleaning."

"What?!" she shrieked. "You are cleaning Rob's apartment?" This provoked a long shrill diatribe, "Don't you spoil him. . . . Don't you mother him. . . . Don't you let him control you."

"But Mama," I argued, "he's doing my therapy. This is the least I can do to help him."

When she met Rob for the first time, she inspected him carefully.

Later, when he was absent, she asked, "What is that?" referring to a large knot in Rob's tangled ponytail. "Doesn't he comb his hair? Why does he wear earrings?" Mama was just culturally backward. Long hair and earrings in men were completely acceptable in American culture, especially in the music industry.

"Mama, I don't care what Rob looks like, if his hair is messy. He has so much inside. He communicates and shares his feelings . . . better than Dad ever did." I paused and blurted, "I think he's my soul mate, Mama."

"Oh my goodness," she said. "He does not have an education. He cannot even support you if you are too sick to work!"

"*Ach,* Hatsuko," Dad interjected into the conversation, "It doesn't matter. He has a good heart, and that is most important." Dad was softening up with age. "He is a fine sturdy fellow who can take care of Ana in other ways."

Mama grudgingly accepted Rob and began subtly encouraging him to pursue his education. After a year, Rob enrolled in college to pursue a degree in addiction studies and counseling.

I'm so tired, I think I'm going to pass out. I'm so numb because I'm so tired. Here goes another day. Every day, go, go, go. No stopping, you can't stop, you have to keep going. One more day, I'll rest tomorrow.

—Ana, age twenty-one

In the winter of 1999, my lung capacity fell to a record low of 16 percent after I caught an aggressive flu. My 104-degree fever would not break, and my breathlessness kept me up at night. A river of mucus was drowning me from within. Broken, I surrendered again to the hospital.

It was a blow to my steadfast commitment to work, my futile hope to prove to my employer that I was worth hiring despite my having CF. A cloud of inadequacy followed me to my hospital room, as I abandoned my patients and burdened my coworkers by an inevitable two-week absence. But I had no choice. I had to be brought to my hospital room in a wheelchair, too weak to walk from the admitting department to the ward. My admission papers read, "Advanced stage cystic fibrosis. Early stage respiratory failure." I dreaded being among the ranks of the end-stagers.

I could not lay flat in my hospital bed. I was panicked by shortness of breath, feeling like I was suffocating. Elevating the head of the bed could not ease my breathlessness. I adjusted the part of the bed that usually propped up a patient's knees and then lay backward, with the knee-rest supporting my heaving chest. Only in that position could I feel comfortable.

I worried about Rob. "So this must be all *déjà vu* for you," I said. "Doesn't this remind you of Sonya?" I lay there dusky and wasted, curled in a fetal position, with oxygen hissing up my nose.

He smiled weakly, the light in his eyes dim. "Yeah, but it's okay. I'm alright with this."

"You know," I replied, "you don't have to be in this. You can leave. You can turn around and walk out of here and not have CF be a part of your life. A lot of men would do that."

"No . . . no," he said. His hands held mine tenderly as he caressed my blue fingertips. "I can't do that. You're too important to me. You're my love, and I'll be with you always, no matter what happens."

"You're crazy." I muttered. "Look at me. I feel like shit. I look like shit. Why do you want this?"

"You're my soul mate. Besides, it all makes sense to me now," he explained. "God put Sonya in my life to prepare me for you. He was testing me to see if I could handle CF. And I learned that I could . . . I think great things are in store for us. I know it."

He leaned toward me and kissed me on the forehead.

I said, "I'm so sorry to put you through this. You deserve so much better . . ."

"Shhh . . . ," he replied, putting his fingers on my lips. "Don't be sorry. I'm here with you. I don't want to be with anyone else but you."

As my health worsened, Rob put up with all the hassles that came with having a sick girlfriend. During sex, I'd push away from his embrace, suffocating, "Stop. . . . Sorry. I can't breathe. I need air." My toes tingled from the lack of oxygen. He'd get up from bed, his naked body smooth and muscular, go to the oxygen tank, and turn it up to five liters. Then he'd slip back into bed without speaking. In the middle of passionate foreplay, I'd say, "Hold on, the tubing is crimped. I'm all tangled up."

"How kinky! Tangled up in tube," he'd say, laughing, playing on the words of a Bob Dylan song.

Sometimes when I came, the pressure caused the blood vessels in my sick lungs to burst, and I interrupted our closest moment by coughing up blood. "Sorry, Rob," I apologized, getting up, reaching for Kleenex. My sex appeal was dwindling as fast as my lung capacity.

Like me, Rob looked forward to the prospect of the lung transplant that would free us from the CF predicament. We waited thirteen months on the transplant list, and he kept his word. We cherished each day together despite my declining health.

"This could be the best it can be," he said. "So let's just enjoy what we have now."

Chapter 26

Dying to Work

Ana

My passion to live was now fueled by Rob and by my work. Even as I got sicker, I continued to do my job. Every day I slipped off my oxygen, plastered blush on my face to hide my paleness, colored my blue lips with plum lipstick, donned earrings and a formal outfit, and spent four hours each afternoon working as a genetic counselor.

Genetic counselors work with individuals who have genetic disorders or couples at risk of having a child with a birth defect or genetic disease. The profession combines teaching, counseling, and science by providing information and support, coordinating testing, and connecting families with community resources. Genetic counselors do this with a keen awareness of the psychological issues surrounding pregnancy, reproductive risk, genetic disease, and loss.

On a typical day, I met several patients, most commonly to discuss prenatal diagnostic tests such as chorionic villi sampling (CVS) or amniocentesis, invasive procedures in which fetal cells are removed from the early placenta or amniotic fluid, respectively, and tested for chromosome disorders or genetic diseases. I counseled women about various reproductive concerns: women over thirty-five whose babies were at risk for chromosomal abnormalities, women exposed to medications during pregnancy, blood-related couples, couples with a family history of genetic disease, and women whose ultrasounds had revealed abnormalities.

My office at the Perinatal Diagnostic Center sat across from the fetal monitors. Their familiar hum provided a soothing background sound of life in the making.

Sitting on my desk was the chart for the patient I was to see that morning. I opened the chart. *CF Carrier*, it read. Routine screening done as part of the patient's first-trimester blood tests had found that she was a carrier for delta F508, the most common genetic mutation causing CF.

The woman, named Jill, and her husband, Paul, arrived moments later. They were a young, attractive Caucasian couple, both affluent Silicon Valley engineers. I invited them into my office. As soon as Jill sat down, she burst into tears. Paul reached over to hold her hand.

"I can't believe this," she sobbed. "This is just horrible news. I've been an emotional wreck all week."

I tried to console her. "I know this news is very scary." I reached into the Kleenex box I always kept on my desk and handed her a tissue.

Jill dabbed her eyes. "As soon as I found out, I read about cystic fibrosis on the Internet and I didn't like what I read. It's a horrible disease. People die from it!"

She was right, I thought. *CF is a horrible disease . . . but it's so much more, too.*

Paul said, "We don't want a child with CF. We are not in a position to care for a sick kid. We'd rather have a kid with Down syndrome than one that's coughing all the time."

I swallowed his comment with a nod. "It sounds like you've already thought through the 'what-ifs.' That takes a lot of courage. We need to test you, Paul, first to see if you're a carrier. Only if you are would your baby be at risk."

I pulled out my genetics diagrams and illustrated for the couple how CF was inherited, that it was recessive and both parents had to carry the gene for their child to have the disease.

Jill's emotions consumed her. *Was she hearing me at all?* "I just don't understand how I can be a carrier. No one in our family has ever had it."

"Over 90 percent of patients with CF have no family history. The CF gene can be passed down for generations in some families without ever revealing itself."

"What did I do to become a carrier? This is all so unfair." She blew her nose.

"This is not your fault. We have no control over what genes we carry."

I thought about CF: the irony is that carriers have an evolutionary advantage, being resistant to cholera, and that's why the gene has propagated through time.

I went on, explaining to Paul about carrier testing and the limitations of a DNA test that had a 90 percent detection rate. I discussed the option they had for prenatal diagnosis through amniocentesis should Paul prove to be a carrier.

Paul shifted in his seat. He rubbed his face with the palm of his hands. "Let's get to a difficult question." His blue eyes peered at me. "Tell me how we can terminate the pregnancy if this baby has CF."

I crossed my legs as I sat back. "Well, we can certainly talk about that . . . but remember, you haven't been tested yet. And the odds of you being a carrier are 1 in 25. We may be jumping the gun here. . . . The odds of you having a child with CF are about 1 percent at this point."

"I realize that. But I just want to know. Like I said before, we cannot raise a child with CF. That's just unacceptable." He waved a firm hand in my direction.

"Okay," I said. "The choice to end a pregnancy for genetic reasons is available up to twenty-four weeks in California. So we have some time. And it is a surgical procedure done with minimal risk right here in this hospital." I hesitated to go further. Tears were welling up in Jill's eyes again. She looked down at the floor; her arms were folded across her chest.

"That's enough information," Jill said. "I just can't think about that right now."

"Sure. I know this is hard information to hear." I turned to Paul. "If you are found to be a carrier too, we can meet again. Then, if your baby is affected, we can revisit the details about your options. Let's cross that bridge if and when we get to it."

Jill sighed. "All I want is a healthy child."

"Of course. That's so natural, that's what we all want." I used 'we,' holding up a facade of normalcy. Toward the end of our session, I asked Jill if she had any siblings.

"I have a sister," she replied.

"Well, if you're a CF carrier, then there's a 50 percent chance that she's also a carrier. You may want to share this information with her so that she can get tested."

"You're right. But her husband's Chinese. Does that matter?"

"It does," I said. "CF is extremely rare in Asians. So, the fact that they are an interracial couple decreases the chances that their children would be at risk."

"Well, that's reassuring. I guess she doesn't need to worry then."

Paul did get tested. He carried the delta F508 CF mutation as well. I saw the couple back again, and amid more tears, Jill chose to have an amniocentesis. I kept my fingers crossed for them during the two-week wait for results. Three-fourths chance, no CF; one-fourth chance CF. *Please God, let them be spared,* I prayed.

Two weeks later, the results came in. The report read: *Homozygous delta F508. Fetus affected with cystic fibrosis.* Damn.

I called the couple in the evening, hoping to speak to them directly in the privacy of their home. Paul answered the phone. I identified myself. There was silence. He knew. I asked that Jill be put on the other line, and I shared the news over the telephone that their baby had CF.

The following day, Jill and Paul entered my office again. The humming of the fetal monitors could again be heard through my office door. For this couple, those once-joyous sounds were now a harsh reminder of shattered dreams.

Jill's eyes were red, her face flushed. "I can't believe this is happening. It's like a bad dream."

"I'm so sorry to have to share this difficult news with you. It's not what we were hoping for." There was little I could say to alleviate the distress.

Paul spoke, "You know from our previous discussion how we want to proceed. Tell us how we can make an appointment for an abortion as soon as possible."

Jill put a hand out and rested it on her husband's knee. She turned to him. "Wait . . . I know you're sure. But I'm not . . . things are different now. I'm feeling the baby kick. I'm almost eighteen weeks. I just . . . I just need to think about it." She buried her face in her hands.

"It's important that you really think this through. There is some time. Your options are not only to end the pregnancy. Some people continue their pregnancy and use this time to prepare, both emotionally and medically, for having a baby with CF. That way the baby can start treatment right away. Plenty of studies have shown the benefits of early treatment." I paused. Their eyes were sullen.

"What we can offer you is information about CF, including meeting with a CF specialist so you can learn what to expect. We can introduce you to other parents who are raising children with CF if you'd like. That way, you can be the most informed before deciding. Some people take us up on this; some people are sure about their decision. It's up to you."

Jill was eager for information and she was ready with questions: How long do people with CF live? What kind of treatment is involved? How do we know how sick our baby will be?

I described for her, as objectively as possible, the symptoms of CF and emphasized its extreme variability and our inability to make long-term predictions based on genetic testing. I refrained from flooding them with the information about the resources that I knew so readily. I wanted to say *Join the CF community! Meet the wonderful families I know!* But I knew a diagnosis like this was the beginning of a long process, and inundating them with too much information at this stage would be counterproductive.

Following my recitation of the treatments available to babies born with CF, Jill said, "Well, I want to talk to a CF specialist. I want to know what it's like to live with the disease, I mean, like quality of life. He probably knows more about CF than you do." I bit my tongue. Keeping my professional distance and anonymity at this time when the couple was facing a decision was critical.

Ultimately, Paul and Jill chose to end their pregnancy. Deep down, I was sorry that the couple was turning away from all the gifts that CF could offer. But they were also sparing their child a lifetime of daily therapies, hospitalizations, stomachaches, needle pokes, and breathing difficulties.

A friend of mine with CF once said, "I don't know how you do the work you do. I could never do that. I mean, isn't it just a slap in the face every time someone aborts a baby with CF?" I often wondered if I was sending a horrifying message to the CF community: that the only real "cure" for CF lay in the prevention of the birth of people with CF.

But I trusted the best intentions of each set of parents, and I accepted their decisions. I was grateful that my parents never had to face these choices. Things seemed a lot simpler back in 1971, when Mama carried twins with CF without even knowing it. Was her pregnancy a happier, more enjoyable one?

Fortunately, most couples who undergo prenatal diagnosis end up having healthy babies. Yet, every day I witnessed the anxiety and fear of an unfavorable outcome and the sorrow of losing a wanted pregnancy. In this world, I secretly appreciated being spared the angst of parenthood, since I chose not to bear children who would be motherless at a young age. A patient once lashed out at me in her state of angry grief, "You have no idea what it's like not to be able to have children."

Actually, I do, I thought, *and I'm fine with it.*

Six months later, Jill called me. She was pregnant again.

"Congratulations," I told her over the telephone. "How does it feel?"

"Better . . ." she said. Her voice was calm and confident. "We used in vitro fertilization and did preimplantation genetic diagnosis. I really feel like this baby will be fine."

Preimplantation genetic diagnosis (PGD) is a technology in which embryos created through in vitro fertilization are tested for a genetic defect like CF first, and only unaffected embryos are implanted into the mother. For this couple, it was a way to avoid the 25 percent chance of having a baby with CF. It was, in essence, a way to circumvent fate.

I scheduled an amniocentesis for Jill to confirm that the baby was really unaffected, since PGD can have false negatives. She arrived for the test a few days later.

"I just wish I could know that everything will be okay," she said. Although the amniocentesis results confirmed that the baby did not have CF, I knew there were other potential problems that could arise: chromosome abnormalities, other birth defects, delivery complications. There were no guarantees, not for Jill, not for any expectant mother.

I knew my career choice would require me to confront society's views of CF. A strong unspoken message pervaded my work: that illness, disability (be it mental or physical), and death are to be feared and avoided at every cost. But illness ultimately makes its way into all of our lives and has the potential to teach enormously valuable lessons that one can learn no other way. These lessons have inspired many resilient families to rise to the occasion and become dedicated advocates and caretakers for their children with genetic diseases. Indeed, those are the lessons my family and I learned so well. I hoped that in my job I could stand before couples, secretly demonstrating that people with genetic diseases could contribute to society and carry a wealth of unique perspectives.

My bout of the flu had served as a reminder that one infection could deal a crushing blow to my lung capacity. After the flu subsided, I struggled to keep my numbers above 30 percent. More than ever, I looked forward to the call for the lung transplant. Life was becoming increasingly difficult. Panic attacks from air-hunger disrupted my sleep. Showers were a dreaded ten minutes of suffocation. My whole life existed in a narrow self-centered tunnel made up of chores of subsistence: breathing, coughing, treatments, home IVs, filling oxygen tanks, sterilizing nebulizers, visiting the doctor, taking medicines, and trying to consume enough calories to keep from wasting away. Ironically, working four hours each day was the only bit of "normal" left in my existence—a brief respite of daily denial. It suddenly didn't matter that CF had given me a bountiful life of unique opportunities and perspective. I hated CF because I just couldn't breathe and that was all I wanted to do.

One rainy January evening, I realized I was slowly killing myself. After exiting my office, I walked through the darkness, gulping the fresh cold air, taking each step toward my car slowly and deliberately. I craved the delicious stream from the oxygen tank that I had left in the car. I finally arrived, gasping and desperate after walking just half a block to my handicapped space in the parking lot. My heart was pounding, screaming at me for refusing to wear oxygen at work because I was too embarrassed. The nasal cannula felt like a long-lost friend, and I sipped the oxygen until my headache diminished and the fog in my head lifted. *Ah, relief.* I looked in the rearview mirror and saw blue-tinged lips. *I'm such a fucking masochist.*

I drove to my new apartment in Redwood City, sucking on a nebulizer in the car. At home, I slipped into my pajamas and crawled into bed. My body sank into the mattress, weighed down with fatigue. My eyes were heavy, and within minutes I drifted off.

The ringing of the phone woke me. I heard Isa's voice on my answering machine. "Ana, do you want dinner? I'm making *tonkatsu*. Give me a call . . ."

I reached for the phone. "Hi, Isa." I cleared my throat.

"Are you okay? Did I wake you?"

It was just our voices in a sea of darkness. "It's okay. I should get up. What time is it?"

"After seven. *Heiki*? You okay?"

"I'm so tired. I came home straight from work and went to bed." I could hear myself panting into the receiver.

"That's not right. I'm worried about you. Let me bring you dinner." By then, Isa had graduated from Berkeley and had moved with Andrew to the same apartment complex where I lived.

Later, as we devoured the fried pork and rice in my apartment, Isa started nagging.

"Ana, you should quit your job." She poured *natto* over her rice, our favorite side dish of fermented soybeans and green onions that resembled a slimy ball of goo and reeked of spoiled cheese. I found it delectable; it was one of the few foods I could still enjoy. When Isa served herself, the stringy beans separated, and threads of fermentation lingered in the air like spiderwebs.

"Don't start with your nagging," I glared.

"Look at you," she said. "You're breathing so hard. I can't believe you're still working. You're withering away." Her voice was reminiscent of Mama's. "If you quit your job, you can spend more time and energy taking care of yourself."

"It's not that easy. I don't have a rich fiancé to depend on," I snapped. "I have to work. How would I pay rent?" I took another bite of pork. It was hard to chew. I drank it down with an Ensure.

"There are options. Mama and Dad could help you. There's disability."

"I can't. That would be so pathetic." I slouched on my elbows.

My mind swarmed with worst-case scenarios. If I quit my job, I'd lose my health insurance. It would take months to get disability. I'd be forced to default on my loans. I'd have to leech off my parents.

Isa continued, "Why not? There are plenty of CF adults who rely on their parents, or on social security disability."

"I just couldn't do that. I can barely afford anything now, and getting disability would be worse." I was living the catch-22 of so many with CF and other chronic illnesses: caught between sacrificing one's health to remain independent and using up all of one's assets to qualify for a measly disability income that was barely sufficient to sustain oneself.

"Isa, work is all I have left that is normal. I need it to keep going." I was getting full, and it was hard to breathe.

Isa pointed her chopsticks at me. "You're doing exactly what Michael did." Michael, who also had CF, had refused to give up his job until it was too late. What a legacy, to be remembered after one died as someone who put work before health. People would talk: "If she just took better care of herself, if she just didn't take that trip, or didn't work so much, if she just wasn't so stubborn." Blah. Blah. Blah. I wanted to be remembered as someone who did everything right, and still, still, CF got the best of me.

I coughed.

"If lungs don't come by the summer, I'll reconsider," I said. "I promise . . ." I exhaled.

Isa was my conscience. She saw things that I didn't, and I trusted her judgment. It *was* getting harder to just get through a regular day, and I didn't know how much more of this I could take.

A few weeks later, I went out to dinner with my former CF camper. Amy was now a college freshman, and she was vibrant, energetic, and beaming with youthful beauty. She shared stories of her first year of college, her aspirations, and her new boyfriend. It was refreshing to see her doing so well. But I was ashamed to struggle just to show up and get enough air in the claustrophobic restaurant. *Look at me,* I thought. *I'm so sick, I can barely work; I'm waiting for a transplant, and I can barely eat.* I was no longer a role model and was merely setting an example of what lay ahead. Driving home, I sobbed. I had failed Amy.

While I waited for new lungs, I bargained with God: *If I get new lungs, I won't ever complain. I'll be the best person I can. I'll give back. I'll never take anything for granted.* I knew very well that I could die waiting for lungs. So I asked God to let me face death as boldly and courageously as Bob Flanagan had.

I put all my affairs in order in preparation for the sudden call for new lungs: a phone list of people to be notified, e-mail passwords shared among family members, and bank account access for Isa. I wrote instructions for my funeral, just in case. I checked my pager several times a day.

On hopeful days, I made lists of things to do after transplant: learn Spanish, take trapeze lessons, travel to Alaska. The prospect of life without CF, a new life, was visible in the distant horizon, and I was chasing it. I had to keep going.

Chapter 27

A Marriage Comes Full Circle

Isa

Andrew and Isa: It is a rare privilege to look into the eyes of a couple and know that when they promise to be together for better or for worse, that they have already begun the living of those vows. Through the challenges you have faced you have learned what many have yet to discover—that every moment of life is a cherished gift from God, not to be squandered but savored, slowly, deliberately, joyfully, thankfully. Your faithfulness to one another, your joy in the midst of adversity, your reconciliation in the midst of estrangement, your enduring hope—you, my friends, are the proclamation of God's enduring love.

—Rev. Maurice Charles, Stanford Memorial Church, June 27, 1998

Wedding planning dominated my last year in graduate school. My parents and I had no idea what an American wedding was like. Bridesmaids, "something borrowed, something blue," and a father-daughter dance were foreign to us.

Mama suggested, "Isa-chan, don't you think it would be nice for you to wear a kimono on your wedding day?" Her eyes lit up. "Mama has a wonderful idea. Why don't you have some *taiko* drumming at your reception?"

"Mama, that's embarrassing. I want a real American wedding. Nothing with token Japanese stuff. It's too exotic."

She kept her suggestions to herself after that.

My parents adored Andrew, and our wedding vibes rubbed off on them. They began to share nostalgic stories of their wedding. Mama even retrieved her wedding ring from the safety deposit box, had it resized, and wore it again, after almost twenty years.

Although Dad never wore his ring because he worked with electricity, he had become more affectionate with Mama. Mama and Dad seemed strangely content together. We even spotted Dad kissing Mama one night. It felt weird, but we were pleased. Dad summarized his marriage to Mama: "First she was cute. Then she was annoying. Now, she is cute again." They were far from romantic, but the years of animosity had faded, and their union had transformed into a committed friendship.

Six months before the wedding, Andrew's parents came to Los Angeles to meet my parents. My mother prepared a gorgeous Japanese feast, trying to impress the future relatives. Amid cocktails and hors d'oeuvres, the Byrnes and Stenzel parents eagerly discussed the upcoming wedding and chatted about their own wedding days. Dad and Mr. Byrnes talked about their university careers while Mama and Mrs. Byrnes talked about the dresses they would wear to the wedding.

During the meal, Mama received a phone call. I couldn't hear what she said, but I noticed that her tone became serious.

"Is everything okay?" I asked, when she returned to the dining room.

Mama smoothed out her black silk skirt as she sat down, glancing at the Byrneses.

"Yes, it was nothing," she dismissed, and our lighthearted discussion continued.

After Andrew and his parents left for the evening, Mama told us the truth. "That phone call was my doctor. He said Mama's routine blood count came back low, and another test may be positive for colon cancer."

"What? Cancer?" A wave of panic spread over me. How could she hide this through dinner?

"How can they be sure?" Dad asked, his eyes wide.

"They are not. I will have to go to Kaiser tomorrow for more tests. Let us not worry about it now," she said, but from the expression on her face, I sensed her anxiety.

That night, I lay in bed thinking the worst. I could not imagine life without Mama.

The following week I returned to Redwood City and received updates from Mama by phone. Numerous procedures confirmed that Mama had stage 3 colon cancer. She was scheduled for surgery and chemotherapy that was to finish a few weeks before the wedding.

Mama's illness came as a complete surprise. Ana and I had been so self-absorbed with our health that we had never thought of our parents' mortality. They were always the caregivers, strong and invincible. An unexpected curse of our longer lives was witnessing our parents age and suffer their own health problems. We weren't supposed to outlive our parents; Mama's cancer was a stark reminder that we might.

A few months earlier, Ryuta had returned from Japan to start business school at nearby Pepperdine University. He was living at home again and helped care for Mama.

"I have faith Mama will be fine," I told Ryuta. "She's strong. She'll get through this."

"You didn't see her all shriveled up in bed and weak after her surgery." Ryuta's voice was shaky. I had never seen him so concerned. "She looked like hell."

My parents' marriage had its cracks, but they certainly upheld their marriage vows when it came to supporting each other "in sickness and in health." Mama's illness crushed her fierce independence. When she was too weak to cook or run errands, Dad learned to appreciate how much she did and that he needed her, too. It was good they hadn't divorced. My parents relied on each other during this vulnerable time as they had for years during our health crises.

A few months into her treatment, I visited Los Angeles again and accompanied Mama to a cancer support group. Mama's wrinkled face was dry and her lips chapped from the chemotherapy. Despite her expensive black wig, she looked like she had aged a decade. Adults, old and young, sat around the table crying about their fears surrounding their diagnoses. Mama, never hesitant about disregarding my privacy, spoke up, "This is my daughter, Isabel. She and her sister have cystic fibrosis. I have been around illness their whole lives so this is nothing new to me. It is just part of life."

On June 27, 1998, Andrew and I married. After eighteen months of detailed planning and tension with Ana, fairy tales and Disney magic could not compete with the glorious perfection of my wedding day. Mama had finished her chemotherapy, and her recovery was going smoothly. Ryuta was a loving, proud groomsman. Dad overcame his social anxiety to give a short but warm speech welcoming the guests. My Uncle Jürgen gave a drawn-out but touching speech about Oma and Opa's wedding on June 27, exactly sixty-two years earlier. Obachan was healthy enough to travel from her new residence in Hawaii with Uncle Juichi to attend. The whole family was together.

Most important, Ana had found Rob, making her adjustment to my marriage much smoother. She had agreed to be my maid of honor. She had not been called for her transplant, something I had selfishly feared would steal the show. I was relieved.

At the reception, Mama approached and hugged me. "Isa-chan, this wedding is not only a celebration of your commitment to Andrew but also a celebration of your life."

She was so right. I had made it to adulthood.

I reflected on all those prayers that I had made growing up: the wishes that I had made every time I blew out the candles on my birthday cake (they were, in fact, double wishes because I knew Ana made the same ones); the wishes that I had made when I spotted the first star at night, when I broke a wishbone, or when I dropped a shiny penny into a well; all I ever wished for was a cure for CF, so I could live a long life. The wishes continued with each passing birthday cake until, around my twenty-fifth birthday, I realized the number of candles could barely fit on my cake, and it hit me; I was *living the cure*. My wedding day validated that even more. The cure wasn't something on the horizon, way off into the distance. It wasn't something that I would always be reaching for, desperately trying to grab. The cure was happening *right now*.

Chapter 28

Giving Back

Isa

The emotional sensitivity and understanding I have gained from my involvement with the CF community enables me to openly and compassionately discuss delicate issues such as mortality, self-esteem and quality of life. . . . I've learned how a negative aspect of one's life, namely, illness, can be channeled into a positive attribute if appropriate support and coping mechanisms are provided. The lessons I have learned have given me a strong will to share this philosophy as a practicing social worker.

—Isa, graduate school application, age twenty-two

I chose to pursue social work because, through the years, my emotional resilience and the support system of family and friends were my primary sources of strength to deal with my illness. While I couldn't always control CF, I could control who was around me and my attitudes about coping with CF. I wanted to help families who had children with serious medical problems, so I found a part-time job at the same children's hospital where Ana was working. Even as professionals, we seemed to follow each other.

On my first day, the inevitable happened.

"Hi, Ana," a stranger in a white coat greeted me as we passed in the hall.

"I'm not Ana, I'm her twin sister, Isabel," I corrected.

"Oh, my God," the coworker exclaimed, laughing loudly, "you guys look exactly alike! How cute! And you both work here?"

Another time, I entered an exam room to meet young parents with a medically fragile newborn. "Hi, my name is Isabel, and I'm a social worker."

"Wait . . ." the mother paused awkwardly. "You look just like the genetic counselor we saw when I was pregnant. I thought your name was . . . was it Ana?" Once more, I explained myself. I hadn't anticipated that Ana would meet the families before birth, and I would see them after birth!

In my role, I met with families and conducted psychosocial assessments, asking about how they were coping with their ill child, whether they had social support, what their financial and practical resources were, and whether they had a strong marital relationship. I made sure families had access to resources such as transportation, health insurance, community agencies, and disability programs. I conducted support groups for parents and chronically ill teens.

At work, I could escape my health problems and try to give back to others. But work was emotionally draining. Being a social worker meant getting used to feeling helpless. On a single day, I might be referred to an abused child, a mother on the verge of eviction from her home, a child whose condition had worsened so that a discussion of hospice was in order, and an illegal immigrant who needed cash assistance. I was constantly reminded of how comparatively easy our family had it. As a social worker I was a mere speck in a large bureaucracy, and often I could do little to "fix" a family's problems. I had to find contentment providing help in little ways: a phone number to a mother's club, a letter to an employer, a bag of donated baby clothing, or a meal ticket for the cafeteria.

I spent my first three years at work trying to keep my two lives separate. I wanted to tell patients and colleagues that I had CF and genuinely understood life with a chronic disease, but professional distance kept me from disclosing my situation. I also feared being taken less seriously or being pitied by my colleagues. I didn't want to be known as "the social worker with CF."

During my first year at the children's hospital, I started to receive my care at its world-renowned CF Care Center, courtesy of Andrew's health insurance. Sometimes, my CF doctor would catch me in the halls talking to a colleague or family member and stop to say, "Hi! How are you feeling? Are the new meds working?" I would smile awkwardly and meekly reply, "Yeah, I'm doing fine. See you later," and continue with my conversation, hoping no one would decipher the exchange.

On one occasion, I visited a depressed teenager with severe arthritis to ask about resources. In the middle of our conversation, her roommate exclaimed, "Hey! I know you! Don't you have CF?"

I stopped and responded, "Yeah, I do," and continued questioning my patient.

After I finished the assessment, I left the bedside of my patient and approached the roommate. I asked, "How do you know me?"

She said, "I remember you from CF camp! I'm Diane."

My mind flashed back to CF camp in the early nineties. I remembered Diane as a quiet preteen. I hardly recognized her. She was now a bright, chubby adolescent with braces. We talked for a while and reminisced about camp friends. As we spoke, I imagined a spotlight focusing on me. *What will my patient think about my having CF? Will she tell anyone?* It occurred to me how silly I was to assume that those around me knew or cared about my secret life. The girl with arthritis remained motionless in her bed, absorbed by her own misery. Why would she care about my fears?

Sometimes, I provided one-on-one counseling to patients who were having difficulties adjusting to their illnesses.

"I just want to be normal!" a teenager with lupus confessed to me during her dialysis treatment. "Like you!"

"I know, I know." If only she knew.

Through the years, I felt the intense demands of my job slowly sapping my energy. My lung infections, which occurred more frequently now, correlated directly with my level of exhaustion. I had initially worked four days a week; then I cut back to three, but my health still fluctuated like a roller coaster. I struggled to squeeze in time at work to eat lunch, let alone do a nebulizer treatment in the bathroom or flush my IV line. After home IVs, I usually felt much better and energized, but several months later, I would find myself again exhausted and needing another round of antibiotics. I often postponed IVs because of my work schedule. All other aspects of my life—my social life, CF community commitments, exercise, cooking, cleaning, and recreation—became an effort.

Finally, I approached my boss. "I need to reduce my hours," I confessed. "I'd like to work twenty hours a week."

"Have you ever thought about vocational rehabilitation?" he asked. Vocational rehab was a program for disabled people who needed help finding jobs.

My face flushed. "I am your colleague, not your client," I said. "I have a job, I just need some accommodation."

That night, I lay over a pile of pillows waiting for Andrew to give me therapy. My body ached. I felt thoroughly depleted.

"Ready for your beating?" he chimed as he sat down.

I moaned. "I'm so exhausted. . . . Why am I so weak?"

He began his rhythmic pounding. "You're tired, sweetheart. Work is too much."

"Do you think I should quit?"

"I think it's getting too much for you. If you want to quit, you can. I mean, we can manage financially."

"But I don't want to let my colleagues down."

"Don't worry about them. Do what's right for you."

I let out a deep sigh. "All I want is to be normal. . . . But what if work keeps me going? I'm so pathetic. I can't believe I had four years of graduate school and I can barely work for three . . . what a waste of a higher education."

"Love," Andrew stopped pounding and looked me in the eye, "don't beat yourself up! There's nothing more important than you taking care of yourself. You didn't waste your education. Maybe there's something else you can do that's less taxing." Andrew's reinforcement stopped my moping, at least for the moment.

All the signs told me to slow down, but I was determined to prove to myself and to others that I could be a functional, normal professional despite having CF.

Chapter 29

A Day of Intensity

Isa

To all donors and their families, everywhere. Past, present and future. We give thanks.

—Letter to Ana and Isa from Nahara Mau, CF adult, age forty-four

The door swung wide open in the darkness. "You guys! Wake up!" a deep voice yelled from the doorway. My pulse leapt into high gear, and I opened my eyes to see Andrew kicking the covers off and screaming, thinking it was a burglar.

"Andrew!" I yelled at him. "It's just Rob!"

"Get up. Ana got called." Rob's voice was quivering but composed.

"Oh my God, oh my God," I said, running over to him. It had been a terribly hot night, and Andrew and I had left the windows open and worn only our underwear in an attempt to stay cool. I clutched my blanket to my chest. "Is this it? Is this really it?" Rob and I hugged, and I felt his large smooth hands against the skin of my back.

It was 4:30 in the morning on June 14, 2000. Right at the starting line of the twenty-first century. Right in the middle of the year. Right during the longest and hottest days of the summer.

Rob rambled on about the drama of the last hour. The transplant surgeons had tried in vain to reach Ana by phone at her home. Then they had tried her pager, which lay at the bottom of her backpack accidentally set to "vibrate" mode. Next, the surgeons had sent the police to Ana's apartment, but when she did not answer the door, the police had left a note. Finally, the doctors called Rob's apartment, where Ana was spending the night. When Rob picked up the phone, he heard, "Hi, this is Dr. Reitz. We're looking for Ana." And he knew. It was time.

I threw on clothes and ran downstairs. The predawn air was heavy and warm, approaching 80 degrees even before the sun rose. It was a saving grace to live in the same apartment complex. Ana had just hopped out of the shower.

"I'm so ready! I'm so ready!" she said, ecstatic.

She was dancing around the living room without her oxygen, thrilled by the perfect timing of the call. I laughed at her joy.

"Are you sure you need a transplant?" I joked, amazed by her sudden burst of energy.

I called Mama and Dad.

It was nearly 5 A.M., and Mama's voice was hoarse and sleepy. "Halo?"

"Mama, it's me, Isa." After so many years of waiting to deliver this message, I broke down. I said, "Mama, Ana got called for her transplant. This is it. She needs to go to Stanford right away."

"Oh, my goodness." She paused. "Why are you crying?"

"Because, because I'm . . . scared."

"Isa-chan," she comforted in a steady voice, "you know there is nothing you can do now. It is out of your control. Do not be afraid. You must be strong."

Her confidence and composure amazed me. She was right; I needed to pull myself together. I needed to support Ana.

Ana and Rob drove to Stanford minutes later, and Andrew and I stayed to finish my therapy. Mama and Dad immediately gathered what they would need and left Los Angeles by car. Andrew and I arrived over an hour later at the ambulatory treatment unit, where Ana received an X-ray and blood tests in preparation for surgery. Then she had to wait all morning to see if the donor's lungs were in good condition for transplantation.

As soon as the morning sun rose, it became apparent we were experiencing a heat wave. The television news report in Ana's room warned that temperature records were breaking all across California. God was sending all the universe's energy down to my sister.

Ana was calm. She lay on the gurney, wearing her oxygen nasal cannula and smiling contently. "I am so ready for this. I am totally alright with my decision." Her shoulders jutted out from her loose hospital gown, and they bounced with her rapid breaths. Her cheekbones and chin seemed too sharp for her face. All the signs made it clear that the timing was right.

Why was I so terrified? I was so much healthier physically, yet inside I felt tremendously fragile and needy. Rob obviously felt the same way. He sat next to her dressed in baggy shorts and a worn T-shirt that read *No Fear*. His tense face nestled next to Ana's as he whispered soothing words.

Rob, Ana, and I prayed. *Please, God, please let this be the real thing, and not a "dry run"* (where the lungs end up being damaged and cannot be transplanted). *Please let Ana accept the lungs and be strong.*

I laid my hands on her chest, feeling her warmth. "*Yokunare, yokunare.* Heal. Heal." I chanted.

Time crawled as we waited, and each passing hour seemed like a lifetime. After lunchtime, Andrew had to go to work. He hugged and kissed Ana, wishing her well. "Be strong," he told me before leaving.

We were told that the lungs had been recovered from a male donor in his late twenties in Oregon, flown to a local military base, and brought by ambulance to Stanford.

"Are you sure they won't spoil in this heat wave?" I asked the surgeon.

"They are packed carefully on ice," he reassured me.

There was so much to worry about. The nurses at Stanford were on strike. I wondered if the scab nurses knew how to handle transplant patients.

Ana was finally wheeled into the operating room at 2:30 P.M. She received a narcotic to sedate her and began to laugh hysterically as the operating room doors opened. Rob and I were left behind, hugging each other, crying, fearing what might happen.

Just as we left pre-op, Mama and Dad ran up to the doors. Mama's face was bright red, her wiry hair tangled in an unruly mess. Her right arm was badly sunburned. Dad looked just as overheated. *Great,* I thought. *The only parents in the world who would drive through California's Central Valley on the hottest day of the year in a car without air conditioning.* We asked a nurse if they could see Ana quickly, but it was too late.

"Then tell her for us, *gambatte!* Endure!" Dad called to the nurse, and she agreed to do so.

Now the real waiting began. After a quick late lunch, I hurried to my office, where I was to lead a childhood chronic illness workshop that evening. The ovenlike heat was excruciating. It was 111 degrees in Redwood City. I prayed that God would infuse my anxious mind and exhausted body with some of the sun's energy, but the heat drained me even more. I had spent eight months preparing for the seven-week-long workshop starting that night. I conducted the opening session frazzled and distracted. Afterward, I rushed to the intensive care waiting room and met my family. It was 10:30 P.M. I had been up for sixteen hours.

"Did it happen? Did she actually have the surgery?" I asked Mama and Rob.

"The surgeon said one lung is in already," they replied.

Wow. *This is really it!*

Just then, Ryuta arrived. He had flown up from Los Angeles, where he was working in marketing for a clothing company. He carried a tray full of food from the cafeteria.

"Alright!" He beamed. "Let's party. Hot dog, anyone?"

Andrew had also arrived from work, and we did therapy in the empty waiting room. Around midnight, the surgeon came out and announced that Ana was out of surgery and doing well. She had endured a lot of bleeding as they removed her scarred lungs, and she was critical but otherwise stable. We could see her.

I was terrified of spreading my germs to Ana. We had discussed with the doctors our need to be separated initially because of Ana's severely immune-compromised state. Like most advanced CF patients, I was growing three strains of multidrug-resistant *pseudomonas aeruginosa* and the fungus *aspergillus* in my lungs. In other words, I was a walking biological threat to Ana. If I ever spread these bugs to Ana and she died, I could never live with the guilt. We had agreed to avoid all physical contact in the first several months after transplant.

But now that Ana had survived the surgery, I wanted to see her. I needed to see her. With the doctor's permission, I washed up, gloved and masked myself, and walked into her room.

She lay on a raised bed, ghostly white. The ventilator was breathing for her, slowly and steadily. She seemed comfortable but artificially sustained. Her eyes were slightly open, but she was totally unconscious. There were two IV poles bearing at least two dozen bottles and bags, all infusing tubes into various lines in her arms and neck. A nurse sat at a computer with a spreadsheet open on the screen, organizing Ana's medication doses, times, and drug levels. Everything seemed terrifically complex.

All that buildup and the surgery, the hardest part, was over. My strong, strong sister. Her CF lungs were gone. The new, fresh, clean lungs were breathing inside her, giving her life. I held her foot. It was cold and paler than the sheets she lay on. I had a flashback of Karen, lying on her bed, her cold white foot sticking out of the sheets. "Stay strong, Ana. Hang in there. You did it." I wished she could hear me.

Andrew and I returned to our apartment at close to 1:00 in the morning. A gust of hot air welcomed us after the day's heat wave, a reminder of the poor insulation on the second floor. Our indoor thermometer read 105 degrees.

As I nestled my weary, overheated body into bed, the chest pain started. I felt a tightness at first, then a dull ache. I first attributed this to anxiety, but it persisted all night. *Dear God,* I prayed, *heal Ana's chest. I feel her pain. Let me breathe deeply for her.*

I spoke to Ana: *Ana, please be strong. You can pull through this. We can get through this together.*

My mind raced as I rubbed my chest. I hurt as she hurt.

Chapter 30

Wings of a Butterfly

Ana

My heart pounds softly
As the new lungs within
Breathe easily
Expanding like the wings of a butterfly
Having escaped the surroundings
Of an old rusty cocoon.
The lungs are fragile yet safe
Within my chest
I have survived.

—Ana, age twenty-eight

I awoke in a strange delirium, free of pain. I felt like I was floating underwater in a pool, hearing muffled voices from above.

So this is it. It's done. I've got my new lungs. I'm alive!

The mechanical breathing of a ventilator interrupted my sigh of relief. I gagged on the tube in my throat, coughing. My body was immobilized, tied down by tubes and wires emanating from every orifice. I was hot and sweating profusely; only a light cotton hospital gown loosely covered my torso. Beeping, slurping, and buzzing machines surrounded me. Weakly, I opened my eyes and squinted against blinding white light.

Is this Heaven?

I motioned for a pen and paper with my left hand, the hand free of IV tubing, the pulse oximeter, and arterial blood-gas lines. *Take it out, please,* I scribbled illegibly, as I was normally right-handed. *I can't breathe.*

The nurse said something I couldn't comprehend.

I blacked out again, freed by the sedation of morphine. I awoke several more times, pulled to semiconsciousness by the sound of voices. I began to hallucinate, seeing scaled fish dancing on the white ceiling and hearing the southern drawl of the traveling nurse at my bedside. "Anabel, can ya' move yo' toes?" Suddenly, I thought I was in Savannah, Georgia, and the Civil War had just ended. My thoughts were jumbled, delirious. *Where am I? What day is it?*

I blacked out.

A while later I awoke to the familiar sound of my parents' voices: a soothing German accent harmonizing somehow with a high-pitched Japanese screech. I couldn't understand them. I stared at my father, absorbing his tanned features and his sandy brown hair, wispy over his forehead. Our eyes met.

Later, I felt Rob's soft hands. I saw his blurred outline beside my bed. With a trembling hand I wrote, "Sorry I look like shit. Thank you for coming."

My arm reached across my chest, caressing the bulky bandage that cradled my breasts like a strapless bra. I needed to feel the proof that the surgery was over. *Oh, my God. There are a dead man's lungs inside of me.*

I gasped. The heart monitor above my bed beeped. My family hovered over my bed, celebrating this gift of life, while another family, somewhere far away, hovered over the corpse of their dead son. I imagined them grieving, desperate, torn up inside, yet so generous. That was too much to think about right now.

I blacked out again.

I had heard stories about the "Great Awakening," that first deep breath of fresh air after a transplant, as if one were coming up for air after a deep-sea dive. But my first breath off the ventilator hours after surgery told me this "rebirth" would not be easy. Deflated during their trip from Oregon, my new lungs expanded slowly, like a butterfly's wings emerging from a rusty old cocoon. I lay there more breathless than ever. I imagined these foreign lungs—delicate, unsettled, hanging loosely off the stitches that bound them to my trachea. *Are these lungs really working? How do I use them? Breathe, just breathe. It's going to get better.*

One night in the intensive care unit, I bolted up into a sitting position. My chest burned as I strained my incision. I had yanked on the chest tubes that carried oozing blood from the stitches. Various machines beeped unhappily at my abrupt movement. I cried out, "I can't breathe! I can't breathe! Help!" I was hyperventilating, tears streaming down my cheeks.

The nurse approached my bedside. She rubbed my back. "You're alright. It's okay. Just calm down. One breath at a time. Slowly . . . slowly . . ." A psych consult, a panic-attack diagnosis, and a dose of Ativan later, I was composed.

I donated my old CF lungs to the laboratory of Dr. Jeff Wine, a renowned CF researcher at Stanford whom I had the privilege of knowing throughout my undergraduate years and from CFRI. The lungs were a mass of sickness, blackened and hardened by scar tissue. The trachea had expanded to three times the normal diameter with each desperate gulp of air. The lungs weighed over five pounds, filled with green pus and fluid. The graduate student who saw the specimen had to excuse himself, nauseated by the decrepit sight.

"How could anyone live with these?" Dr. Wine asked in disbelief. "Whoever received a transplant today was surely on her last breaths." A tag was stuck to the specimen.

He turned and read *Anabel Stenzel*; he gasped.

After three long years on the waiting list, I could finally feel my donor's lungs settling into my chest cavity. But now there was more waiting. Waiting for the lungs to expand. Waiting for the medications to do their thing. Waiting for the scar to heal. To eat again. To walk again. To start living again.

After surgery, my body was racked by the effects of countless medications—painkillers, steroids, diuretics, and supplements—as well as by several blood transfusions. All of them caused relentless side effects. Anti-rejection medications suppressed my immune system so that it would not attack the foreign lungs. Antibiotics, antifungal, and antiviral medications minimized my chance of catching infections. Other medications acted as stimulants, leaving me feeling like bugs were crawling on my legs. I closed my eyes, trying to relax and accept whatever was to come my way, to envision the "big picture" reason for a transplant: to enjoy life.

Ironically, a great sadness consumed me. One night, at three in the morning, I began crying and couldn't stop. I cried and cried, my rib cage burning with each heaving sob. I cried over the tragedy of needing a transplant at twenty-eight just to live and over the exhausting battle I had fought to stay alive until I could get the transplant. I cried because my precious lungs had failed me and were gone forever. I also cried in gratitude that I had received this enormous gift, elated that I was guaranteed not to die from CF. And I cried because a young man had lost his life, and somewhere out there his family was crying, too. *Who was he? Does his spirit know his lungs are pulsating inside of me?* I closed my eyes, feeling his presence, and spoke to him. *I'm so sorry you died. Please know that I accept your gift. I will savor each breath. I will live for you if you allow me.*

My recovery in the hospital was uncomplicated. I was allowed to go home after only twelve days: the shortest hospital stay of my life. During the early weeks at home, everything felt new. Even showering felt different. My body felt cleansed as the warm water flowed over the broad scar. It was a beautiful scar, just a thin horizontal line shaped like a bra's underwire. My body felt fuller and heavier because of the fluid retention. For once, the contours of my body didn't feel emaciated. I was growing.

It's amazing what effect the antirejection medications had on me. I found it increasingly difficult to concentrate, as if my mind were underwater, murky and dense. I was absentminded and unable to participate in intellectual conversations. Cyclosporine, a powerful antirejection medication, caused excessive hair growth and oily skin, while prednisone, a steroid, caused my face to swell. My face seemed to change daily in the first few weeks. Dark hair the texture of peach fuzz grew on my nose, earlobes, and cheeks. My eyebrows became dark and bushy, forming a unibrow. The hair on my head became drier and thicker; one strand even formed a corkscrew curl that stuck out from my otherwise straight hair. Pimples erupted like bubbling lava from my oil-drenched skin.

I stood in front of the mirror one day, crying. Words from my genetics training flooded my mind: *cushingoid, dysmorphic, synophyrus.* "I look awful!"

Mama stood behind me. She had moved in for three months to serve as my caregiver. "Don't you worry about that. You don't look so bad. It's a small price to pay to be able to breathe."

Almost overnight, the disciplined medical regimen that had consumed my life with CF was over. No more daily therapy, washing nebulizers, or home IVs. Antibacterial products, disinfectants, masks, and gloves replaced the familiar tissue boxes, paper cups, and oxygen tubing. Now, I had no control. I was at the mercy of my own cellular mechanisms to reject this lung, to succumb to infections, or to develop cancer. For so long, the desire to preserve my body so that I could survive the transplant had fueled my passion for living. I had made it, and I was in a state of limbo wondering "What now?"

I was left with a feeling of emptiness, at a loss over what to do with all the spare time I had, time I had never had before. Too weak and disoriented to pursue any new hobbies or even read books, I fumbled for things to do, for a purpose, a reason to get up each morning. Being immunosuppressed, I was afraid to leave my home. Intense cravings for Mama's Japanese home cooking, combined with an enormous appetite caused by the prednisone, could not be satisfied because of a strict low-salt diet. I felt more restricted in this new life than in my former one.

The hardest adjustment after my transplant was the forced separation from Isa. We couldn't even touch each other and had to visit from a distance, wearing masks or seeing each other in open air outdoors.

"I miss you," I called, as I looked through my apartment window at Isa. She stood in front of me, outside, wearing an old CF camp T-shirt. I held my hand up to the glass. She held her hand up to the same place, and we each pressed against the glass. Tears welled up in my eyes.

Isa missed me too. It was hard to believe we would never do therapy for each other again. I asked her if this transplant was worthwhile if we couldn't be together. She reassured me that our separation was just for the first few months when I was the most susceptible. We didn't want to take any chances.

I stared at Isa. The image didn't look like me. "You look so beautiful, like the old me," I said. "We're no longer identical."

For the first time, we were living different lifestyles and taking different medications. Someone else's cells were inside of me. We breathed from genetically distinct lungs. *Were we still twins?*

A few months after my transplant, Ryuta moved to the Bay Area for work and became another caregiver. "C'mon, Ana!" he protested when I resisted going out for a hike. "What's your problem? You gotta get out and walk. It'll make you stronger." I was touched by his persistence. Several times a week, Ryuta dragged me out to local parks to hike, encouraging me to "snap out of it."

"One more mile," he'd say. "We're almost at the end."

"You sound like Dad," I would reply, huffing and puffing up a redwood-lined path. My lungs inhaled deeply, but the rest of my body trudged along.

Despite the support I received from my family, I felt disillusioned. Fatigue clouded my world. At times, I wanted to fall asleep and never wake up. There were days that I wished I could turn back the clock and have my old life back. *I should be happy that I received this gift,* I thought. *Why am I so miserable?*

"Your problem," Dr. Theodore told me, "is that you don't know how to be well because you never have been. You're just feeling sorry for yourself. You've got to get on with your life."

I resented his remarks. *Who the hell are you to say such things? How would you know?* I was determined to prove him wrong.

"Smile!" He hollered at me during another visit. "You have something to be happy about. You're doing great, physically, at least. You've just got posttransplant depression. Over 80 percent of our patients get it. Some of it is due to medication, and some of it is just because of what you've been through." He seemed nonchalant.

Depression? Is that what this is all about? Off I went to the psychiatrist for a prescription for Zoloft to add to the handful of pills I was taking twice a day. With the "happy pills" working on my brain chemistry, I found myself more motivated. My mind was emerging from the water.

Ten weeks after my transplant, I had built up enough strength to ride my bike for ten miles. Although my muscles burned with each stroke, the ability to exercise without coughing, gasping for air, or breathing from an oxygen tank was a grand novelty. I sailed through my first ride, holding my head up toward the sunshine. Insatiable, I gulped down the fresh summer air, feeling my lungs soak in air so deeply that it was filtering down to my toes. It was my first glimpse of joy in my posttransplant life.

After five months, I forced myself to return to work. My neurons had to rewire themselves for the intellectual detail that my job required.

Through the entire process, Rob's love for me shined. When I received the call that a donor's lungs were available, Rob cried like a baby, fearful that he would lose me. He gave me my last percussion treatment and drove me to the hospital. The touch of his soft lips on mine was the last thing I felt before I was wheeled into the operating room, giddy from sedation. I heard him whisper, "You're going to make it."

After my surgery, he stood at my bedside, encouraging me to breathe deeply, to take my first steps. He even washed my hair in the sink in the intensive care unit. He still told me I was beautiful. Rob encouraged me to smile, to exercise, to talk to him, when I was in the midst of the dark depression.

Now, I could work longer hours, go out with friends late into the night, and travel without Rob. I was no longer the weaker partner, fragile and dependent. I took charge of the home, the vacations, the social calendar. Instead of spending time in the hospital or doing therapy, we discovered hiking, biking, and jogging together. Best of all, we could now make love free from oxygen tubing, bleeding lungs, and coughing fits.

Rob took advantage of his extra time by completing a program in alcohol- and drug-addiction counseling; he started working as an adolescent recovery counselor. He acquired an admirable reputation at work and continued to advance his education. Even my mother finally acknowledged that Rob was exceptional.

A few months before our thirtieth birthday, Isa and I went camping with Andrew in a local state park. It was one of my favorite activities, although Isa's advancing CF meant that we were more encumbered by oxygen tanks and portable nebulizers. The enormous redwoods enveloped our campsite, the sweet scent of their branches made the air pure. The coastal fog was rolling in, bringing an unusual chill to the October evening. Our breath rose like floating smoke in the autumn darkness. Bundled in our winter coats, we sat on mats around the campfire. The flickering glow of the fire alternately illuminated and cast shadows on Isa's face. A few embers popped and floated into the sky, looking like fireflies.

I looked up, admiring the stars that glittered in the night sky.

"Wow. How beautiful," Isa said. I could hear her rapid, heavy breathing.

"Can you believe we're going to be thirty soon?" I asked.

"I can't . . . we made it to the twenty-first century." Isa put an arm around my shoulders. We had become comfortable enough to touch each other again. It was a risk worth taking.

She continued, "We're so lucky to still be together. We've lived eleven years longer than Karen. She'd be so impressed."

The bright moonlight turned the redwood trunks to silhouettes. I thought about the tension we had suffered in Berkeley and with Andrew. It had all worked out in the long run. So much worry, so much fear. And life just unfolded perfectly.

"At least you're reaching thirty on your own," I replied. "I've cheated with my new lungs. As far as CF statistics go, I'm dead. But you . . . you're still hanging in there with your nasty lungs. That's amazing."

"Please . . ." Isa rolled her eyes, "you've survived in your own way. Don't minimize that." She slapped at a mosquito on her leg.

The stars absorbed me. "We're only alive because we have each other. Think of all our friends who've died. They're somewhere up there, a star for each of them."

Mama used to say we were born under lucky stars. She was right. God had been good to us.

Later that evening, Isa went into her tent to do therapy. I heard the music of CF again: Andrew thumping Isa's back, the coughing, the sputter of inhalers, the hissing of the oxygen, reminding me how it took so much work, once upon a time, just to breathe. I sighed, in an effortless, comfortable exhalation. *Ah, breath.*

Our lives were so vastly different now. I pinched myself daily, wondering when I would awake from this magnificent dream. I was like a child in a candy store. I filled my days with bountiful energy to live hard—to see and do as much as I could to make up for lost time. I got more involved with Cystic Fibrosis Research, Inc. (CFRI). I became a volunteer for the California Transplant Donor Network (CTDN), the regional organ procurement center that coordinates transplants, to raise awareness for organ donation. I worked almost full-time and pulled myself out of the financial misery that had plagued me as a sick person.

One day I told Rob, "I'm going out with Michelle tomorrow. I have ballet class on Tuesday. On Saturday, I have a CFRI board meeting."

"Look at you go! The social butterfly. Did you ever think you'd have this much energy?" Rob celebrated. "But . . . when are we going to spend time together?"

Our time together was outdoors. With a lung capacity that surpassed 100 percent, I became like Dad and embraced the beauty of nature. Rob and I hiked the red rocks of the Arizona high desert against a backdrop of blue skies and swaying yellow aspen trees. We smelled the clear summer air of the Sierras at an elevation of ten thousand feet as we stood atop a mountain pass in Sequoia National Park. We felt the cool waters of a Northern California river, rafting down its rapids with my fellow transplanted CF friends. I blew soap bubbles for my donor from the top of Half Dome in Yosemite. With each adventure, these scenes overcame me; I wanted to hold onto every sight, sound, smell, and taste forever.

My overbooked calendar meant less time with Rob. We began to live parallel lives. CF had been the spark of our relationship; now that it had died, we needed new kindling to fuel the fire. Our love was being tested.

One day, I received an anonymous letter from my donor's family via CTDN. My donor was a young man named James who had passed away just short of his thirtieth birthday. His family told me a bit about him—he loved the outdoors, AC/DC, and pumpkin pie—and they told me they deeply loved and missed him. I never knew how he died, but that didn't really matter. I knew only that I had to live for him and to enjoy life that was cut short for him.

Another lung transplant recipient once said, "We are living on overtime." So, each extra day accompanied by good health warranted a celebration, an acceptance of whatever lie ahead. I drank the juices of life with such desperate thirst, knowing that posttransplant complications, now the second leading cause of death among CF patients, could extinguish my party at any time. When these lungs fail, there will be no more second chances, for retransplants of lungs are rare and usually unsuccessful. Having tasted normalcy, there will be more to lose then. Getting a transplant was the icing on my delicious cake of life. My fate had not changed; it had merely been postponed. My mantra became, "Today, I'm okay." I tried not to think about what could go wrong tomorrow. No regrets.

Chapter 31

It's My Turn

Isa

I'm almost thirty—and succeeding at survival—
. . . I'm almost ready if the end would come
To say I've lived an almost perfect life.
Almost.

—Isa, *www.thebreathingroom.org,* age twenty-nine

Within a few years after her transplant, Ana became the quintessence of health: she worked almost full-time, and she could run several miles, swim one hundred laps, and backpack over ten miles. She was even training for the United States Transplant Games scheduled for June 2002. The games were held every two years in which over twelve hundred transplant recipients competed in various sports. I couldn't believe she could swim and run without coughing. Our roles were reversed. She was the strong one who had to slow down for me to catch up with her when we hiked. She made meals for me when I had to nap. She had paid her dues, and I wanted more than anything for her to enjoy life.

"So when are you getting your transplant?" people would ask me, and I'd roll my eyes. My CF was progressing, but I was in no hurry to go through what Ana had. Besides, my life was full, and I didn't have time for a transplant.

Hyperbusyness was the cocaine of the twenty-first century, and we were addicted. Andrew worked sixty hours a week. I was working twenty-five hours a week, leading educational workshops, exercising, and volunteering compulsively for CFRI. The events of September 11, 2001, happened and shocked the nation. Our belief in the goodness of humanity was shattered, and we joined in the country's heightened sense of stress. Yet Ana and I admitted that finally ordinary people might confront their mortality and realize the preciousness of life. Despite the national turmoil, Andrew and I took advantage of an economic downturn in the Bay Area housing market and decided to buy a house in Redwood City. At the end of 2001, our otherwise restful weekends became packed with house-hunting, financial planning, and shopping for carpets and hardwood floors. Little did I know that amid our obsession with the house, life was slowing draining out of me.

On a chilly Saturday in January 2002, we returned home after signing papers at the title company. As I walked up the stairs, the gurgling began—another lung bleed. I knew this was a sign that I had overdone it. "I always bleed when I'm tired or stressed," I said to Andrew.

That night the bleeding continued. In forceful coughs, I filled one, then two five-ounce paper cups with blood.

The next day, I called the doctor.

"Come in right away. You'll be admitted through the Emergency Room."

"A little lung bleeding isn't a big deal. I can't afford to come into the hospital right now. We're moving in two weeks, and I have to go to Santa Cruz for work on Monday." I hung up and went on an evening walk with Ana.

That night, after several more heavy bleeds, I finally admitted to myself that it was time to take this seriously and surrender to the hospital. I hated letting my colleagues down and calling in sick, but I could not work with hemoptysis. I was a time bomb waiting to spew blood.

"Babe, you can go to work. I can drive myself to the hospital," I told Andrew the next morning.

"Don't be ridiculous, love. I'll drive you, I insist." He put on his trench coat and grabbed his keys.

The cool morning air felt refreshing as I walked to the car. As soon as I got into the passenger seat, though, a gushing force of salty liquid erupted from my mouth. Luckily, I had placed some paper cups in the cup holder and was able to spit into one. My chest rumbled loudly, and the pressure to cough overwhelmed me. Andrew quickly pulled into the street and drove.

"This is bad," I muttered between coughs as I filled one, then two, cups in less than a minute.

Andrew panicked and floored the accelerator.

"Andrew!" I screamed, "let's not get ourselves killed!" I didn't have time to put on my seatbelt, and the last thing I wanted was to die by flying through the windshield.

Suddenly, numbness engulfed my toes; the sensation crawled up my legs like spiders running over me. I remembered the feeling from over a decade ago during my last major bleed after Karen's death, when I had gone into shock.

"Andrew! I'm going numb!"

I placed a filled paper cup into the cup holder and grabbed another. I was drowning. I tore open my jacket because I had started to sweat profusely.

"Shock, Andrew!" I said, panicking. I couldn't breathe. I hurriedly rolled down the car window. I needed air. The cool wind felt good. As I poured more blood into another cup and yet another, my head seemed lighter and lighter. I spilled one of the cups, and Andrew reached back into the passenger section where I had left a jar of trail mix as a snack. He tore open the jar, and I spewed gelatinous blood over the trail mix, coating each nut and raisin in bright beautiful redness.

I couldn't move anymore. My arms were tingling, and I was fading. I glanced at Andrew, who was bent over the steering wheel crying hysterically. I could hear screeching tires and feel the rough motion of Andrew's driving. He was praying; it sounded like Hail Mary, but he wasn't even Catholic. He honked constantly, trying to get the cars in front of him to speed up or move out of the way.

My eyes closed. *Is this really how my life will end? What about the carpets? What about the furniture we just bought? Was I not meant to live in my new house?*

As I faded in and out, I countered those thoughts. *I'm not meant to die, yet. Please, Jesus, let me live.* I pleaded. *Keep me breathing.* I cultivated all my physical and spiritual strength to do one thing: breathe. I could no longer inhale to cough. I could only gasp.

I hung my arms and head out the window. I opened my eyes to see my blood-stained hands dangling over the car door. I gulped in the force of wind. I looked up and saw a bus driving alongside our car. *Are those passengers watching me die?* I thought. *Just keep breathing. Stay alive. Don't fall asleep. Breathe. Breathe.*

The car screeched to a stop, and I heard a door slam. Then I heard Andrew shrieking, "I need a doctor, quick! I need help! Please!"

I was pulled from the car and placed in a wheelchair. My body slumped like a rag doll. I had no control. I remember being wheeled briskly into the familiar trauma room, where I had worked a few shifts during my social work internship. I was lifted onto the gurney, and someone was tearing off my clothes, cutting apart the T-shirt I had received for completing two hundred Jazzercise classes.

"Oxygen!" I begged desperately.

A nurse put a large mask on my face, and immediately my vision cleared. The room was crowded with people, some working around me while others watched as if they were seeing a circus act.

The doctor tried to get me to lie down.

I protested, "Can't breathe!" My back arched and my shoulders lifted with every attempted breath.

"Miss," the doctor said gently, "we need to put a tube in your throat so you can breathe better."

I turned slightly toward him. "No!" I paused, gathering in air to speak. "No! . . . CFers die . . . CFers die . . . on vents!"

My mind had raced back to the memories of my CF friends who had spent their last days speechless and motionless on ventilators. Once an end-stage CF person is placed on a ventilator, there is little chance he or she can come off it. But then I thought of my other friends who had survived major bleeds and gotten off the ventilators when their bleeding had stopped.

The doctor calmly said, "We'll take good care of you. You are working too hard to breathe right now, and the ventilator will help you." I agreed. I turned to a nurse who was holding another mask, and after a few breaths, I was out.

Later I found out that I had thrashed and coughed violently during the intubation, spraying blood all over. The team had suctioned a large amount of blood out of my lungs. Once on a ventilator, I was sent for a CT scan to identify the areas of the lung that had been bleeding and finally to surgery for a bronchial arterial embolization (BAE), which involves entering the arteries through a catheter in the groin and inserting small plastic plugs to block off the fragile bleeding arteries. I had five BAE plugs placed in my lungs.

Back in the ER, Andrew was an emotional wreck. He collapsed, sobbing and screaming, believing that I had died. The ER social worker quickly isolated him, and he spent the next hours raw and tearful. The social worker called Ana at work, and she immediately came to support Andrew and get an update on my condition.

"She'll be all right, Andrew. She's strong, a survivor. I can feel it," she told him.

Hours later, I woke up in the intensive care unit. I had no concept of time or where I had been. I could hear the pumping and beeping of the ventilator. I lifted my hands and saw the dried blood caked on them. I looked up and saw several bags of blood. *Wow, my first transfusion. Cool!*

Two nurses stood at the doorway of my room chatting.

"Did you see *A Beautiful Mind*?"

"No, Alan and I are going to see it this weekend."

"Oh, it was amazing. Russell Crowe was powerful."

Such vast irrelevance. If I had died, the world would have gone on without me. Movies would have been made, people would have seen them and continued on with their routine lives.

Later, Ana and Andrew visited. Ana wore a mask to protect herself from hospital germs. I signaled for paper and a pen and scribbled, "Did I almost not make it?"

Andrew, tearful and pale, said, "I was so scared, baby, at how close it was."

He was getting queasy and had to step out of the room, and Ana and the ICU doctor explained to me about my procedures. That night, Ryuta visited me, and I wrote to him, "Can you bring me doughnuts?" Within an hour, I had a bag of doughnuts on my table, even though I couldn't eat them. He told me he had washed my car. *My brother had washed my car!* Though grateful, I pitied him for having to see the mess.

The following day, Mama, Dad, and Andrew's parents flew in to be with me. The ventilator was removed, and I moved out of the intensive care unit into the regular CF ward. It was January 8, 2002, my thirtieth birthday. Hallelujah. I had made it to thirty. Barely.

I had lost 10 percent of my lung capacity, and the embolizations impaired my oxygen absorption. I needed supplemental oxygen twenty-four hours a day, at a flow rate of up to seven liters per minute. The bleeding stubbornly persisted, and I underwent another round of BAEs. I received steroids to decrease the inflammation in my lungs, which gave me diabetes, a common problem in adults with CF. After two months in the hospital, I had to quit my job.

When I was finally discharged, Andrew drove me to our new home. As he opened the door and I crossed the threshold, I saw that the house was in disarray with boxes stacked everywhere and furniture placed randomly. In the corner of the living room stood our newest furniture, two large liquid-oxygen tanks reminiscent of R2D2. I unplugged the tubing from my portable tank and hooked myself up to them.

"I'm so glad I survived to enjoy these new hardwood floors!" I told Andrew, as I inhaled the smell of fresh polyurethane. I walked through the halls, dragging my fifty-foot oxygen tubing behind me and enjoying the freedom of being home.

I began my thirties rehabilitating, getting myself on the lung transplant list, and organizing and decorating our new home. I also started the humiliating task of applying for disability and filling out the paperwork to discharge my federal student loans due to total and permanent disability. I had robbed Uncle Sam.

"Do you have your cell phone? How full is your oxygen tank?" Andrew would ask as I left the home for errands. He routinely shot up at night when I coughed, asking, "Are you okay, are you bleeding?"

One night, Andrew spontaneously started crying. "I just don't want to lose you," he said.

I embraced him. "I don't want to leave you, either," I said. "I'm so sorry to put you through this."

Andrew held on to me tightly, as if he were cupping a flickering flame in the wind. "I love you."

"I love you, too."

We told each other this more and more, as if to remind ourselves that we were still together.

I began to live as an end-stage CF patient, like Ana had lived two years earlier before her transplant. I slept ten to fourteen hours a day. I spent five hours a day on therapy. I lugged my oxygen tank to Jazzercise, my aerobics class, where I yanked on the cord with each vigorous dance move like a stubborn dog pulling at a leash. Exercise was torture, but with oxygen I could maintain a certain level of fitness that I would need for the lung transplant. The oxygen became an umbilical cord that nourished me, a security blanket that would save me if I bled again. When I felt well, I removed my oxygen, but it was never far from my side; I was like a toddler testing her independence from her mother. I tried to stay active and volunteered to walk dogs at a local animal shelter. I soon found a beloved basset mix and adopted her as a much-needed companion. As I walked my dog, my oxygen walked me.

For years, I had feared becoming unproductive and dependent on Andrew. But my expected feelings of loss and shameful surrender over quitting work did not lead me to depression. Rather, I accepted that I had fought all I could and had pushed myself against the odds to live a full, normal life. I would never be a powerful career woman, or a mother of six, or change the world. But at thirty, I reflected on my childhood experiences—life at Kaiser, CF camps, T-shirt painting, Stanford, Japan, marriage, and social work—and I felt satisfied. With the little energy I had, I enrolled in writing classes and began my lifelong quest to write a memoir with Ana. This project provided an opportunity for life review, a highly therapeutic exercise that gave me purpose and perspective. My life had been full of quality and meaning, and I had no regrets.

CF had been my teacher, my source of self-love and reflection. It made me proud to be different but not too different. CF cultivated my faith in God

and my love and compassion for others. As my body had slowly suc-
cumbed to disease over the years, my spirit had grown stronger, wiser, and
more capable of higher forms of strength.

Six months after my lung bleed, Obachan decided to visit our new home
for a week. "This is my last trip to the mainland," she said. "It is getting too
difficult to travel." In her late eighties, she had even given up trips to Japan
and settled into a simple routine living with Uncle Juichi in Hawaii. Spending time with my grandmother was a unforeseen benefit of being on disability. We talked about the simple pleasures of natural beauty, kind
friends, and good food. Like me, she never took health for granted.

As Obachan and I sat on my couch, I compared my body to hers. My skin
was smooth and tanned, and apart from my rapid breathing, I was a picture of health. Yet, Obachan and I were united by a common struggle: our
bodies were slowly withering away.

Obachan sagged everywhere. Her eyes, dulled over the years, were sunken
behind thinned eyelids. I held her wrinkled hand, admiring her loose *mochi*
skin, so pliable that I could pinch and play with the peaks and valleys.

In broken Japanese, we talked openly about death.

"*Yappari* (overall), I am ready to go to Heaven," she said, adjusting herself on the couch. Her thin legs, on which the skin clung to the bones, were
tucked under her. Her little round belly protruded, a reminder of way too
many Bud Lights and nightly shots of whiskey and sake.

"Are you sure?"

"I have lived long enough. Almost ninety years! I just wish for a quick
death. I don't want to be on a machine for months, with tubes coming out
of me and suffering. Too many friends have died that way."

"I agree. Sometimes, I feel like my life is complete, and it would be okay
if I died too," I confessed.

"Don't you say that! You are too young. I pray every day to God that you
and Ana-chan stay healthy and have a long life."

"Thank you, Obachan . . . I am glad you are still with us. You are lucky
to have such a long life." I looked at her intently. "But . . . aren't you afraid
to die?"

She smiled. "Not at this age. I have escaped death many times, so when
it happens finally, I will have no fear."

She leaned back, sinking deeper into the sofa cushions. Looking outside,
she continued, "I remember one time when I really was afraid of death. We
were in Korea, waiting for the Japanese ships to take us back home after the
war ended. The Russian soldiers broke into the boarding home where we
Japanese refugees were living. I could hear the screams of women next door

as they were raped by the soldiers. I knew they would come for me next. I put on my best kimono so that if I was raped or killed, at least I would die in my best clothing." She spoke like the event had occurred just yesterday.

"Then, a Russian soldier kicked down the door, waking the children. Your mother and uncles ran to me and clung to my side, crying in fear. The soldier stared at me and the children. I was so afraid to die at that moment, but mostly because I didn't want my children to be left alone."

She continued, "My neighbor entered the room and stood between the Russian soldier and me. She said, 'Take me, instead!' He grabbed her. I still remember her eyes looking at me as the soldier pulled her downstairs. I wonder what ever happened to her. God saved me at that moment. When I married, my husband said his only wish was that I outlive him. And here I am." She sighed. "I don't know why I am so lucky. Sometimes, I can't believe I'm still alive to see your beautiful smile!" She reached over to pat my cheeks, and I blushed.

"Me, too! What an amazing story. You have been through so much. You have strong genes to live through those times. And you've given them to us to survive with CF," I said. "We both understand death, Obachan."

"Yes, I have been to many of my friends' funerals. And so have you. It is not easy to be the one left behind."

"Just promise me, Obachan, that you'll stay healthy if I stay healthy. *Yubikiri.*" I reached over to her hand and linked my pinkie with hers in a twist. This was a solemn promise.

I looked out into the garden. In the corner, between the young Japanese persimmon and the flowering cherry trees, stood the *Lindenbaum,* or linden tree. Its lime-colored leaves hung low in the summer heat. I had planted a cutting taken from my parents' tree, which, in turn, had come from Oma's tree in Bremen. Hers came from a tree at the home of my great-great-grandmother in Berlin. It is a family heirloom, a constant reminder of my German roots.

I reflected on the struggles of my grandparents and parents. The physical strength it had taken to survive the war amazed me, but I was more moved by the emotional strength they had shown in persevering, rebuilding their lives, and going on. As immigrants, my parents endured alienation from their families and isolation in a new foreign land. They were given sick children and did their best to raise them.

Neither my grandparents nor my parents dwelled on their struggles. They had no Prozac or Valium to help them cope. Rather, they relied on pure human resilience to get through their difficulties. My family culture rested on *gaman,* the ability to endure challenges. The tools to do this had been passed down through the generations: *Mobilize support. Rely on each other. Strengthen the family bond despite relationship strife. Stay positive. Ask for help. Focus on productive projects. Work hard. Enjoy life. Be kind to others in need.* Compared to those of many, my life had been easy. I had been blessed with a stable family and a comfortable financial situation in a free country, where I had equal opportunities to those around me. My only struggle was my health and the fear of impending death.

In my fight against CF, hope became my ultimate motivation. Perhaps that was what had gotten my grandparents through the darkest hours of World War II. Hope had also enabled my parents to start a new life in America. Hope had sustained their optimism that our family would remain intact and their children would survive. And now hope gave me visions of growing old with Andrew and leading a more active, better life after transplant.

The time had come to be evaluated for a lung transplant. I felt a strange *déjà vu*. I had been through this process with Ana six years earlier, but this time, it was all about me.

I told Andrew, "I refuse to do what Ana did and work myself to the ground waiting for a transplant." Months after quitting my job, I continued to rationalize my decision.

"I don't want you to do that either. In many ways, having the lung bleed was a blessing because it forced you to quit work." He was right. I was so stubborn; only something dramatic could make me stop pushing myself.

My health stabilized in the year after my bleed. Coordinating insurance approval and medical testing slowed the process of getting listed for a transplant. But I felt stronger and had no sense of urgency to speed it up. In the spring of 2003, a year after I had started the process, the Stanford Transplant Program accepted me as a candidate.

My lung function was around 45 percent of normal, on the higher end for those pursuing a lung transplant.

"My numbers are so good, I don't think I'm ready for one," I told my new doctor at my next clinic visit. Dr. Noreen Henig was a CF-adult physician who conveyed expertise in a warm but firm manner.

She tucked her curly red hair behind her ears. "We look at much more than just your numbers to decide whether you're ready for a transplant, Isabel. With your history, you run the risk of having another life-threatening bleed at any time. Transplant is an option to avoid that. And, honestly, your oxygen requirements worry me."

I crossed my arms and looked down. "I know. I don't know why I need so much oxygen. But when I wear it, I feel fine. I can still hike, go to Jazzercise, walk the dog . . . enjoy life."

"Good. I'm glad. Keep that up! Transplant is something you need to be absolutely ready for. You know the risks. It's a tough decision." She had a calm, respectful aura that put me at ease.

"Sure, I can't work, and I sleep a lot. And I do need a lot of home IVs. But on a day-to-day basis, with oxygen, I still feel strong." I needed to persuade Dr. Henig, as well as myself, that I was way too healthy for a transplant. Besides, I was too busy writing a book. I didn't have time for a transplant. And so, despite being approved, I stayed off the transplant list.

Ah, the power of denial. CF was distorting my own definition of quality of life. I didn't want to admit to Dr. Henig that, in between my daily activities, my life revolved around the next opportunity for a nap. I found happiness in simple things: good food, my dog, natural beauty, productive projects, and meaningful relationships. I asked for no more. With the distractions, I forgot about my shortness of breath and fatigue.

"If Ana's doing so well," my friend Ashley asked at the time, "doesn't that just make you want to get a transplant and get it over with?"

Yes, Ana's transplant had been a resounding success. But there was no guarantee my outcome would be the same. Three of our CF peers who had received transplants the same year as Ana were dead. Magical thinking overcame me: if Ana had a harder life than I did, then it would be only fair if my transplant wasn't as successful as hers. I sought guidance from Ana.

"Believe me," Ana told me, "you'll know when it's time to get listed. Your whole life will be defined by CF, and you'll be miserable. Then go for it."

Her advice confused rather than consoled me. We were identical twins, but she had experienced a gradual decline. My health status had plummeted after my severe bleed. Even though I was still active, I walked a tightrope, risking a deadly fall in the form of another unexpected bleed. Would I really see a sign, an intrinsic feeling that it was time to get listed?

I doubted that I possessed Ana's willpower. She had pushed herself to work, live independently, and support herself financially, all while her lung function hovered around 20 percent. Ana had been running around Stanford and Japan when her lung function was at what I had now. Self-doubt overcame me. *Could I be stronger? Why can't I just push myself harder?* Perhaps my dependence on Andrew had made me weaker.

I struggled with the same concerns that Ana had faced. The survival statistics—50 percent after five years—had not improved since her evaluation seven years earlier. Lung transplants were still the least successful solid organ transplants. I dreaded the side effects of the medications. Cyclosporine and steroids caused high blood pressure, high cholesterol, diabetes, osteoporosis, cataracts—in essence they advanced the aging process by several decades. Weren't those things worse than the life I had now?

Like Ana, I was guided by the lessons I had learned from friends with CF who had pursued lung transplants. The cruel failure of Hayley's two transplants still haunted me. I thought of Liz, who had functioned so well at 30 percent lung function that she believed she was too healthy to get listed for a transplant; a virulent and sudden infection wiped her out in a matter of weeks. Sandy, who waited to be listed until her lung function was 20 percent, died gasping for air as a massive lung bleed suffocated her before the ambulance arrived. I remembered Kim, who had received her transplant call on her deathbed. After surgery, she had gotten married, bought a home, and enjoyed a fulfilling career in the six years she lived after her transplant. I stood over Terry's bed the night before they removed his ventilator after a vicious infection destroyed his new lungs only two years after his transplant. But none of their experiences could determine my course. I had to simply live it out and see where the cards fell. I prayed to God to guide my future.

By December 2003, my lungs had become increasingly infected, but I decided to travel to Florida for the holidays with my in-laws, whom Andrew and I had not visited in three years. I needed more oxygen than usual, was using oral and inhaled antibiotics, and accepted that I would need a tune-up in the hospital upon my return home. Andrew helped me with aggressive therapies, and I slept long hours and minimized my activities. We went to Disney World for two days during the New Year holiday; to save energy I used a wheelchair and three liquid oxygen tanks to survive the twelve-hour days. The Byrneses were extraordinarily understanding, but it was clear I was in trouble.

I was admitted to the hospital shortly after my return from vacation and placed on IV antibiotics. I hoped that the hospitalization would be a typical two-week tune-up and that soon I would resume my normal life at home. But my infection raged on. Two weeks into the stay, my lung function had dropped from 45 to to 30 percent. Despite being exhausted, I had a hard time sleeping because of shortness of breath. The struggle to breathe terrified me. Ana was right. I knew it was time.

On Friday, January 23, 2004, I decided to get listed for a transplant. Andrew supported my decision.

"We'll get through this, love." He was leaning against my bed, wearing an old Stanford sweatshirt, giving me chest percussion to help out the respiratory therapists. His strong, penetrating whacks felt healing on my tight chest.

I coughed heavily and stopped to catch my breath. "Dr. Henig said with my blood type and height, I could get called sooner rather than later. Can you believe it? It has been exactly two years since my bleed, and I've finally processed everything. I'm really ready."

"I think it's time, sweetheart. I hope it comes soon. I'll be by your side." Andrew pounded away, and my lungs burned.

"We have to believe everything will be okay." I took it upon myself to stay positive, to counter my own fears. "You know, I want to grow old and gray with you!"

Andrew laughed. "Great! What else do you want to do? We have to start planning. I, for one, want to go to Europe, maybe see your relatives."

"And we've gotta go to Japan again. And I think we should join a choir. You miss singing, don't you? We have to go camping. To the Sierras. With the dog," I added, giggling.

Andrew groaned. He hated camping. Too much dirt, too little routine, and too much exertion.

"Well, okay, after your transplant, I promise to go camping. Aren't I nice?" He bent down to kiss my cheek. I reached up to caress his thinning hair. I had caused his hairline to recede considerably over the years.

I laughed and paused to catch my breath. "I dream of cuddling with Ana without worrying about cross infection. I want to laugh our heads off without cough attacks, and I want Ana to show me how to backpack, rock climb, and swim with new lungs. We can become middle-aged together, go through menopause, and wear bifocals as transplanted twin sisters!"

Silence hung momentarily as we reflected on the possibilities. I looked up at him, and the fluorescent ceiling light blinded me.

"Andrew, we are so blessed to have this option. I can't imagine how depressed I'd be if this was it; if I didn't have a second chance."

"I don't know how I'd go on either, love."

"But it's kind of bittersweet. While we're planning for a new life, somewhere out there is a person who has no idea he or she is going to die, suddenly, and his or her generosity will save my life. Whose shoes is it harder to be in now?"

"I don't know, love. I don't know."

Chapter 32

The Miracle

Ana

. . . Isa is not doing so great and asks for your prayers and positive energy. Her shortness of breath has gotten progressively worse and she is
very anxious, as are Andrew and I. One day at a time . . . one breath at a
time. Easier said than done. My twin-gut-vibe tells me she'll be okay.

—Ana, post on a CF online chatboard, age thirty-two

She lay there, just trying to breathe. Her chest heaved up and down like
an accordion; her closed eyes were obscured by the face mask of the BIPAP
(bilateral positive airway pressure) machine, a preventilator device to help
force air in and out of her damaged lungs. Cool air flowed into the room
from the open window. I sat by her bed holding her hand. Through the rubber glove I wore I could feel the warmth of her skin. Beads of sweat clung
to Isa's forehead as she worked so hard, as if she were running her last
marathon, just to breathe. I shivered in the cold room.

I stared at her in the darkness. Was she awake, or was she finally asleep?
The hissing of the BIPAP machine blowing pressurized air into the mask
created a soothing background hum, interrupted by occasional explosive
coughing fits. When she coughed, her chest vibrated, tightening in squeezing motions as copious blobs of foul mucus poured out of her lungs, making sounds like shoes stepping in deep mud.

"I'm coughing," she'd manage to say, signaling me to step away, and I would move back from the bed, giving her space to cough. There was no more muffling of the noise with cough towels, no modest covering of dirty tissues. It didn't matter anymore. All that mattered was expelling the peanut butter–like goo that was solidifying her lungs. It took everything she had to cough, exhausting her so that she was barely able to hold the paper cup to spit into.

She relaxed again. "Ana," she said, "just rub my chest. I'm so sore. It hurts."

I put my hands beneath her T-shirt and again absorbed the heat of her skin. I could feel the smoothness of her chest, the chest that I had pounded for so many years. The sinewy muscles were firm, the expanded rib cage hard. I put my hand firmly on her chest, repeating Mama's mantra, "*Yokunare, yokunare*" (Get better, get better).

"My stomach," Isa whispered. "Rub my stomach."

I slid my hands down to her belly, the smooth, flawless belly free of a scar. I felt the dimple created by her protruding belly button surrounded by her proud six-pack abs. The muscles were contracting heavily, as if she was doing sit-ups every second, her diaphragm pumping just to breathe.

Just to breathe. All she wants to do is breathe. Such a simple task had become so momentous in such a short time. A routine hospitalization for another tune-up last month had led to an unexpected, relentless, downhill decline.

"What happened? When did I become end-stage?" Isa kept asking. It was only a *Pseudomonas* infection, not a virulent new strain of bacteria or a virus that we had feared. So why weren't the five potent IV antibiotics working?

The signs were staring me in the face. The BIPAP machine. The panic attacks. The cessation of eating and sleeping. The commode. The Depends. The Gatorade. The darkness of the room. The plea to make the room colder because she was burning up. The way she was breathing, or not breathing. I had seen it with Bob Flanagan, with Karen, and with so many others. Was this really happening? Was it her turn in line? I stared at Isa in the darkness. No, this can't be happening to Isa. We were supposed to be at the end of the line—the dreaded line we were all standing in, just waiting for our turn to die from this fucking disease. We were supposed to write a book together. She had unfinished business. My denial kicked in, and I heard voices in my head. *She's strong. Those Stenzel-Arima genes will keep her going. She'll pull through. This is just a bad spell.* Rob had said Sonya was like this, and then she'd snap out of it and be okay for a while. I trusted Rob.

There was a knock on the door. It was the respiratory therapist. Time for another treatment. They came every two hours for an exhausting hour of aggressive chest percussion in a last-ditch effort to remove her lungs' putridity.

"Isabel, treatment time," remarked Tom, the tall, burly man that Isa had requested for his strong percussion skills. He towered over her bed, his large frame casting shadows on her body.

Isa opened her eyes. She turned to him, almost whispering, "Later, not now. I just want to sleep."

This is the ultimate sign, I thought. *She's refusing therapy. Oh my God. Maybe this is it.*

"You need your treatments," Tom replied. "I'll come back in half an hour. We have to get this crap out of you."

"Yeah," she whispered, "half hour. Just let me sleep."

A few moments later Isa awoke, her wide eyes staring at me as she shouted, "There's going to be a miracle!" Then, her body relaxed, and she closed her eyes again. I didn't know what she meant.

Later that night, Isa awoke again, this time shouting, "Praise God! Praise God!"

I watched her unusual religious proclamation and prayed that God was with her. Just a day before, Isa had told me, "I'm having a spiritual epiphany."

Sometime later, there was another knock on the door. It was Dr. Henig. Andrew, pale and unshaven, was at her side. I stepped into the hallway with them. The warmth, after the cold of Isa's room, soothed my chilled bones.

Dr. Henig spoke in a low voice, explaining how grave Isa's condition had become. "I believe," she said, "that your sister is at the end of her life. Without a transplant, we need to seriously discuss compassionate care."

I blocked out the words. My mind swam with a million reasons why Dr. Henig must be wrong, that the Stenzel twins were somehow an exception to the ultimate CF death sentence.

I was losing my twin. She lay there, just as Bob Flanagan had before he died, a contorted skeleton in a fetal position, destroyed by this disease. Her face was squeezed from the mask, her cheeks swollen from fluid retention.

"My family! Where's my family?" Isa shouted.

Andrew rushed in, his eyes watery and puffy. "We're here, sweetheart. We're here. We just stepped outside to talk to Dr. Henig so we wouldn't wake you. You need your sleep, baby."

Dr. Henig and I stood by Isa's bed.

Her eyes were closed. She mumbled weakly, "I don't want to be alone. I'm afraid. I want you to watch me."

"I'm so sorry, dear. I won't leave you again. I'm right here."

Isa opened her eyes and saw Dr. Henig standing at the foot of her bed. "Are you here to give bad news?"

Dr. Henig smiled. "No, but we need to talk."

She began a discussion about whether or not Isa wanted to be on a ventilator.

Isa perked up, salvaging the energy she had left to sit up in bed. She resisted, "I don't feel like I'm dying. I'm still strong. I'm still coughing tons of stuff up."

Dr. Henig explained that if Isa's lungs continued to fail, she would be taken to the intensive care unit to be put on a ventilator.

Isa protested, "I don't want to go to ICU. I don't want to be on a ventilator. Then I couldn't cough. I know what all that means."

"If you're on a ventilator, you'd be able to get more rest. I'm concerned that you're not sleeping, that you're exhausted, and that's not helping the situation." She sat down on Isa's bed and took her hand.

"I think there's going to be a miracle," Isa said.

"I hope so," Dr. Henig acquiesced. After a pause, she asked, "Why aren't you sleeping, Isa?"

"If I sleep I won't wake up."

"Are you afraid you'll stop breathing?"

Isa nodded.

"You need your sleep. We'll watch you. No one will let you stop breathing while you sleep."

"Okay." She was calmed by Dr. Henig's soothing, gentle tone. Isa reached out and held my hand.

"I'll watch you, Isa," I said. "I can see you breathing, strong and hard. I'll wake you, I promise, if you don't breathe."

A few minutes later, Ryuta arrived. He could see we had been crying. Isa woke briefly, holding out her hand to him. "Ryuta," she mumbled, "I'm sorry to put you through this. I'm sorry you have such sick sisters."

"No," Ryuta replied, his voice composed, "it's all right."

"I wish you had normal sisters."

"No, you're better than normal sisters." His face was blank.

She gripped his hand tightly. "I love you, Ryuta."

"Love you, too."

The night before, Ryuta had slept at her bedside so she wouldn't be alone. Worn out by recurrent panic attacks brought on by the torturous sense of suffocation and impending death, she had broken down and sobbed in front of Ryuta and the respiratory therapist. "I just can't breathe. Is this the end?"

Ryuta had stroked her back as she continued, "If I'm dying, take care of Andrew. Take care of the dog. Tell Mama and Dad I love them. I don't want to die yet." He fought back tears, trying to focus on the moment, trying to calm her. Each sob strained her breathing more as her chest heaved, wrenched, her muscles twisted in an effort to get air.

"Just breathe. Just concentrate on breathing. You'll be okay, you'll pull through. You gotta fight. You're strong."

"I want you to have my German gold coin, the one from Oma."

"Shh. Don't talk like that. Just keep fighting. You're gonna win."

Now, Dr. Henig and Ryuta stepped out, and Andrew and I were left alone with Isa. It had been over three days since she had slept. Just when it seemed like she had drifted off to sleep, Isa spoke: "Haven't we been here before? Haven't we done this before?" followed by an apologetic whisper, "I'm so confused. I'm delirious."

Andrew and I looked at each other in the darkness. Our red and swollen eyes exchanged glances of disbelief.

I couldn't imagine life without Isa. She was part of my everyday consciousness, my every move. "Isa, does this outfit match? Isa, what should I get Mama for Christmas? Isa, do you want me to make you dinner? Isa, what do you think about what I wrote?" Her guidance permeated every aspect of my life, and I envisioned a life without Isa as one filled with unfathomable emptiness.

I bowed my head and wept silently, holding her hand. My tears and runny nose soaked the masks covering my face—the masks that had separated me from Isa for over three years because of the risk of cross infection. Fuck cross infection. It wasn't going to keep me from spending these last days with her.

Isa turned to Andrew. "Babe, I want you to love again. I want you to marry again, to have a child, to be happy."

Andrew buried his head in his hands, shaking his head, sobbing, "No, only you . . . No . . . No, never . . ."

The pain of watching him lose his love gave me images of heart-wrenching agony, and even psych consults, Prozac, and suicide attempts.

For a moment, there was immense peace in the room. The night sky outside the window was dark. There was a soft drizzle of February rain tickling the leaves of the trees outside. A few stars peered through the clouds. A gentle breeze swayed the flowers in the garden outside the window, like the night itself was exhaling. It was quiet.

For what seemed to be hours, we sat there: Andrew, seated at one side of the bed, holding Isa's hand, and I at the other, our sniffles muffled by the humming of the BIPAP machine. The moment embraced us with dread and beauty.

Isa was dying. *Dying. Dying. No fucking way. I can't believe this. What happened?* There's so much left to do together. What about our aspirations to hike, travel, write a book together after our transplants? I had always envied her. Was it some cruel justice that I was meant to live with new lungs and she wasn't? I felt sick at the thought of Isa dying without ever having experienced life without CF. Would God be so cruel?

Isa turned to her side and began to cough. I stepped away. After a few seconds the coughing became a shallow, wheezy, empty exhalation. Then silence. Andrew and I watched. More silence.

"Isa?" Andrew said in a loud voice. No response. He peered at her and noticed a small stream of blood oozing out of her mouth.

"Oh, my God, get the nurse."

He reached for the emergency call cord and yanked it from the wall. I ran to the door, flinging it open and shouting as loud as I could, "Help!"

Within minutes, the room was filled with a dozen medical personnel hovering over Isa's limp body. Bright lights were flicked on, a crash cart wheeled into the room, and alarms beeped, all while a voice repeated over the intercom, "Code blue. Ground floor. Room 41."

Andrew and I were escorted to the corner of the crowded room by a nurse. "You need to step aside."

"Isa!" I shouted over the commotion. "We're here! Hang in there!" Could she hear me?

She began to speak loudly with a fervor I hadn't heard for days. "It's okay," she called out. "I'm all right; this is not a big deal. I'm fine. I'm okay."

Then she became confused, "Am I having my transplant now?" The doctors worked over her, pulling out tubes, syringes, measuring this and that. I noticed her hands were a deep magenta.

"Twins! We're twins!" she continued. "We're writing a book!"

I shouted back. "Yes, we are twins. Hang in there. We're right here!" Tears streamed down my cheeks. My muscles trembled like I was seizing. Andrew and I held each other, terrified. He sobbed, "Oh my God, it's happening. No, no, no . . . please, God, no." I began to hyperventilate. I saw Isa's face turn a deep purple, her hands and legs began to contort. *She's dying right in front of me.*

A few seconds later, Isa's whole body began to contort like she was riding a wave; her legs flew back and forth wildly.

"Woooowwwww," she cried out. "This is ammaaaazzzing! This is beauuttifulll!" She giggled. It was as if she were flying somewhere far away, admiring the view. "Ammaazzing!!"

She was crossing over. Then she called out, "Bob Flanagan! Bob Flanagan!" as if she saw him and was greeting him.

She laughed, "Ooooh, it's sooooooo bright!"

A respiratory therapist working on her yelled, "Isabel, stay with us! Don't look at the light. Stay here, sweetie!"

I was trembling. Panic swept over my body like a torrential rain, and I felt faint.

"You need to step outside," the nurse said again.

I stepped away, dazed, as though moving through a fog. *This is it. I can't believe it.* From the hallway, I peered back into the room at the team of doctors and respiratory therapists working over Isa's body. I heard the suction machine, the hissing of oxygen, the shouting of a doctor, "We need a face shield."

A chaplain approached us and stood by my side. Suddenly, I felt more religious than ever before. I prayed. *I'm sorry I'm such a shitty Christian, God, but please, please, help Isa. Please bring her back. Please let this not be the end.*

In the flurry of people entering and exiting the room, I saw the faces of the respiratory therapists who had worked so hard for Isa in the days before, doing therapy on her until their arms burned, acquiescing to her demands for longer and harder therapy as she desperately fought to save herself. Looking into their faces, I could tell that they had watched this scene play out all too often. How did they do it day after day, code blue after code blue, CF patient after CF patient, always with the same result?

Later than night, Isa was put on a ventilator, the machine she had argued against just a few hours earlier in her last coherent conversation. She did not die. She was heavily sedated, so that she would not fight the tube in her throat. She was finally resting.

She had seven days. After seven days on a ventilator, Stanford deemed a patient too sick to survive the lung transplant surgery. Most people wait on the list for over one year and Isa had been listed only two weeks earlier. We were told there were 211 people waiting for lungs in the Bay Area. The odds were unbearably slim. I mentally wrestled with denial and hope: denial that she would die and that I would be left behind, and hope—visions of her telling me someday, "I don't know why everyone was so freaked out, I told you there'd be a miracle."

Mama and Dad arrived late that night, and we embraced. "I have been dreading this moment all of my life," Mama said, tears welling up in her eyes. "I thought I would be prepared, accepting. But I'm not ready to lose Isa-chan." The last time I had seen her cry was when Karen died.

The next day things were grim. Our family besieged the ICU, making the waiting room a base camp of hope and mourning. I watched Isa, my mind numb. I felt disoriented; I had lost all track of time. It didn't matter. Isa's pale, thin body lay motionless, her belabored breaths the only sign of life. She developed a fever, and Dr. Henig began to worry about her lung infection spreading to other organs, a condition called sepsis, which would really signify the end. Throughout the day, friends streamed in and out of the waiting room in a seemingly endless outpouring of support and love. Despite the somber mood, there was beautiful energy in the air, like love was talking and people were listening.

Later, I stood by Isa's bedside alone. Her eyes were half-open, and she stared at me. But her eyes were glassy, blank, and her pupils trembled like dancing beads. She was absent, but I spoke to her anyway.

"I love you. Hang on, Isa. You're strong. We're all praying for you." I looked at her jugular vein, which was bouncing like a pinball in her neck. "If you want to stay, hold on . . . stay strong, fight, give it everything you've got." She moved her arms. Could she hear me?

"But if you want to go, it's okay. I don't want you to suffer. I'm here with you either way." Tears soaked my mask again. "It's okay to let go if you need to."

I held her hand, watching her. Suddenly her chest vibrated and her face became red. She seemed to be coughing, her chest erupting into the closed ended tube of the ventilator. I looked at the monitor. Her oxygen saturation was 92. Then 88. Then 73.

I turned to the nurse. "She's de-satting. Can you check her?"

The number was now 62. *Oh my God. She's letting go. Now, it's really happening.* The nurse ran to the door and shouted out to the nurse's station, "We need some help in here."

I stepped aside as a flurry of medical personnel entered the room again. The nurse unhooked the ventilator tube and began pumping air into Isa's ventilator using a plastic bagging device. I left the room, panicked, scurrying toward the waiting room in tears.

"She's de-satting!" I blubbered to the audience of family and friends. "I was talking to her, and her sats began falling. I told her it was okay . . . that if she wanted to stay, she should fight . . . but if she wanted to go, that it was okay . . . " My voice trailed off.

Andrew stood up, his face darkening and tears streaming down his face. He yelled, "How could you say that?! You have to be positive. You have to give her encouragement. If you tell her she can go, you're killing her!!"

"Andrew, we have to give her permission. She'll decide. We're being selfish by wanting her to be here. She's suffering . . . do you want to prolong her suffering?" He didn't understand. He had never been around death before.

"No!" he screamed, "You shouldn't say such things. Not yet." He fell onto the sofa, cradling his head in his hands, his face beet-red and his hands shaking.

"Isa and I talked about it. I know what she wants. I can tell her anything." I turned to Rob. He knew; he'd been there. "Don't you think it's okay? It's okay, isn't it? People need to hear that it's okay to let go, or they'll keep hanging on for the sake of others." Rob nodded and put his arms around me.

The room was filled with statues, everyone frozen by the volatile exchange they had just witnessed. I looked around at the tearstained faces, and then I looked back at Andrew. A knot of resentment swelled inside me. I hated Andrew, yet I loved him because we were in this together. I plopped down on the sofa, my back turned to him. My body was consumed by fatigue, and my head ached from dreadful emotions.

Death happens every day for so many reasons. I tried to find comfort in the idea that if others had gone through this then it would be easier, but I was not finding this to be true. I envisioned Isa's funeral, what we would do with all of her belongings, and wondered if I could even return to work, or my CF community involvement, without Isa as my sidekick? I just saw myself crawling into a big hole and not coming out for a very long time. Would my broken heart roll me into organ rejection, and would I die soon after her?

A while later Andrew, my parents, and I approached her room. She lay calmly now. The respiratory therapist explained that Isa had begun to cough, and that had moved mucus up into her main airways, and they had been able to suction out a large amount. Her oxygen saturations had improved. So it hadn't been something I had said. It had been Isa's deliberate attempt to keep fighting, to cough the poison out, to clear her lungs. I was relieved.

Dr. Henig approached the room, a tall man in a white coat at her side. Her eyes were sunken under her dark-rimmed glasses, her frizzy red hair hung above her brows. She looked exhausted. She spoke in a serious tone. "We need to examine Isabel. Can you excuse us?"

The four of us staggered back to the waiting room, dazed. It was close to six in the evening. I watched as nurses walked nonchalantly down the hall with their belongings, having finished another workday, going on with their lives.

Outside, the sun was setting behind cumulus clouds; the puffy white cotton balls floated in a fading blue, their edges silhouetted against the illuminated pink and purple streaks. The sun sets every evening, but it is funny how I remember this sunset in particular, the day Isa was dying. The first blossoms of spring were emerging, and gentle petals were beginning to cloak the barren brown branches of plum and pear trees in the hospital courtyard. It reminded me of Japan.

Later that evening, Dr. Henig entered the waiting area followed by the tall man in the white coat. Under his coat, he wore hospital scrubs, and he had a surgical cap on his head. On his name tag, I glimpsed the words *Cardiothoracic Surgery* next to his name.

Dr. Henig's eyes were tearful, her face reddened behind freckles. "We have lungs available for Isabel," she announced, her face coming to life with a smile.

I gasped in disbelief as my family and friends around me cheered as if the Stanford football team had just won the Big Game. The transplant team from Stanford was on its way to the donor's hospital to examine the lungs. For a moment, I mentally tiptoed around my exuberance since there was a small chance that the lungs were not suitable. But then I suppressed that slim "what-if" and grabbed onto faith: God would not put us through all of this for nothing.

In an instant, the ominous cloud of impending death was lifted, and the rainbow of hope shone through with brilliant light. Our prayers were answered. The sunset outside turned brilliant.

Isa was taken into the operating room at 4:30 that morning. By two in the afternoon, the surgery was over and was a success. Dr. Reitz, who had also done my transplant, reported that Isa's carbon dioxide before surgery was 140, and he had never known anyone to survive with such a high level.

That evening, I peeked into the ICU. Isa was still on a ventilator, completely sedated, similar to how she had been the night before. But this time, there was no straining at each breath, no heaving chest moving up and down like a piston. Instead, her breathing was peaceful and calm, a gentle inspiration and expiration like the movement of a butterfly's wings. Her lips and nail beds were pink.

Back in the ICU waiting room, I held Mama's hand. "Congratulations," I said, "you are now guaranteed not to have your children die of cystic fibrosis lung disease."

She smiled back, squinting through the tears of relief and awe.

"Now aren't you glad you didn't have triplets?" We laughed.

Epilogue

Isa

I could hear my own breathing, a heavy panting, louder than anyone's around me. Sweat droplets tickled my forehead, and my muscles burned. *Just keep going. Just focus. Push. Push. Push.*

A crowd was cheering. I squinted as the low morning sun cast its warm rays on my face. I spotted Mama and Andrew in the bleachers and feigned a smile despite my physical misery.

"Go, Isa!" Andrew yelled. "You're almost there!" Always the cheerleader.

The finish line was visible as I picked up my pace. The cheers reached a crescendo, and the applause invigorated me.

Mama's high-pitched voice cut through the buzz: "Be careful! Don't you overdo it! It is too much!"

I laughed aloud. *She's still nagging me,* I thought.

I looked straight ahead and saw Ana recovering at the finish line, breathing heavily, her skin shining with perspiration. She held her arms open as I used all my might to speed ahead, keep my form, and make it to the end. I finished the 1,500-meter racewalk in fifth place, after thirteen minutes, my best time. We embraced—a power hug—and didn't want to let go. "Oh, God, we did it! Praise God, we did it! The power of two survives! Ah-ha!"

Five and a half months had passed since my eleventh-hour double lung transplant. I was now participating in the United States Transplant Games in Minneapolis, Minnesota. There were 1,800 athletes whose stories were similar to mine, living testaments to the immense blessing of organ donation.

I had survived. Visions of my death had haunted me since I was a little girl, and finally the end had come. It had all happened so quickly that I hardly had time to stop, take in the moment, and wonder in disbelief that I was going to die. I never imagined my CF could take over so suddenly, that within weeks my health would spiral to critical condition, and that the rampant war inside my lungs could so easily overcome my will to live.

The night I coded, I had died but been brought back. It had been a purely physical struggle, one of utter exhaustion, a grotesque mortal wasting, a total bodily shutdown. Days before my death, I had turned off emotionally. I was in survival mode, and feelings didn't matter. I could share my wishes directly with my family and could express myself with composure.

Spiritually, though, I was fully alive; my dying was peaceful, soothing, safe. I saw the light, and I no longer needed to fear death. I felt a tremendous divine calm, a reassurance that everything would be okay. I repeatedly told those around me that there would be a miracle. They may have dismissed these affirmations as mere delusions, confusion caused by pain medication, or proof of the power of denial. But there was a presence that uplifted me in my final hours. As I began to cross over, the presence gave me elation and ecstasy that made the process of dying almost pleasurable.

I still don't know what the future holds, but I will carry this sense of security about my dying until the final end. I was not in control of when I would die. It wasn't my time. I was still meant to be. To be with Ana, Andrew, and my family.

Seven months after my transplant, our family gathered in Lake Tahoe for our first family vacation free from CF. As we hiked among golden aspens and alpine meadows, Ana and I raced ahead of the others, oblivious to the high elevation.

"This is awesome!" Ana exclaimed, holding her hands high above her head.

I took in a deep breath, my lungs expanding, and felt the fresh air permeate my entire being.

Mama, Dad, and Ryuta followed us, and I could hear Mama panting.

"Wait up!" Mama cried from a distance. "You are too fast!"

"Yeah," Ryuta said, wheezing. "Some of us are still on our first pair of lungs."

It was supposed to rain, but the clouds parted long enough to allow the occasional ray of sunshine through on a cool spring Saturday. I was at Chabot College in Hayward for the Donor Recognition Ceremony on April 22, 2006. I had been anticipating the meeting since receiving a call from the California Donor Transplant Network a month before. My donor family was going to attend, and they wanted to meet me. When I heard the phone message, I unexpectedly broke down. All I could think was *I'm so sorry. I'm so sorry.* Even after two years, all I knew about my donor was that he was male and from Fresno, about three hours south of the Bay Area. I had written two anonymous letters to my donor family, one for each Thanksgiving since my transplant, but I had not received a response. I had prayed that if it was God's will, I would hear from them. But I never expected the first communication I would have would be an invitation to meet.

Shortly after noon, Mama, Andrew, Ana, Ryuta, and I were told the donor families had just finished an hour-long workshop on grief in a nearby tent. Scores of families exited the tent and began crossing the lawn in the center of campus. All I had been told was that my donor had been eighteen years old when he died and that his mother, Martha, and identical twin sisters, Yvonne and Yvette, would be attending, and that Yvonne was seriously pregnant. I looked out eagerly for a pregnant woman.

From out of the bustling crowd a good-looking young man approached me. Behind him came a trail of people. "Excuse me, are you Isabel?" he asked. I looked at his name tag, and it read *Anthony, Xavier's friend.* At that moment, I learned my donor was indeed Xavier Cervantes, one of the dozen names of possible donors we had cut out of the February 2004 obituaries in the *Fresno Bee* and saved in my transplant scrapbook. I nodded to Anthony and immediately reached out my arm to give him a hug. "I'm Xavier's friend, and this is his family," he said, as he turned toward a group of seven others. I noticed everyone was wearing matching T-shirts. On the right side was a photo of a sharp young man in a tuxedo, standing, jacket slung over his shoulder, in front of a sunny green Central Valley field. On the left was a photo of Andrew and me that I had sent the family with my first letter. We were standing in the Black Hills of South Dakota, where we vacationed five months after my lung transplant.

Tears began to flow as I scanned the group, eyeballing the name tags. My eyes caught the name "Martha" and I looked up, overcome, as I found my donor's dear mother. We embraced and sobbed, as I told her how sorry I was for her loss. She nodded and told me how grateful she was to hear how healthy and fully alive I had been in two years. I felt like I could hold on to her forever. She told me she knew it was me in the distance amid the crowd, because she could *feel* my presence. Martha was a petite, beautiful woman with warm, big eyes, and ruffled, dark long hair. I met Xavier's sisters, his stepdad, his aunt, his niece, and his other best friend, Daniel. In the buzz my family began talking to each of Xavier's family members, sharing both laughter and tears.

We exchanged gifts almost immediately. Martha presented me with a neatly folded high school T-shirt with "Class of '04," and showed us photos of Xavier at his winter formal, held just two weeks before his death. She gave me an enlargement of his senior portrait, where he sits casually in jeans and a stylish black shirt on a draped stage, behind a 2004 block marking the best and worst year of his life. Gazing at the image, I see that he had dark eyes just like those of his mother. His nose was triangular and broad, just like mine. He has a wide forehead just like Ryuta's. He sported a trendy buzzed haircut with bleached spiked tips. His youthful smile was the only reminder of his childhood, because his body exuded a grown-up manliness. I felt the heavy weight of sorrow.

I presented Martha with the gold medal that I had won in the 2004 Transplant Games in volleyball, telling her how this medal belonged to Xavier because he allowed me to be healthy enough to participate. My mother said her brief but genuine words of gratitude to Martha and presented her with a gift, a tear-shaped pearl pendant passed down from Obachan, which symbolized something beautiful that came out of a hard piece of sand. Andrew tearfully thanked Martha for saving my life and told her what it was like at the moment on February 5, 2004, when the doctors told him lungs were available for me.

I focused all my attention on Martha, who had a bubbly personality and a smile despite her tears. Martha's energy was contagious as she announced that she wanted us to visit her home and meet all of Xavier's other friends. "This visit is just the beginning, and as far as I'm concerned your family is part of our family," she said.

We laughed and talked about donor-recipient similarities. Martha said that from my letters she had known that I was just like Xavier, full of energy, plans, and activities. He could just "go, go, go." Ana told Martha about my auditory hallucination in ICU shortly after my transplant, when I heard Latino music and a male voice asking for his father in Spanish. I simply *knew* my donor was of Latino heritage. I asked Martha if Xavier had liked fishing, because since my transplant I've had a strong urge to go fishing. I learned that Xavier and his buddies would often go fishing. I also learned that Xavier had loved the outdoors and "mudding" with his truck, and that he had wrestled and played football in high school and helped with local construction projects. He had a sweet personality, was happy all the time, and always wanted to make people happy and cheer them up. He was dedicated to friends, really popular, and had three hundred friends visit him in the hospital.

Xavier suffered a head injury in a car accident. He had been reaching for his cell phone in the backseat when he lost control of the car. Desperate measures were taken to save him, including brain surgery. Martha shared how grateful she was that she had four days with Xavier in the ICU while he was somewhat conscious before he died. The day he died, she was singing at his bedside, and he nodded his head for her to stop, tears flowing down his face. She asked if the angels were coming for him, and he nodded yes. The swelling in his brain ultimately caused brain death later that day.

Martha told us how Xavier wanted to be an organ donor, and that he had shared this with her two months before his accident. He had signed up to be a donor at the DMV when he got his license. So it was a natural decision for the family to fulfill Xavier's wish.

Our families separated for the ceremony that started at 1:00 P.M. We all clapped extra hard when Xavier's photo appeared on the large screen during the memorial slideshow and again when his family went onstage to receive a special donor medal. Over twelve hundred donor family members and friends were honored that day.

After the ceremony, we found each other again and spent another two hours together. I wanted to know all about Xavier and to tell Martha how *hard* I was living posttransplant; how I had traveled to Japan, Norway, Germany, and Spain, how I was writing a book, how I had joined a community choir with Andrew and sung at Carnegie Hall, and that I was now learning to play the bagpipe. I had plans to climb Yosemite's Half Dome and was training for the 2006 Transplant Games. I told Martha that my lung volume from my pulmonary function test showed 109 percent of normal, thanks to Xavier's healthy young lungs.

Martha talked about the depth of her despair during the year after Xavier's death. But, she said, everything changed for her when she received my first letter. She suddenly saw a new purpose to Xavier's unfair death. She became a Christian and learned that God had a special plan for Xavier and he was meant to be in a better place. She has come a long way in her grief and did not seem to have any unhealthy expectations that I somehow represented Xavier in living form. She simply stated over and over again how grateful she was that I was alive and enjoying such a wonderful life because of her son's gift.

The psychology of this union is indeed complex and multifaceted. While Martha and her entire family had had two years to process their grief, I left that afternoon in deep mourning. It was so unfair that someone so healthy and strong and with so much potential should be robbed of life in one moment. My disease was natural—Darwinian—making it almost okay if I were to die young. A healthy young man dying in a freak accident is not the natural order of things. But my balanced donor mother said we should not focus on the sadness of death but on the life Xavier lived and the life I could now enjoy.

Having seen the pleasure I gave Martha with my newfound health, I feel an overwhelming sense of responsibility to stay alive and healthy for Martha, to keep her son's memory alive. I feel proud to know my donor was Latino, making me now triracial and proving that people of different races have the same blood because I have not rejected these lungs. I feel immense joy that Martha will soon see the birth of a grandchild and the cycle of life continues. I am so grateful that Xavier's family had the courage to confront their grief by meeting me, because I am the privileged one who has only gained from their tragedy. I feel incredible love for Martha, already, as if I am loving my third mother.

I left my donor family reunion with an intense gratitude for this stroke of fate. My miraculous resurrection seemed planned. As Xavier and I lay dying on ventilators in two intensive care units 250 miles apart, there was a profound connection that was meant to be. This is the only explanation for the implausibility of finding a match after being on the list for only two weeks. Over a year after my transplant, in May 2005, the rules governing lung allocation were changed, allowing the sickest patients to be bumped up to the top of the waiting list. The main goal of these new rules was to decrease deaths on the waiting list and even out waiting times across the country. More lungs have become available, thanks to increased organ donation awareness and improved techniques to remove and preserve lungs from organ donors. Now, it is not uncommon for critically ill patients to receive their transplants in a matter of weeks or even days. I am tremendously relieved that future patients with very end-stage lung disease, as well as their families, may be spared the close call that I had before they receive their call for lungs.

This stranger, Xavier, has become a real person to me about whom I think every day. He *is* my savior. Believing that he died for me is too great a burden to bear. I must accept that he died a tragic death, but through his passing he was able to allow me to live, and for that I will be forever grateful. Martha said it best in her note to me: "God blessed our family so much when he chose you to continue breathing life for our Xavier."

Epilogue

Ana

It was Easter Sunday, 2006, and I had just returned from a week in New Orleans. I, along with other genetics professionals, had volunteered to interview family members of persons missing since Hurricane Katrina and collect family history data for DNA-identification purposes. Back home, the mail was piled high, and as I sifted through solicitations and advertisements, the return address on an envelope suddenly caught my eye: Pacific Northwest Donor Bank, Oregon's organ procurement organization. I tore it open, wondering if it could possibly be a response to my third anonymous letter to my donor family. I had written to them in February, five and half years after the death of my donor, James. I wanted to share with them how I was still alive and truly living well because of them.

The Pacific Northwest Donor Bank's social worker wrote that my donor family was interested in meeting me. My face grew hot as I fought back tears. *Who are they? What would I say to them?* I called the social worker the next day, informing her that I would be in the Portland area in late April for a regional genetic counselors' conference. She cautioned me that the process of a donor family meeting the recipient was an emotional one and that the family might need more time. I shouldn't get my hopes up. Having met Isa's donor family only one week earlier, I was well aware of the impact of this reunion on donor families.

Late April arrived, and within twelve hours of arriving in Portland I received a call from Fred, James's eldest brother. His voice was calm and soothing, but that did nothing to stop my hands from shaking so much that I could hardly hold my cell phone. We arranged to meet briefly during a lunch break at my conference. It was located at a brewery-turned-conference-center encompassing gardens, outdoor cafes, and hotel rooms. I anticipated meeting Fred with butterflies in my stomach. After five and a half years, I thought, maybe this won't be as emotional as the meeting with Isa's donor family, where Martha's grief was so raw.

I was walking toward the facility's restaurant shortly before our scheduled meeting time when a man passed by me, then looked back at me, and asked, "Ana?" I looked up at a tall man, in his fifties, with schoolteacher-like spectacles and sparse golden hair.

"Fred?" I asked. He smiled and held out his arms. Instantly I fell into them and lost control of my emotions, tearfully thanking him over and over for saving my life. His wife, Jan, stood by, a thin and gentle-looking woman, also teary-eyed. I embraced Fred as I would an old friend—it was as if I knew him and he knew me. He later said he felt a pull in my direction and felt instantly who I was.

We spent over an hour talking—he shared stories of James's life with me, and I told him about my life. There were more tears and a gift exchange. I sat before a weeping older gentleman, holding his hand as he recounted the life and death of his brother James Dorn. James's parents had died years before his death and thus been spared the grief of losing one of their sons. Fred was twenty-two years older than James, and he had four other siblings, all but one of whom lived in the Portland-Eugene area.

James had died suddenly from a brain aneurysm. He had been a healthy man, content with his life, who suddenly developed a severe headache. Brain scans revealed an aneurysm, and he underwent emergency surgery to correct it. While James was recovering from surgery, his siblings visited him in the hospital, and they were able to spend the last days of his life healing old family conflicts. Then James unexpectedly took a turn for the worse. His brain swelled, causing brain death, and his family was left with a difficult decision. When asked about donating his organs, the family did not know his wishes. James had never talked about organ donation, but after much discussion, they decided in favor of it. Fred told me about his ambivalence, which was resolved when he received letters from the recipients of James's liver, kidney, corneas, heart, pancreas, and lungs.

Our time was cut short, as I had to prepare for a lecture I was giving that evening. As we said our goodbyes, Fred presented me with a photo of James. There he was—the man I had thought about every day for the last five and a half years—a blond, camera-shy man in a baseball cap with a Mona Lisa smile. It could have been the guy next door, but it wasn't; it was the man whose lungs I was breathing with, hiking with, running with—*my donor*. Like Isa, I was humbled by feelings of gratitude, guilt, and a sense of responsibility to live for this man in the picture.

An hour after we parted, I received another call on my cell phone. It was Fred again. He said there just hadn't been enough time together, and he wanted to see me again. I invited him back to talk more and to listen to my lecture. I was a panelist for an evening talk on genetic counselors with genetic conditions. Within an hour, Fred and Jan had returned, amid pouring rain typical of the Northwest spring. As we spoke more, two worlds were becoming one, and we were each intrigued by the other's. In an e-mail after our meeting, Fred wrote, "There is no way I can convey my meeting with Ana . . . it was a life changing experience."

We made arrangements for me to meet the other siblings in Eugene, Oregon, that fall. The trip was full of symbolism and reflection. Isa and I flew to Portland in early October and headed south on Interstate 5 toward Eugene. As we fumbled with the radio in the rental car, the first song that came on was by James's favorite band, AC/DC. Just then, the clouds opened up, and rays of sunlight broke through like fingers reaching down from the sky.

We arrived in a rural town on the western outskirts of Eugene and found our way to a large home perched on a broad hillside. As we drove up the long, dusty driveway, the morning sun shone on a backdrop sprinkled with yellow, orange, and red droplets of fall. Fred met me in the driveway, and we embraced. His smile was familiar and comforting, and I felt like no time had passed since April. Then James's older sisters came out onto the porch. There was Beth, the eldest and the mother of three redheads; Janice, who owned the ornate and cozy home with her wise-guy husband, Neil; and Kristin, James's closest sister. All three women wore eighties-style glasses and bore a striking genetic resemblance—they were robust women with thin blonde hair hiding their ears. We embraced with smiles and moist eyes, as if we were celebrating a happy occasion. I felt a sense of peace and knew that it would all be okay. That began a long day of sharing pictures, stories, and tears. We all sat in Janice's living room, surrounded by lace curtains and family photographs, and as the day wore on, more people from James's life came by—his best friend, Chad, and his niece and two nephews and their children. It was the first time Chad had seen James's family since his funeral. His eyes lit up when he saw me; he had had no idea he would be meeting the lung recipient. He shared stories about James that none of the siblings knew—about his ability to drive skillfully while intoxicated, his ability to control an all-terrain vehicle, his giftedness in car mechanics, his broken heart at a failed engagement, his sensitive, private, and stubborn side. I learned quickly that James had been a strong, independent, and determined man, who, at age twenty-nine, was content with his life. Maybe some of our shared characteristics were what had kept me from ever having experienced organ rejection.

I learned about his family—descendants of German and Scottish immigrant farmers who had moved west from Nebraska. They shared photos of James as a child—a skinny kid with yellow hair and a wide mischievous smile that made him look like he should have been in the cast of *Home Alone*. I soaked it all in, sometimes feeling like a fly on the wall, wanting to know him, to imagine him, to smile when I heard his name. Strangely, James came alive in that living room that day, in the curious way that people who have passed do on the lips of those who carry their spirit within them.

After sharing stories, we went outside to pick tomatoes and grapes. In the autumn sun, a family of five reunited after tragedy to harvest the abundant fruits of another passing year, and as I worked beside them, their brother's lungs breathed within me.

James's family was vastly different from the Stenzels. They had American roots: they were blond, blue-eyed, churchgoing Lutherans who ate apple pie, coleslaw, and Jell-O salad and whose grandparents wore overalls and drove tractors. They were a large, affectionate family, counting forty-four descendants from the five siblings alone, many born after James's death in that inevitable circle of life. Though not highly educated or immensely wealthy, they provided comfortable homes for their families and always left one another with the words "I love you." They exuded down-to-earth human goodness, and they opened their hearts and homes to Isa and me, welcoming us with smiles and warm embraces. They showed us generosity and kindness as genuine as that they expressed the day they made the difficult decision to donate James's organs.

I learned that James's ashes had been scattered over a river in the Willamette Valley, nestled between Oregon's Coastal Range and the Cascade Mountains. He, too, had loved the outdoors. When Isa and I were leaving, I hugged Kristin, and I apologized for her loss. She whispered back, "It's okay. We're okay," and I felt immense relief that time, as it always does, had healed some of Kristin's grief.

I cried myself to sleep that night, listening to Christy Nockels's "Breathe" on my iPod: " . . . This is the air I breathe. / Your holy presence / Living in me." Just like I had broken down in the intensive care unit six years earlier, I found the floodgates of emotion opening again. I cried for James, for the stranger-turned-self, for the heartache of his family, for the love he never knew and the children he never had among a family of many. I cried for the wishes he was never granted and the unfairness of it all—the strange twist of fate that I should live but he should not. In the midst of my emotions, I felt more alive than ever.

I left Oregon the next day with a yellow rose from the family's garden, a delicate bundle of soft petals curled in a teardrop shape, about to bloom.

One thousand origami cranes sit on my corner table in an enclosed case, reminding us every day that wishes do come true. We recall the guardian angel who visited us under the blossoming plum tree in Japan, the old man with the long beard who predicted that we would see the twenty-first century. And years later, we rejoice that our family is still intact, alive, and well despite years of our expecting otherwise. Even Obachan sits in the Hawaiian sun each day, reminiscing on her ninety-one years.

Our family has persevered. Like the generations before ours, we have adapted to hardship and become stronger. The way that our family coped with adversity was not always ideal. There were harsh words said, kind words left unspoken, and things done and left undone that we regret. But we did the best we could.

In 2006, Mama retired from sixteen years of practice in medical social work at Kaiser Hospital in Los Angeles. She has transformed her own depression and struggles into altruism. She has helped countless families dealing with chronic and life-threatening diseases such as diabetes, cancer, and CF, often in the very same hospital corridors that we once called our second home. "We would be nowhere without the help of others. Mama would like to do the same," she says often.

Now our empty bedrooms in Pacific Palisades are rented out to UCLA graduate students, mostly foreign students, who, as our parents did decades ago, are seeking better educational opportunities in America. Finally, after thirty-eight years in America, Mama gave up her Japanese citizenship and became American. This country has brought her far. For a project, Mama wrote:

Today, I feel we have won this difficult life that was offered to us, as if we swam across a tough, harsh, complicated river. We are standing at the other side of the river and reminiscing about the past. How fortunate we are. I have become the luckiest mother in the world. No words can express our gratitude for the gifts of the donor families. When the end finally comes to my daughters, I will surrender to our destiny with grace and dignity. I will celebrate and enjoy every moment with joy, peace and appreciation for my experience, which has carried me to my maturity.

Dad will retire within a few years, and then he will really be free to roam the Sierra Nevada Mountains at his leisure. In 2003, he completed a sixteen-year quest to ascend the 247 most famous peaks in the Sierra Nevada Mountains for the Sierra Club's mountaineering group. He was one of only sixty-three persons to accomplish the feat. His name is etched in mountain peak registries among famous climbers such as John Muir. He climbed Mount Whitney five times. He has made his mark in science with significant contributions to the field of plasma physics while being an admired, though austere, professor to aspiring physicists. He remains private and humble, and among those physicists who recognize his name, few are aware of our family struggles. Dad has become softer and more emotional throughout the years. He reflects on the challenges of his marriage with feeling-laden comments like, "Your mother and I have come far." His latest hobby is surprisingly romantic: ballroom dancing with Mama twice a week. Like Mama, Dad turned in his green card after thirty-eight years and became an American citizen.

Ryuta is an incredible man—compassionate and strikingly handsome. He has transformed from the mean older brother into one who shows guidance and concern. Though he carries some of our father's emotional inhibition, he shows his love through kind deeds and continues to be a source of humor in our family. He has matured into a hardworking professional in business marketing and demonstrates the business savvy and the drive that both Opa and Uncle Juichi passed onto him through genetic traits, modeling, or a combination of both. As we spend more time together, he has witnessed our lives with CF and made more effort to be involved, to encourage my transplant recovery, and even to mourn with us the losses of our CF friends.

When our parents first settled in America, they sought the American Dream. When Isa and I were diagnosed with CF, they never imagined we would survive to live over three full and productive decades. This country gave us the medical advances to survive with CF, and now to have a second chance through transplantation. Our ordinary family was saved by two extraordinary American families. That is their true American Dream.

Resources

Cystic Fibrosis Research, Inc.
Bayside Business Plaza
2672 Bayshore Parkway Suite 520
Mountain View, CA 94043
(650) 404-9975
Fax: (650) 404-9981
Web site: *www.cfri.org*

Cystic Fibrosis Foundation
6931 Arlington Road
Bethesda, MD 20814
1-800-FIGHTCF
Fax: (301) 951-6378
Web site: *www.cff.org*
E-mail: info@cff.org

United Network for Organ Sharing (UNOS)
700 North Fourth Street
Richmond, VA 23219
(888) 894-6361
Web site: *www.UNOS.org*

California Transplant Donor Network
1000 Broadway, Suite 100
Oakland, CA 94607
510-444-8500 or 888-570-9400
Fax: 510-444-8501
Web site: *www.ctdn.org*

Transplant Recipients International Organization, Inc.
2100 M Street, NW, #170-353
Washington, DC 20037-1233
(202) 293-0980 or 800-TRIO-386
Web site: *www.trioweb.org*
E-mail: info@trioweb.org

Make-A-Wish Foundation
3550 North Central Avenue Suite 300
Phoenix, AZ 85012-2127
(602) 279-WISH (9474) or 800-722-WISH (9474)
Web site: *www.wish.org*

The Breathing Room: The Art of Living with Cystic Fibrosis
Featuring Through the Looking Glass—Images of Adults
    with Cystic Fibrosis
Web site: *www.thebreathingroom.org*

Transplant Games
Web site: *www.transplantgames.org*
Sponsored by the National Kidney Foundation
Web site: *www.kidney.org*

Lung Transplant On-line Support Group
Web site: *www.2ndwind.org*

To sign up to be an organ donor in California, please visit
www.donatelifecalifornia.org

To sign up to be an organ donor in other states, please visit
www.donatelife.net

Recommended Reading

Alex: The Life of a Child, by Frank Deford (New York: Viking Press, 1983).

Bob Flanagan: Supermasochist, volume 1, People series (San Francisco: Re-Search Publications, 1993).

Cystic Fibrosis: A Guide for Patients and Families, 3rd edition, by David Orenstein (Philadelphia: Lippincott, Williams & Wilkins, 2003).

The Lung Transplant Handbook: A Guide for Patients, 2nd edition, by Karen Couture (Victoria, British Columbia: Trafford Publishing, 2001).

The Nicholas Effect: A Boy's Gift to the World, by Reg Green (Sebastopol, CA: O'Reilly Publishing, 1999).

Taking Flight: Inspirational Stories of Lung Transplantation, compiled by Joanne M. Schum (Victoria, British Columbia: Trafford Publishing, 2006).

Index

Permissions

Listed in order of their appearance in the text

Lyrics from the Indigo Girls' song "Power of Two," written by Emily Saliers, courtesy of Hal Leonard Corporation and EMI Virgin Songs, Inc. and Godhap Music. ©1994. All rights reserved.

Photographs and poems entitled "Therapy" (©1998) and "Symbiosis" (©1996) from the project "Through the Looking Glass," reprinted courtesy of The Breathing Room. All rights reserved.

Lyrics from "Tomorrow," from the musical *Annie*, written by Martin Charnin, and published by Charles Strouse Publishing, courtesy of Hal Leonard Corporation. ©1977. All rights reserved.

Lyrics from Kinky Friedman's "Old Ben Lucas," courtesy of Jimmy Perkins at Why Are You Following Me Music, LLC. ©1992.

Lyrics from "Brand New Tennesse Waltz," courtesy of Jesse Winchester and Keith Case and Associates. ©1970. All rights reserved.

Lyrics from "Remember Me," words by Gus Kahn, courtesy of Alfred Publishing and EMI Robbins Catalog, Inc. ©1933. All rights reserved.

Quotations from *Alex: The Life of a Child*, courtesy of Frank Deford. ©1983. All rights reserved.

Andrew and Isa's wedding photo, reprinted courtesy of Howard Auzenne of Photographic Expressions. ©1998. All rights reserved.

Photo of Xavier Cervantes, reprinted courtesy of Lifetouch National School Studios, Inc. ©2004. All rights reserved.

Quotations from Bob Flanagan's poem, "Why?" courtesy of Sheree Rose. ©1993. All rights reserved.

Lyrics from Christy Nockels's song "Breathe," written by Marie Barnett (©1995 Vineyard Publishing), courtesy of Music Services, Inc. All rights reserved.